Praise for Rebuild Manufacturing

"Rebuild Manufacturing" represents the latest installment of Michele Nash-Hoff's tireless efforts to promote the strengthening of U.S. manufacturing. The book demonstrates her encyclopedic knowledge of the problems that have beset manufacturing but, more importantly, presents manufacturers, policymakers and other readers with insightful recommendations for actions that will improve U.S. industrial competitiveness and the American economy."
Steve Minter, Sr. Editor, Industry Week

"Michele's latest book is a "Master Work" and a must read for those who wish to know the UNVARNISHED FACTS concerning the impact of 'Global Free Trade Agreements' (FTA's) upon America and American Workers over the last generation. Her book is loaded with Charts and References which portray a compelling story of the failure of the existing FTA's, and why it is now necessary to return to an 'Americans First' Manufacturing Policy as opposed to an 'Everyone Else First' Policy."
Den Black, President of the American Jobs Alliance

At a given level of demand there are only two ways to rebuild manufacturing: export more or import less. Importing less, reshoring, is much the easier to achieve. Michele has been an active and effective reshoring advocate, helping to launch the trend in 2010."
Harry Moser, founder & President of the Reshoring Initiative

"Michele Nash-Hoff has long been the top spokeswoman for restoring American manufacturing and a fierce advocate for trade reform. Her informed opinion is critical to anyone wishing to understand the restoring movement and the seismic shift in American politics it has promulgated."
Greg Autry, PhD, Assistant Professor of Clinical Entrepreneurship at the University of Southern California and co-auth~~~~~~~~~~ 'hina

"For many years Michele Nash-Hoff has been unwavering in her support for U.S. manufacturing. In her latest book, she not only presents the challenges facing U.S. manufacturing and the national security issues that arise when we offshore so much of our manufacturing capabilities; she also continues to provide insight and ideas to reverse the harmful trend of a globalized economy."

Steve Cozzetto, President, Century Rubber Company

To my aunt, Doris Bernard, with all my love,
for being my role model and mentor

COALITION FOR A PROSPEROUS AMERICA 2012
Published by the Coalition for a Prosperous America
700 12th St. NW, Suite 700
Washington, DC 20005

ISBN 978-1976430565

Book Cover Design: Paola Masman

Acknowledgments

I want to thank my friends Darity Wesley, Lisa Newmeyer, Judy Lawton, Cari Vinci, and Sheila Washington for encouraging me to write this book, and my husband, Michael Hoff, for providing the love, patience, and encouragement to keep me going when I thought I would never get it finished. I want to express my gratitude to all the people who provided me with data, stories, and permission to use material they had written previously (too numerous to list, but you know who you are), as well as the hundreds of people I have interviewed in the last five years. I especially want to thank my test readers, who provided me with good feedback and editorial critiques as I wrote the book: Peter Polgar, Alan Douglas, Dave Sulli, Kim Niles, Sidney Wildesmith, and Steve Cozzetto. Special thanks go to Paola Masman for transforming my idea of a book cover into exactly what I had envisioned. Last but not least, I want to thank Michael Stumo, CEO of the Coalition for a Prosperous America for his continuous support of my work and agreeing to publish this book. Without the help and guidance of my "team," it would not have been possible to finish writing this book and get it published.

Preface

One of my ancestors was Paul Revere, who became famous for his midnight ride to warn that the British were coming. Since the first edition of my previous book, *Can American Manufacturing be Saved? Why we should and how we can,* was published in 2009, I started calling myself "Paulette Revere" because I felt I was on a modern-day journey to warn people that we will lose our freedom if we don't save American manufacturing.

I am the president of ElectroFab Sales, a manufacturers' sales representative agency for job-shop companies that perform custom fabrication, which I founded in 1985.

From 1985 – 1990, I doubled business every year over the previous year and I served on the board of the San Diego Electronics Network, a professional organization for women in electronics, becoming its president in 1988. I also served on the board of the San Diego Chapter of the Electronics Representatives Association (ERA) and became its first woman president from 1989 to 1991.

Then the recession of 1991-1993 hit, and our bookings dropped. We had to make the painful transition from defense to commercial. We were successful in making this transition by acquiring companies to represent that could competitively perform fabrication services for the commercial industries of our region.

During this recession, the San Diego region lost more than 30,000 manufacturing jobs, 17,000 of them as a result of two divisions of General Dynamics being sold and moved to another state. This was such a shock to the economy that it captured the attention of business leaders and elected representatives at all levels of government in the region.

While serving as board chair of the San Diego ERA from 1991 to 1993, I became president of the High Technology Foundation, a non-profit organization our ERA chapter founded to promote high technology in San Diego. I recruited industry, government and media members for a High Technology Advisory Council and spoke publicly about the importance of high-tech manufacturing to the regional economy. In 1992, we sponsored a forum on "What's Being Done to Save Manufacturing in San Diego?" We lobbied elected officials at the local, state, and federal levels to improve the business climate by reducing the local business tax, eliminating state regulations that overlapped federal regulations, reducing the capital gains tax, and increasing the R&D tax credit.

In 1993, the foundation formed a coalition of 18 organizations, called the High Technology Council, to plan and produce the first High Technology Summit at the San Diego Convention Center. The purpose of this summit, held in March 1993, was to ensure that elected officials and business leaders were aware of the importance of high technology to the economy of San Diego and address ways to improve the business climate at the state and local levels. The council produced a white paper on the issues affecting San Diego's tech industries, which included recommended actions to be taken at the local, state, and federal levels.

However, as the San Diego economy began to prosper in the boom years of 1995-2000, most of these volunteer civic efforts stalled or ceased to exist. So, in 1996, I ran for San Diego City Council, against a three-term incumbent, in an attempt to spread my message about the importance of high technology manufacturing to the economy of San Diego to a greater audience. My low budget, grassroots campaign was unsuccessful, but as a result of that experience, I was recruited to run for the California State Assembly in 2000. I easily won the primary for this open seat, but after a hard-fought, 14-month campaign, I lost the general election. The campaign did give me a great opportunity to talk about the importance of high technology to the economy of San Diego, the need to save manufacturing jobs, and ways to improve the business climate of California.

Then came the dotcom bust of late 2000 and 9/11 in 2001, leading to a recession. The 2001-2002 recession saw an unprecedented pruning of prospects, customers, and competitors in the region. This cut across all sectors of manufacturing. It witnessed key Original Equipment Manufacturers cutting back to a fraction of what they once were, going out of business entirely, moving out of the area, or sourcing their manufacturing out of the area and even out of the country. In my more than 20 years of sales and marketing in San Diego, I had never seen it this bad.

The loss of companies didn't make local headlines, as the departure of General Dynamics had in the early 1990s, because these were mostly smaller companies, with fewer than 100 employees. Buck Knives' announcement about their intent to move finally made the headlines in 2003, and they moved to Post Falls, Idaho in December 2004. The loss of Tyco Puritan Bennett in 2002 should have made the news, as they had more than 1,000 employees in 2000, but it didn't.

I started keeping a record of the companies that had moved out of state or gone out of business since January 2001. In the spring of 2003, several legislators with whom I had campaigned asked me to provide them with the list. I turned the list into a report in an effort to make these legislators, and other key policymakers aware of the seriousness of the situation. I disseminated this first report in March 2003 to legislators, local elected officials, industry leaders, and local news media by email. The report got attention from a local radio talk show host, Roger Hedgecock, who invited me as guest on his show. I prepared two more reports later that year and was invited on his show after each report was released.

I published two to three reports every year from 2003 to 2010, and was a featured guest on other radio shows, like the Hugh Hewitt show. I became a "go to" expert on the state of San Diego's manufacturing industry and was frequently quoted in the San Diego Union-Tribune and San Diego Business Journal. Some of my reports were republished by other media and organizations, such as VoiceOfSanDiego.com and the e-newsletters of the American Society of Quality, the American Purchasing and Inventory Control Society (APICS), and SME.

In 2006, my reports expanded from a focus on what was happening in San Diego manufacturing to issues affecting manufacturing in the nation as a whole. As I read about the downslide of manufacturing, it became my passion to do what I could to save it. I firmly believe that if we don't save manufacturing in this country, we will lose our middle class because manufacturing jobs are its key foundation. After e-publishing a report in May 2007 subtitled "Can U.S. Manufacturing be Saved?" I decided it was time to write a book on the topic. I started writing my book in July 2007.

Since the release of the first edition of my book in May 2009 with my keynote speech at the Del Mar Electronics & Design Show, I have spoken to trade organizations; business and professional groups; service clubs like the Kiwanis, Rotary, Lions, Optimist, and Soroptimist clubs; several regional trade shows; and one national conference. I started submitting articles to a local e-Newsline, San Diego News Network (SDNN.com) in August 2009. In April 2010, I started writing weekly blog articles, which I sent out to a database of several hundred people (now about 1,500), posting them on my website, and submitting them to a local e Newsline. In 2011, I started blogging for the Huffington Post, Industry Week, and the Coalition for a Prosperous America's Trade Reform Blog. After I was offered my own column on Industry Week in 2014, all of my articles are now published on their e Newsline.

In 2012, I became the chair of the Coalition for a Prosperous America's California chapter, on the board of directors for the San Diego Inventors Forum, and a director on the national board of the American Jobs Alliance.

In the past five years, I have given hundreds of presentations on topics related to how we can save American manufacturing and how we can return manufacturing to America using Total Cost of Ownership Analysis as an authorized speaker for the Reshoring Initiative. I've worked with the Coalition for a Prosperous America (CPA) to plan and produce five manufacturing summits: two in San Diego, two in Orange County, and one in Sacramento. I've been to Washington, D. C. for the CPA annual fly-in five years in a row, and visited the offices of every Congressional Representative from Bakersfield and Santa Barbara south to the border multiple times.

By the end of 2015, I realized that I had written over 150 articles since the 2012 edition of my book came out, so it was time to write a sequel to incorporate all that I have learned in the past five years. I started to write this book in December 2015, and I am happy that it is finally done.

Please sign up to receive my blog articles at www.savingusmanufacturing.com

Contents

Chapter 1

What is the current state of U. S. manufacturing?

Rather than give my personal opinion on the current state of American manufacturing, we will consider what has happened to the manufacturing industry over the past few decades, what is the current state, and how the future state appears.

For over sixty years, American manufacturing dominated the globe. It was responsible for turning the tide for the Allies in World War II and defeating Nazi Germany and Japan. It helped rebuild Germany and Japan after the war and enabled the United States to win the Cold War against the Soviet empire, while meeting the material needs of the American people.

Manufacturing is the foundation of the American economy and was responsible for the rise of the lower working class into the middle class in the 20th Century, in which the average daily wage rose from $2.50 per day in 1900 to $96 per day in 1999.

High-paying manufacturing jobs helped spur a robust and growing economy that had little dependence on foreign nations for manufactured goods. American families and communities depended on a strong manufacturing base to improve our quality of life.

American companies like General Motors, Ford, Boeing, IBM, and Levi Strauss became household names. American manufacturing became synonymous with quality and ingenuity. In more recent times, IBM sold their computer line to Chinese company Lenovo, and Levi jeans are made in China just like most every other brand of jeans.

We lost 5.86 million manufacturing jobs from the year 2000 through February 2010 in the depths of the trough according to the Bureau of

Labor Statistics. This was about 20 percent of manufacturing jobs, and we have only recouped about 880,000 jobs through January 2017 or 7 percent since the low in February 2010.

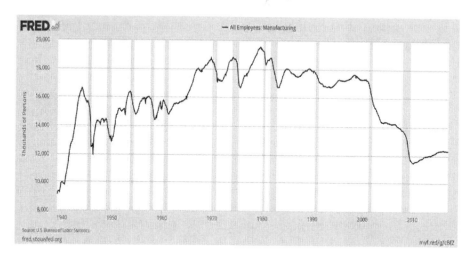

Source: https://fred.stlouisfed.org/series/MANEMP#0

According to Wikipedia, [1] "The largest manufacturing industries in the United States by revenue include petroleum, steel, automobiles, aerospace, telecommunications, chemicals, electronics, food processing, consumer goods, lumber, and mining...the United States leads the world in airplane manufacturing."

Manufacturing is the key engine that drives American prosperity. Federal Reserve Chair Ben Bernanke said, on February 28, 2007, "I would say that our economy needs machines and new factories and new buildings and so forth in order for us to have a strong and growing economy."

Similarly, in 2011 the Center for American Progress released a report entitled "The Importance and Promise of American Manufacturing: Why It Matters if We Make It in America and Where We Stand Today," by Michael Ettlinger and Kate Gordon. It asserts that: Manufacturing is critically important to the American economy. For generations, the strength of our country rested on the power of our factory floors—both the machines and the men and women who worked them. We need manufacturing to continue to be bedrock of strength for generations to come.... The strength or weakness of American manufacturing carries implications for the entire economy, our national security, and the well-being of all Americans.

Manufacturing ensures that the U. S. has a strong industry base to support its national security objectives. American manufacturers supply the military with the essentials needed to defend our country, including tanks, fighter jets, submarines, and other high-tech equipment.

In a keynote address "Lessons for a Rapidly Changing World" at the CA World 2003, Dr. Henry Kissinger,[2] former U. S. Secretary of State, said "The question really is whether America can remain a great power or a dominant power if it becomes primarily a service economy, and I doubt that. I think that a country has to have a major industrial base in order to play a significant role in the world. "

Manufacturing employment in the United States reached a peak of 19.6 million in June 1979, representing 22 percent of jobs. During the trough of the Great Recession in February 2010, it had dropped to 11.5 million, representing 11.3 percent of employment. By July 2017, manufacturing employment had increased to 12.4 million, representing only 9 percent of the workforce due to the increase of total jobs.

Manufacturing represented 21.6percent of the Gross Domestic Product (GDP) in 1979 and dropped to 12 percent by the beginning of 2010. After increasing to 12.3 percent in 2013, it dropped back to 12 percent by the end of 2015, but grew 1.6 percent in 2016[3] for a new total of 13.6 percent.

The economic collapse of the real estate and financial markets in 2008 had more impact on manufacturing job losses than the recession of 2000-2001 caused by the dot.com bust because jobs related to manufacturing represented a much higher component of employment than the software/dot.com industry did at the time.

When consumer demand dropped sharply because of so many people losing their jobs and homes, this eliminated the last thing keeping the domestic market floating on a bubble.

Decline of U. S. Manufacturing is Main Reason for Low Growth

At the January, 2017, San Diego County Economic Roundtable, Alan Gin, Associate Professor at the University of San Diego, said, "The big problem is that since the Great Recession, the growth rate has lagged. The U.S. economy has been shrinking at an annualized rate of 8 percent since 2009. The average GDP growth rate from 1947 to the Great Recession was about 3.5percent. While we have touched that rate for a few quarters…we have averaged a growth rate of about 2 percent." This level of growth is not enough to create the amount of jobs we need.

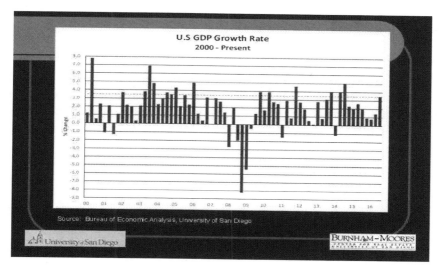

According to Kiplinger,[4] 2017 will see a slight upturn in growth: **"GDP growth in the second quarter bounced up to 2.6%, returning to a level that we expect will continue for a while.** Economic expansion in the second half of 2017 should run at an annual pace of 2.5% or so, leaving growth for the full year at about 2.1%." For 2018, **"GDP growth is likely to be 2.4%."**

Where Did the Manufacturing Jobs Go?

The loss of manufacturing firms and jobs was mainly the result of the fact that a large number of multinational and American companies outsourced manufacturing offshore and/or set up plants in China and other parts of Asia. As originally reported in a Wall Street Journal article in April 2011, U. S. Department of Commerce data shows that "major U. S. corporations cut their work forces in the U. S. by 2.9 million jobs during the 2000s while increasing their employment overseas by 2.4 million."

These multinational companies literally outsourced American jobs in an attempt to compete with the "China price," take advantage of less stringent environmental regulations, reduce taxes, and thereby maximize profits. While the majority of these jobs were lost due to the outsourcing of manufacturing jobs offshore in Asia, increased productivity through the use of automation and robots also played a role.

We lost an estimated 57,000[5] manufacturing firms during this same time period. Unfair competition through currency manipulation, product dumping, and government subsidies by China and other Asian nations were major factors in the closing of so many manufacturing firms.

Top Reasons Why U. S. Lost Manufacturing

- China's Unfair Trade Policies
- Transition to a Service Economy
- End of NASA's Manned Flight Program
- Wind Down of War on Terrorism

Each of these is discussed in more detail below:

China's Unfair Trade Policies

On January 31, 2017, the Economic Policy Institute released a report, "Growth in U.S.–China trade deficit between 2001 and 2015 cost 3.4 million jobs," written by Robert Scott.

Scott explained that when China entered into the World Trade Organization (WTO) in 2001, "it was supposed to bring it into compliance with an enforceable, rules-based regime that would require China to open its markets to imports from the United States and other nations by reducing Chinese tariffs and addressing nontariff barriers to trade."

However, Scott wrote, "China both subsidizes and dumps massive quantities of exports. Specifically, it blocks imports, pirates software and technology from foreign producers, manipulates its currency, invests in massive amounts of excess production capacity in a range of basic industries, often through state owned enterprises (SOEs) (investments that lead to dumping), and operates as a refuse lot for carbon and other industrial pollutants. China has also engaged in extensive and sustained currency manipulation over the past two decades, resulting in persistent currency misalignments."

As a result, "China's trade-distorting practices, aided by China's currency manipulation and misalignment, and its suppression of wages and labor rights, resulted in a flood of dumped and subsidized imports that greatly exceed the growth of U.S. exports to China."

He added, "the WTO agreement spurred foreign direct investment (FDI) in Chinese enterprises and the outsourcing of U.S. manufacturing plants, which has expanded China's manufacturing sector at the expense of the United States, thereby affecting the trade balance between the two countries. Finally, the core of the agreement failed to include any protections to maintain or improve labor or environmental standards or to prohibit currency manipulation."

These trade policies have resulted in an enormous trade deficit with China. Scott, stated, "From 2001 to 2015, imports from China increased dramatically, rising from $102.3 billion in 2001 to $483.2 billion in 2015... U.S. exports to China rose at a rapid rate from 2001 to 2015, but from a much smaller base, from $19.2 billion in 2001 to $116.1 billion in 2015. As a result, China's exports to the United States in 2015 were more than four times greater than U.S. exports to China. These trade figures make the China trade relationship the United States' most imbalanced trade relationship by far..."

He further expounds that "Overall, the U.S. goods trade deficit with China rose from $83.0 billion in 2001 to $367.2 billion in 2015, an increase of $284.1 billion. Put another way, since China entered the WTO in 2001, the U.S. trade deficit with China has increased annually by $20.3 billion, or 11.2 percent, on average.

Between 2008 and 2015, the U.S. goods trade deficit with China increased $100.8 billion. This 37.9 percent increase occurred despite the collapse in world trade between 2008 and 2009 caused by the Great Recession and a decline in the U.S. trade deficit with the rest of the world of 30.2 percent between 2008 and 2015. As a result, China's share of the overall U.S. goods trade deficit increased from 32.0 percent in 2008 to 48.2 percent in 2015." Scott notes that the figures in this paragraph derive from his analysis of USITC 2016 data.

After explaining how EPI calculated the loss of jobs due to the U.S.-China trade deficit, he wrote, " U.S. exports to China in 2001 supported 171,900 jobs, but U.S. imports displaced production that would have supported 1,129,600 jobs. Therefore, the $83.0 billion trade deficit in 2001 displaced 957,700 jobs in that year. Net job displacement rose to 3,077,000 jobs in 2008 and 4,401,000 jobs in 2015.

That means that since China's entry into the WTO in 2001 and through 2015, the increase in the U.S.–China trade deficit eliminated or displaced 3,443,300 U.S. jobs...the U.S. trade deficit with China increased by \$100.8 billion (or 37.9 percent) between 2008 and 2015. During that period, the number of jobs displaced increased by 43.0 percent."

The report calculates job loss by state and Congressional District, stating that "Job losses have been most concentrated in states with high-tech industries, such as Arizona, California, Colorado, Idaho, Massachusetts, Minnesota, Oregon, and Texas, and in manufacturing states, including New Hampshire, North Carolina, and Vermont. Other hard-hit states include traditional manufacturing powers such as Georgia, Kentucky, Indiana, Illinois, Rhode Island, South Carolina, Tennessee, and Wisconsin."

In summarizing the lost wages from the increasing trade deficit with China, Scott stated, "U.S. workers who were directly displaced by trade with China between 2001 and 2011 lost a collective \$37.0 billion in wages as a result of accepting lower-paying jobs in nontraded industries or industries that export to China assuming, conservatively, that those workers are re-employed in nontraded goods industries..."

In addition, Scott wrote, "According to the most recent Bureau of Labor Statistics survey covering displaced workers (BLS 2016b), more than one-third (36.7 percent) of manufacturing workers displaced from January 2013 to December 2015 were still not working, including 21.7 percent who were not in the labor force, i.e., no longer even looking for work."

Scott identifies the following specific problems that require a policy response:

- "Due to the trade deficit with China 3.4 million jobs were lost between 2001 and 2015, including 1.3 million jobs lost since the first year of the Great Recession in 2008. Nearly three-fourths (74.3 percent) of the jobs lost between 2001 and 2015 were in manufacturing (2.6 million manufacturing jobs displaced).

- The growing trade deficit with China has cost jobs in all 50 states and the District of Columbia, and in every congressional district in the United States.
- The trade deficit in the computer and electronic parts industry grew the most, and 1,238,300 jobs were lost or displaced, 36.0 percent of the 2001–2015 total. As a result, many of the hardest-hit congressional districts (in terms of the share of jobs lost) were in California, Texas, Oregon, Massachusetts, Minnesota, and Arizona, where jobs in that industry are concentrated. Some districts in Georgia, Illinois, New York, and North Carolina were also especially hard-hit by trade-related job displacement in a variety of manufacturing industries, including computer and electronic parts, textiles and apparel, and furniture. In addition, surging imports of steel, aluminum, and other capital-intensive products threaten hundreds of thousands of jobs in these key industries as well.
- Global trade in advanced technology products—often discussed as a source of comparative advantage for the United States—is instead dominated by China. This broad category of high-end technology products includes the more advanced elements of the computer and electronic parts industry as well as other sectors such as biotechnology, life sciences, aerospace, and nuclear technology. In 2015, the United States had a $120.7 billion deficit in advanced technology products with China, and this deficit was responsible for 32.9 percent of the total U.S.–China goods trade deficit. In contrast, the United States had a $28.9 billion surplus in advanced technology products with the rest of the world in 2015."

In summary, Scott stated, "The U.S.–China trade relationship needs to undergo a fundamental change. Addressing unfair trade, weak labor, and environmental standards in China, and ending currency manipulation and misalignment should be our top trade and economic priorities with China. It is time for the United States to respond to the growing chorus of calls from economists, workers, businesses, and Congress (Scott 2014b) and take action to stop unfair trade and illegal currency manipulation by China and other countries."

Transition to Service Economy

Another key factor was revealed by the in-depth analysis of national and state data presented in the report[6] "Services, and the Pace of Economic Recovery" by Martha L. Olney and Aaron Pacitti, Berkeley Economic History Laboratory (BEHL), University of California, Berkeley March 2013.

Their hypothesis was: Do service-based economies experience slower economic recoveries than goods-based economies? They argue that they do. They conclude that "service-dependent economies experience longer recoveries because they cannot respond to anticipated demand." Thus, in a service-based economy, the recovery from a recession will take about one year longer than in a goods-based economy.

Why is this? They state, "An economy recovers from a downturn when businesses increase production. Both goods and services can be produced in response to actual demand. But only goods—and not services—can be produced in response to *anticipated* increases in demand, allowing optimistic forward-looking producers to inventory goods until anticipated buyers appear. Services cannot be inventoried. The more services an economy produces relative to goods, the more production is dependent upon only *actual* increases in demand, and the slower the recovery."

Services have to be delivered in real-time by doctors, dentists, lawyers, accountants, web designers, graphic artists, etc. Even in the industrial realm, services such as engineering design, product testing, shipping, and delivery services are performed as needed. These services cannot be produced ahead of the need and "stored." The authors argue that there is a connection between the steady rise of services in the U.S. economy over the last half century and the slower pace of recovery from economic downturns. They state, "…as services become a larger share of output in an economy, more production is dependent on just actual and not also anticipated demand, slowing the pace of recovery from an economic downturn."

The increase in the services share over the past 60 years has been striking. "In 1950, 40 percent of expenditures for U.S. GDP were for services and service-producing jobs were 48 percent of employment. By 2010, services constituted over 65 percent of expenditures for GDP and service-producing jobs were nearly 70 percent of employment." The rise in services in the U.S. has led to longer recoveries, causing the current recovery to last about one year longer than it would have a half century ago.

End of NASA's Manned Flight Program

In 2012, the Commerce Department's Bureau of Industry and Security (BIS) released a report,[7] "National Aeronautics and Space Administration's (NASA) Human Space Flight Industrial Base in the Post-Space Shuttle/Constellation Environment." The official retirement of the Space Shuttle program in 2011 resulted in a 19 percent drop in employment from 2007 to 2010 according to the assessment of the 536 companies in NASA's manned space flight supply chain. Of the 536 companies, 50 percent of them are manufacturing companies, of which 21 percent are based in California, and 9 percent based in Florida.

The report stated that "the Shuttle retirement will impact future NASA programs through a loss of unique skills, capabilities, products, and services by select suppliers." The assessment focused on the "150 survey respondents that identified themselves as dependent on NASA." Within this group, 46 had "reported negative net profit margins for at least one year from 2007-2010… Without continued business opportunities, these companies have the highest potential of shutting down." The report stated that companies that supplied the Space Shuttle program are facing "large-scale layoffs and facility closures across both industry and government."

Near the Kennedy Space Center, more than 7,400 people in Brevard County,[8] Florida alone lost their jobs when the shuttle program ended. The mainly contractor positions cut by NASA accounted for just under 5 percent of the county's private sectors jobs. Thousands of formerly well-paid engineers and other workers around the country are still struggling to find jobs to replace the careers that flourished during the space shuttle program.

The machinery and tools used to support a manned space program are in danger of being discarded. In a separate assessment of the space flight industry, BIS found that 52 companies that were major suppliers (Tier I) had 48,623 pieces of tools and machinery, 91 percent of which had been paid for by the government. This classifies them as "Government-Furnished Property" so that the General Services Administration can process them by being transferred, sold, scrapped, or donated.

The danger is that the U. S. government may never be able to re-establish a manned space flight program to support ongoing missions to the International Space Station once the supplier base of the manned space flight program has been decimated. At the present, the U. S. has no way of sending astronauts to space in its own vehicles, and NASA is relying on the Soviet-made Soyuz capsules to send U.S. astronauts to space station. Thus, the United States may never again be a leader of space exploration.

Wind Down of War on Terrorism

The end of the Cold war with the Soviet Union resulted in a major downsizing of the military-industrial complex in the early 1990s, causing the recession of 1991-1992 and hundreds of thousands of lost jobs. Likewise, the withdrawal of troops from Iraq and the ramp down of troops in Afghanistan had a similar effect on the defense/military industry, with a resulting loss of funding for new programs, cutbacks in existing programs, and job loss. Sequestration compounded the problem when it went into effect in March 1, 2013.

Manufacturing Indicators Rebounding

Finally, during the election year of 2016, manufacturing started to rebound. I don't know whether or not it started on the basis of the hope that a new president would change the direction of the country. But, whatever the reason, one of the key manufacturing indicators turned sharply upward – the Purchasing Managers' Index (PMI) issued by the Institute of Supply Management (ISM). When the PMI is below 50 percent, the economy is contracting; when the index is above 50 percent, the economy is expanding.

Their July 2017 report stated, "Economic activity in the manufacturing sector expanded in June, and the overall economy grew for the 97th consecutive month. The report was issued by Timothy R. Fiore, CPSM, C.P.M., Chair of the Institute for Supply Management® (ISM®) Manufacturing Business Survey Committee: "The June PMI® registered 57.8 percent, an increase of 2.9 percentage points from the May reading of 54.9 percent. The New Orders Index registered 63.5 percent, an increase of 4 percentage points from the May reading of 59.5 percent. The Production Index registered 62.4 percent, a 5.3 percentage point increase compared to the May reading of 57.1 percent. The Employment Index registered 57.2 percent, an increase of 3.7 percentage points from the May reading of 53.5 percent."

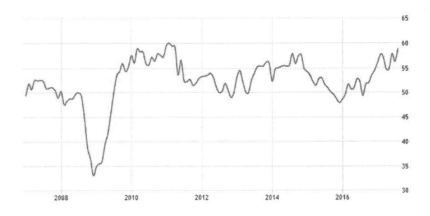

Source: Institute for Supply Management

The U.S. Manufacturing Technology Orders report for June 2017 showed gains for the month and year over year, according to AMT – The Association for Manufacturing Technology.

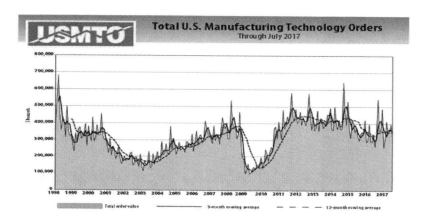

The press release[2] stated, "June manufacturing technology orders climbed 6.5 percent over May, according to a report released by AMT – The Association For Manufacturing Technology. The latest U.S. Manufacturing Technology Orders (USMTO) report also shows a year-over-year increase of more than 10 percent, the fifth consecutive month posting a year-over-year gain.

If the USMTO numbers aren't convincing enough that a recovery is underway, certainly the buzz among our members underscores that a recovery is indeed underway," said AMT President Doug Woods. "Members have shared that the aerospace supply chain in the Midwest is hot; auto orders doubled between May and June; and sales in the Southeast exploded. Over the next six months, they look forward to a broadening of the recovery into areas like agricultural, construction, power generation and off-road machinery industries.

The USMTO data supports the anecdotal evidence from AMT members. Automotive-related orders were up 109 percent from May and the aerospace industry's bookings of new production technology were up 47 percent. While the largest growth by any region is the 42 percent increase in orders originating in the states from Tennessee north to Michigan, the Southeast and West are posting the fastest growth rates year-to-date in manufacturing technology orders."

Upward Trend in Cutting Tool Orders

According to the U.S. Cutting Tool Institute (USCTI) and AMT – The Association For Manufacturing Technology, "U.S. cutting tool consumption totaled $186.57 million in June 2017. This total, as reported by companies participating in the Cutting Tool Market Report (CTMR) collaboration, was down 2.8% from May's $191.93 million and up 6.0% when compared with the total of $175.97 million reported for June 2016. With a year-to-date total of $1.095 billion, 2017 is up 5.8% when compared with 2016.

These numbers and all data in this report are based on the totals reported by the companies participating in the CTMR program. The totals here represent the majority of the U.S. market for cutting tools.

'2017 continues to be a much stronger year for cutting tools than 2016," says Steve Stokey, President of USCTI. "High consumer confidence is a strong indicator that cutting tools sales will continue to improve through the second half of the year.'"

Major Advances in Technology in 2010s

In the January 11, 2016 issue[10] of New Equipment Digest, author John Hitch wrote, "the manufacturing narrative so far in the 2010s has been the major advancements in robotics, 3D printing, and the Internet of Things. These are very different in form and function. The first handles material, the second creates it, and the last is sort of like the force for machines...They do; however, all share quite a few traits: the ability to boost performance, productivity, and profits. Depending on who you ask, they'll make more jobs or take all the jobs, too..."

Hitch cites an example of an exciting advance in additive manufacturing — the introduction of the AgieCharmilles AM S 290 Tooling Additive Manufacturing machine that juxtaposes a direct metal laser sintering machine with a milling machine. The streamlined process could slash cycle times by 60 percent, claims Gisbert Ledvon, director of business development at GF Machining Solutions."

How Does the Health of U.S. Manufacturing Look from an International Perspective?

On January 18, 2017, the Congressional Research Services released a report, titled the "U.S. Manufacturing in International Perspective," by Marc Levinson, Section Research Manager.

Because the decline in manufacturing employment has been of great interest to Congressional members who have introduced hundreds of bills over many sessions of Congress intended to support domestic manufacturing activity, the purpose of the report was to "inform the debate over the health of U.S. manufacturing through a series of charts and tables that depict the position of the United States relative to other countries according to various metrics." The key findings were:

- "The United States' share of global manufacturing activity declined from 28% in 2002, following the end of the 2001 U.S. recession, to 16.5% in 2011. Since then, the U.S. share has risen to 18.6%, the largest share since 2009.

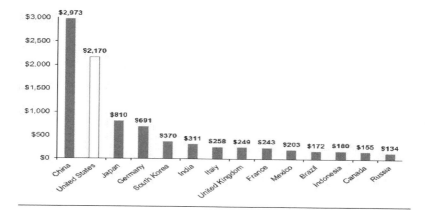

Leading Countries, Value Added in Manufacturing (Billion dollars, 2015)

- China displaced the United States as the largest manufacturing country in 2010.
- Manufacturing output, measured in each country's local currency adjusted for inflation, has been growing more slowly in the United States than in China, South Korea, Germany, and Mexico, but more rapidly than in most European countries and Canada.
- Employment in manufacturing has fallen in most major manufacturing countries over the past quarter-century. U.S. manufacturing employment since 1990 has declined in line with the changes in Western Europe and Japan...
- U.S. manufacturers spend far more on research and development (R&D) than those in any other country, but manufacturers' R&D spending is rising more rapidly in several other countries."
- Manufacturers in many countries appear to be spending increasing amounts on R&D, relative to their value added. U.S. manufacturers spend approximately 11% of value added on R&D, an increase of more than three percentage points since 2002.

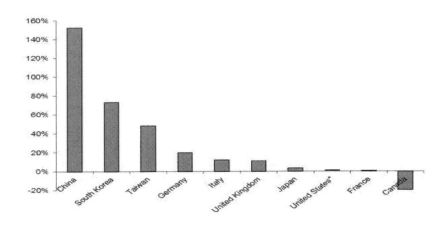

Growth in Manufacturing R&D 2008-2014
Source: OECD STAN R&D database

Is the Recovery Real?

In the Industry Week article,[11] "Is the Manufacturing Recovery Real," by Laura Putre on June 13, 2017, Cliff Waldman, chief economist for the Manufacturers Alliance for Productivity and Innovation (MAPI) said, "U.S. manufacturing got walloped during the Great Recession. It lost 20% of its output and 15% of its workforce. "That's second only to the Great Depression of the 1930s, when it lost about half its total output."

Putre wrote, "And it wasn't an isolated hit. Waldman and economist Mark Schweitzer, senior vice president at the Cleveland Federal Reserve, both say that the economy was still reeling from the recession of the early 2000s. The United States was just coming out of that recession when the terrorist attacks on the World Trade Center in September 2001 shook the economy again. It still hadn't recovered when the U.S. housing market began crumbling in 2008. So much trauma in less than a decade sent the U.S. economy spiraling into the Great Recession. Manufacturing capacity utilization fell 8 percentage points during that time, a significant drop…"

"But it wasn't long before weaknesses in other parts of the world began to take their toll. The financial shock in the U.S. housing sector in 2008 reverberated in Europe and emerging markets beginning in 2009, resulting in the nearly unheard-of event of contraction of the global gross domestic product, not just the U.S. GDP.

While the factory sector still hasn't recovered from the Great Recession, says Waldman, being 4% to 5% lower than its pre-recession peak, it is showing some rallying signs. Manufacturing employment was up every month from January to April 2017 (it dipped slightly in May) and output grew 2.7% in the first quarter of 2017."

Manufacturers' Optimism at 20-Year High, According to New NAM Survey

On March 31, 2017, the National Association of Manufacturers (NAM) released the first Manufacturers' Outlook Survey since President Donald Trump took office. The survey shows a dramatic shift in sentiment, with more than 93 percent of manufacturers feeling positive about their economic outlook. This is the highest in the survey's 20-year history, up from 56.6 percent one year ago and 77.8 percent in December.

The NAM's release of the survey[12] coincided with a meeting of small and medium-sized manufacturers with President Trump to talk regulations, taxes, and infrastructure at the White House.

"Across America, manufacturers' optimism is soaring, in no small part because of President Trump's laser-like focus on pursuing bold action, particularly on rethinking red tape to address regulatory reform, to accelerate a jobs surge in America," said NAM President and CEO Jay Timmons.

"As the survey shows, manufacturers of all sizes are now less concerned about the business climate going forward because they are counting on President Trump to deliver results. Small manufacturers—more than 90 percent of our membership—are among the hardest hit by regulatory obstacles. Regulatory costs for small manufacturers with fewer than 50 employees total almost $35,000 per employee per year—money that could otherwise go to creating jobs. It's encouraging to see an administration so focused on providing regulatory relief to spur manufacturing growth.

"We are grateful for the chance to meet with the president today as we continue to tell the White House directly which regulations are still the biggest obstacles to a manufacturing surge. There is much work to be done, and manufacturers have the solutions on regulatory reform as well as on infrastructure investment, workforce development, bold comprehensive tax reform and a host of other issues."

The survey shows not only a positive outlook but also that concerns about the business environment have dropped. When manufacturers were asked to identify top challenges to their business, concerns about the business environment fell to third place. This had previously been respondents' top concern since the question was added to the survey in 2011.

For the past 20 years, the NAM has surveyed its membership of more than 14,000 large and small manufacturers to gain insight into their economic outlook, hiring and investment decisions and business concerns. The NAM releases these results to the public each quarter."

What is the Future Outlook?

I attended the 2016 FABTECH expo in Las Vegas only eight days after the 2016 election and immediately noticed an atmosphere of optimism. This is the show where equipment, tools, and support systems that are used by manufacturers that perform metal working fabrication services are exhibited. The expo was well attended and companies were receiving orders right on the show floor for new equipment.

This optimistic atmosphere was also displayed at the largest manufacturing-related show in southern California in February 2017 –the Medical Design & Mfg./Pacific Design/Plastics West, etc. held in Anaheim. It carried over to the IPC/APEX show in San Diego, also in February 2017.

The reason for the optimism was the hope that the Trump Administration and Congress would repeal and replace Obamacare, eliminate burdensome over-regulation, and pass comprehensive tax reform.

However, if these policies do not pass this year, manufacturers may become discouraged. What concerns me is that historically, we have eight to ten years from the beginning of one recession to the beginning of another, and it has been almost nine years now since the beginning of the Great Recession. The stock market is at an historic high, over 22,000, and real estate prices have rebounded in some parts of the country, such as California, to the pre-recession peak of 2007.

The question is: Are we at the peak of another bubble that is about to burst? I remember that in the year 2000, no one thought that the bubble would ever burst. As a member of the San Diego Venture Group, I heard from all the local economists month after month that we were in a new paradigm, and the stock market was just going to keep going up and up. Then, we had the dot.com bust at the very end of the year.

We only had less than eight years from the end of the recession of the 2000-2001 recession to the beginning of the next recession, but during that same time period, the decimation of our manufacturing base accelerated dramatically due to the reasons we have discussed above.

We need to do things differently in the future if we want to change our course and rebuild American manufacturing. In the following chapters, we will consider strategies and policies that would help rebuild American manufacturing to create jobs and prosperity. But first, in the next chapter, we will consider the threats to rebuilding manufacturing.

Chapter 2

What are the threats or Obstacles to rebuilding American Manufacturing?

The decline in capital investment is a major threat to American innovation and our nation's ability to rebuild American manufacturing. In October 2013, I wrote an article about the report[13] titled "Restoring America's Lagging Investment in Capital Goods," by Luke A. Steward and Robert D. Atkinson of the Information Technology and Innovation Foundation. The report analyzed trends in private sector investment in capital goods over the previous three decades, investigated the causes of the current decline, and proposed policy reforms designed to spur increased investment growth. The authors warned that this serious decline in capital investment over the last decade is a key threat to economic growth.

The authors state, "Private capital investment is the primary means through which innovation, the key driver of economic growth, diffuses throughout the economy." Business investment in equipment, software and structures grew by only 0.5 percent from 2000 to 2011 compared to an average of 2.7 percent between 1980 and 1989 and 5.2 percent per year between 1990 and 1999.

The authors made a strong case about why capital investment matters in developed, knowledge-based economies like the United States. While innovation powers long-run economic growth, the mere act of innovating is not sufficient to grow an economy. Innovation must diffuse through the economy by being adopted by other companies that seek to improve productivity or the quality of products or services. It is the purchase of machinery, equipment, and software by companies, which is capital investment that spreads the innovation throughout the economy.

"Capital investment acts as a diffuser of innovation because innovation is embedded in new investment. Industrial equipment such as engines, metalworking machinery, and materials handling equipment; transportation equipment like trucks and aircraft; construction machinery, agricultural or mining equipment are now "infused with highly advanced technologies, and each new generation is better than the last."

They concluded that innovation economies require high rates of capital investment in order to be utilized. This innovation economy is also referred to as "the new growth theory, in which investment in new machinery, equipment and software spreads innovation." By high rates of investment, they do not mean a high amount of equipment, software and structures. They "mean that the capital stock is refreshed and replaced with newer and more productive machinery, equipment and software."

They write, "The value of investment is not in acquiring *more* machinery and equipment; it is in acquiring *newer* and *more productive* equipment... A high rate of investment enables innovations to swiftly spread through the economy, bestowing their economic benefits upon their users."

The authors showed that a second reason why "capital investment matters is that it has substantial 'spillover' benefits—that is, benefits not just for the firm making the investment, but also for the rest of society...Many economists acknowledge that investments in the production of innovation (such as R&D) have spillovers, and that this is why policies like the R&D tax credit are important. But fewer recognize that investments in new machines, equipment and software also have spillovers."

The authors concluded: "This stagnation means that business investment rates are actually falling relative to the size of the economy...As a share of GDP, fixed investment was higher in the early 1980s—around 13 percent of GDP—than in any subsequent year. In 2011, fixed investment accounted for less than 10 percent of GDP. Given that it is investment that drives productivity growth, these statistics are sobering. Out of all the fundamental components of GDP—consumption, investment, government, and net exports—a fall in the relative magnitude of investment is the most worrying in terms of future economic performance."

Total business investment in equipment and software grew in the 1980s, boomed in the 1990s, and then stagnated in the 2000s. Between 1980 and 1991, equipment and software investment increased by 37 percent compared to just 2 percent between 2000 and 2011. This means that investment in equipment and software is falling relative to the size of the economy just like total investment.

Not only did business investment stagnate in the 2000s, but investment is "now much more concentrated in a few select domestic-serving services industries, and industries that once powered U.S. investment growth and global competitiveness are now falling behind," such as computers and chemical products.

The investment trends in the computer and electronic products industry are even worse than other manufacturing sectors: "a 36 percent decline in equipment and software investment since 2000."

The authors proposed two possible reasons for the causes of investment stagnation:

1. Decline in the competitiveness of U.S. traded-sector businesses on the global market that has been occurring, particularly over at least the past decade
2. "Short-termism"—the obsession with the upcoming financial report rather than long-range planning—that pervades publicly traded businesses facing stockholder pressures

With regard to "short-termism," the authors mean "the pressure on companies by Wall Street to achieve short-term profits has all too often come at the expense of long-term investment." In other words, executives are willing to "delay new investment projects in order to meet short-term earnings targets, even if it meant sacrifices in value creation."

This report proved that as investment declines, economic growth declines, and as economic growth declines, the capital available for investment and demand for new investment declines. If this trend continues, innovation will slow, competitiveness will continue to decline, and productivity growth will weaken.

Numerous other reports have described the U.S. competitive decline over the past decade, so this report summarizes a few of the key points that have been made in other reports and previous articles I have written. The end result is that the United States has lost its attractiveness as a production location for manufacturing, and when businesses move offshore to other countries, they take their investment along with them. In addition, fewer foreign firms are making investments here in the United States. Thus, investment declines in one industry sector after another.

Defense Department's Globalization of Supply Chain Threatens our National Security

On May 21, 2012, I wrote an article about the release of the Senate Armed Services Committee report[14] on counterfeit parts in the Department of Defense supply chain. The Committee had found over 1,800 cases of counterfeit parts in just the Air Force C-130J and C-27J cargo planes, as well as assemblies used in the Navy's SH-60B helicopter.

To address weaknesses in the defense supply chain and to promote the adoption of aggressive counterfeit avoidance practices by the Department of Defense and the defense industry, an amendment to the National Defense Authorization Act for Fiscal Year 2012[15] was adopted in the Senate and signed by President Obama.

Instead of implementing the requirements of the Act, it appears that DOD "has entered a new phase of its centuries-long development, the latest characterized by globalization of supply chains and the inability of U.S. defense contractors and laboratories to drive technological change" according to Richard McCormack, publisher and producer of the Manufacturing & Technology News, May 20, 2015 edition.[16]

In this issue, McCormack reported on comments made by Bill Lynn, CEO of Finmeccanica North America and former Deputy Secretary of Defense from 2009 until 2011, at the April 29, 2015 meeting of the Center for Strategic and International Studies in Washington, D.C.

The defense sector and the U.S. military have "moved from being a net exporter of technology to a net importer," Lynn stated, adding "When their R&D budgets are combined to total a scant $3 billion (or only 1.6 percent of revenue), the five biggest defense contractors -- Boeing, Lockheed, Raytheon, L3 and Northrop -- would not even make the list of the top 20 global companies that invest in R&D."

Lynn told the meeting, "Those are things where the commercial industrial base is stronger than the defense industrial base and in many ways the key to maintaining our future [defense] technology edge is to be able to import those technologies into our defense industrial base... Since many of the underlying technologies now reside outside of the United States, DOD has to figure out how to deal with foreign corporations and state-owned enterprises that hold the keys to its success."

McCormack noted, "The Department of Defense and its major contractors are now dependent on foreign manufacturers for many of the military's most advanced weapons systems...The defense industry is a shadow of its former self, representing less than 3.5 percent of the U.S. economy, a position that continues to decline as defense budgets reach new lows with no chance of them growing faster than the economy."

Lynn commented that "DOD is slowly catching up to the structural change caused by globalization of technology and supply chains. It is wrestling with the regulatory and procurement systems it has in place to monitor and conduct business with foreign suppliers, but it has little time to waste."

One of these regulations to which he referred is the Buy America Act[17] that was passed by Congress in 1933. It required the U.S. government to give preferential treatment to American producers in awarding of federal contracts. The Act restricted the purchase of supplies that are not domestic products. For manufactured products, the Buy America Act used a two-part test: first, the article must be manufactured in the U.S., and second, the cost of domestic components must exceed 50 percent of the cost of all its components.

After the end of the Cold War and the end of the subsequent Gulf War in 1991, the provisions of the "Buy America Act" were eased to allow purchasing off the shelf commercial parts (COTS) from foreign countries by the Defense Department and other government agencies if they met the same fit and function of parts made to strict military specifications. Previously, parts, assemblies, and systems were required to be substantially made in the United States or in a NATO country, such as Great Britain, France, or Germany.

In the early 1990s, most commercial parts were still being made in the United States, with some outsourcing to the Philippines, Hong Kong, and Singapore, so this change was pretty safe. However, permitting commercial parts to replace Military Specification parts probably drove out of business the small companies that catered exclusively to the military and provided *Traceability of Origin* per Military Specifications for parts supplied to government agencies, military contractors, and subcontractors. This was all done in the name of cost savings. Gradually over the last 26 years, the manufacturing of most commercial electronic components and microchips was transferred offshore, so that now they are fabricated in China, Vietnam, or South Korea. Note that two of these countries are Communist regimes.

The President has authority to waive the Act in response to the provision of reciprocal treatment to U.S. producers. Under the 1979 GATT Agreement on Government Procurement, the U.S.-Israel Free Trade Agreement, the U.S.-Canada Free Trade Agreement, the North American Free Trade Agreement, the Central American Free Trade

Agreement, and the Korea Free Trade Agreement, access to government procurement is granted by certain U.S. agencies for goods from the partner countries to these agreements.

It was reported by Reuters[18] in January 2014 that "The Pentagon repeatedly waived laws banning Chinese-built components on U.S. weapons in order to keep the $392 billion Lockheed Martin Corp F-35 fighter program on track in 2012 and 2013, even as U.S. officials were voicing concern about China's espionage and military buildup."

Lynn stated "that changing perceptions about foreign involvement in the defense industry are similar to what happened in the U. S. auto sector...Americans and their representatives in Congress were skeptical about foreign nameplates. But as foreign auto companies started building technologies in the United States and hiring American workers, the tide turned... "

It is incomprehensible to me to compare what happened to the U. S. auto industry to what is happening to the U. S. defense industry. The whole purpose of the defense industry is to protect our national sovereignty and national security. How can anyone in their right mind want to make our defense supply chain vulnerable to the foreign country, namely China, which has a written plan to replace us as the world's super power? The Chinese are never going to build plants in the U. S. to make parts for our defense supply chain. They have just stolen our technology to build up their own military power as evidenced by the "uncanny" similarity of China's newest stealth fighter, the J-31, as well as the Chengdu J-20 fighter jet, to the F-35 Lightning II advanced fighter jet.

Does anyone believe that we will get any parts and assemblies needed by our defense industry when China has decided we are so weak that we cannot stop their aggression in Asia? We are not even safe to have parts sourced in Taiwan, South Korea, the Philippines, Malaysia, Indonesia, or Vietnam. These countries would all be targets for takeover by China once the Chinese lose their fear and respect for U. S. naval and air power.

When President Eisenhower warned us about the military-industrial complex, little did he know that the military-industrial would be superseded by the consumer-importer complex, which has led to the virtual demise of the military-industrial complex.

Congress must act to strengthen the Buy America Act, not weaken it, eliminate the incentives for offshoring, and provide incentives for bringing manufacturing back to America. We must protect the supply chain for defense and military products and systems, so that the Defense Department can fulfill its primary mission of defending our country.

Chinese Innovation Mercantilism Hurts American Manufacturers

On December 5, 2012, Robert D. Atkinson, President of the Information Technology and Innovation Foundation (ITIF), testified[19] before the House Science Committee Subcommittee on Investigations and Oversight in a hearing on *"The Impact of International Technology Transfer on American Research and Development."* His testimony was based on his book, Innovation Economics: The Race for Global Advantage (Yale University Press, 2012) and the ITIF report,[20] "Enough is Enough: Confronting Chinese Innovation Mercantilism," released February 2012.

Atkinson began his testimony by stating, "A nation's investments in research and development (R&D) are vital to its ability to develop the next-generation technologies, products, and services that keep a country and its firms competitive in global markets. Until recently, corporate R&D was generally not very mobile, certainly not in comparison to manufacturing. But in a "flat world" companies can increasingly locate R&D activities anywhere skilled researchers are located…. the United States has seen its relative competitive advantage in R&D and advanced technology industries decline. While the United States still leads the world in aggregate R&D dollars invested, on a per-capita basis it is falling behind."

He testified that the "decline in America's innovative edge is due to a number of factors, not the least of which are failures of federal policy, such as an unwillingness to make permanent and expand the R&D tax credit, limitations on high-skill immigration, and stagnant federal funding for R&D. But the decline is also related to unfair practices by other nations that collectively ITIF has termed as 'innovation mercantilism.'"

The ITIF report cited above states that these policies "include currency manipulation, relatively high tariffs (three times higher than U.S. tariffs), and tax incentives for exports." In addition, "some policies help Chinese firms while discriminating against foreign establishments in China."

These policies include "discriminatory government procurement; controls on foreign purchases designed to force technology transfer to China; land grants and rent subsidies to Chinese-owned firms; preferential loans from banks; tax incentives for Chinese-owned firms; cash subsidies; benefits to state-owned enterprises; generous export financing; government-sanctioned monopolies; a weak and discriminatory patent system; joint-venture requirements; forced technology transfer; intellectual property theft; cyber-espionage to steal intellectual property (IP); domestic technology standards; direct discrimination against foreign firms; limits on imports and sales by foreign firms; onerous regulatory certification requirements; and limiting exports of critical materials in order to deny foreign firms key inputs."

The report explained that "in the last decade China has accumulated $3.2 trillion worth of foreign exchange reserves and now enjoys the world's largest current account balance. In 2011, it ran a $276.5 billion trade surplus with the United States. This 'accomplishment' stems largely from the fact that China is practicing economic mercantilism on an unprecedented scale. China seeks not merely competitive advantage, but *absolute advantage*.

In other words, China's strategy is to win in virtually all industries, especially advanced technology products and services... China's policies represent a departure from traditional competition and international trade norms. Autarky [a policy of national self-sufficiency], not trade, defines China's goal. As such China's economic strategy consists of two main objectives: 1) develop and support all industries that can expand exports, especially higher value-added ones, and reduce imports; 2) and do this in a way that ensures that Chinese-owned firms win."

The report stated that "because China is so large and because its distortive mercantilist policies are so extensive, these policies have done significant damage to the United States and other economies...The theft of intellectual property and forced technology transfer reduce revenues going to innovators, making it more difficult for them to reinvest in R&D. The manipulation of standards and other import restrictions balkanizes global markets, keeping them smaller than they otherwise would be, thereby raising global production costs...if Chinese policies continue to be based on absolute advantage and mercantilism...the results will be more of the same: the loss of U.S. industrial and high-tech output, and the jobs and GDP growth that go with it."

Chinese mercantilist policies are unprecedented in their scope and size. Atkinson testified, "A principal arrow in China's innovation mercantilist quiver is to force requirements on foreign companies with respect to intellectual property, technology transfer, or domestic sourcing of production as a condition of market access. While China's accession agreement to the WTO contains rules forbidding it from tying foreign direct investment to requirements to transfer technology to the country, the rules are largely ignored."

He added, "Rather than doing the hard work to build its domestic technology industries, or better yet focus on raising productivity in low-producing Chinese industries, China decided it would be much easier and faster simply to take the technology from foreign companies... China's government unabashedly forces multinational companies in technology-based industries—including IT, air transportation, power generation, high-speed rail, agricultural sciences, and electric automobiles—to share their technologies with

Chinese state-owned or influenced enterprises as a condition of operating in the country."

The ITIF report explained that in 2006, "China made the strategic decision to shift to a "China Inc." development model focused on helping Chinese firms, often at the expense of foreign firms. Chinese leaders decided that attracting commodity-based production facilities from multinational corporations (MNCs) was no longer the goal...The path to prosperity and autonomy was now to be 'indigenous innovation'..."

The document "advocating this shift was 'The Guidelines for the Implementation of the National Medium- and Long-term Program for Science and Technology Development (2006-2020)'...to 'create an environment for encouraging innovation independently, promote enterprises to become the main body of making technological innovation and strive to build an innovative-type country.'"

Some 402 technologies, from intelligent automobiles to integrated circuits to high performance computers were included so that China could seek the capability to master virtually all advanced technologies, with the focus on Chinese firms gaining those capabilities through indigenous innovation.

However, China is not alone in trying to force the transfer of technology and R&D from foreign multinationals — Indonesia, Malaysia, India, Portugal, and Venezuela have the same goal.

Why do so many nations engage in innovation mercantilism? Atkinson testified that there are two principle reasons. "First, these nations have embraced a particular and fundamentally limited model of economic growth that holds that the best way to grow an economy is through exports and shifting production to higher-value (e.g., innovation-based) production. Moreover, they don't want to wait the 20 to 50 years it will take to naturally move up the value chain through actions like improving education, research capabilities, and infrastructure, as nations like the United States did. They want to get there now and the only way to do this is to short-circuit the process through innovation mercantilism. This explains much of China's economic policies. The Chinese know that to achieve the level of technological sophistication and innovation that America enjoys will take them at least half a century if they rely on only their own internal actions. So, they are intent on stealing and pressuring as much of American (and other advanced nations') technology as they can to their own companies. If you can't build it, steal it, is their modus operandum."

Atkinson added that the second reason why these nations do this is because they don't believe in the rule of law and the principles of free trade like Western nations and much of Europe do. These nations also "work on the 'guilt' of Western, developed nations. The narrative goes like this: "the West has used its imperialist powers to gain its wealth, including at the expense of poor, developing nations and now it wants to "pull the ladder" up after it. This means turning a blind eye to intellectual property theft and giving our technology, including pharmaceutical drugs, to nations almost for free. After all, we are rich and they are poor because we are rich."

The reality is that forced technology transfer is enabling China and other nations to gain global market share. It is doing "considerable harm to U.S. technology companies and to the U.S. economy, if for no other reason than reducing their profits and ability to reinvest in the next wave of innovation."

He concluded his testimony stating, "Pressured or mandatory technology transfer by other nations has, is, and will continue to negatively impact American R&D and innovation capabilities. It's time for the federal government to step up its actions to fight this corrosive mercantilist practice."

Theft of American Intellectual Property

On May 22, 2013, a report[21] titled, "The Impact of International IP Theft on the American Economy, "was released by the bipartisan Commission on the Theft of American Intellectual Property of the U.S. International Trade Commission. Dennis C. Blair, former

Director of National Intelligence and Commander in Chief of the U.S. Pacific Command, and Jon M. Huntsman, Jr., former Ambassador to China, Governor of the state of Utah, and Deputy U.S. Trade Representative, were the Co-chairs of the Commission.

The day after the release, Forbes published an article[22] about the report, stating that "China accounts for at least half – and maybe as much as 80 percent – of U.S. intellectual property theft." The article briefly discussed the problem of China's Intellectual Property theft and included quotes from the co-chairs, but did not go into any detail about the recommendations of the Commission.

The article provided the link to the 100-page report, which I read. The key findings were:

- *" Hundreds of billions of dollars per year.* The annual losses are likely to be comparable to the current annual level of U.S. exports to Asia—over $300 billion...
- *Millions of jobs.* If IP were to receive the same protection overseas that it does here, the American economy would add millions of jobs.
- *A drag on U.S. GDP growth.* Better protection of IP would encourage significantly more R&D investment and economic growth.
- *Innovation.* The incentive to innovate drives productivity growth and the advancements that improve the quality of life. The threat of IP theft diminishes that incentive."

The report stated, "A core component of China's successful growth strategy is acquiring science and technology. It does this in part by legal means—imports, foreign domestic investment, licensing, and joint ventures—but also by means that are illegal. National industrial policy goals in China encourage IP theft, and an extraordinary number of Chinese in business and government entities are engaged in this practice."

The report stated that existing remedies are not keeping up with the problem because of:

- *Short product life cycles* – "the slow pace of legal remedies for IP infringement does not meet the needs of companies whose products have rapid product life and profit cycles."
- *Inadequate institutional capacity* – a shortage of trained judges in developing countries
- *China's approach to IPR is evolving too slowly* – "improvements over the years have not produced meaningful protection for American IP."
- *Limitations in trade agreements* – there are also significant problems in the WTO process that have made it impossible to obtain effective resolutions. "Bilateral and regional free trade agreements are not a panacea either."
- *Steps undertaken by Congress and the administration are inadequate.*

The Commission recommended short-term, medium-term, and long-term remedies. The short-term measures are immediate actions that are largely regulatory or made effective via executive order and include the following:

- Designate the national security advisor as the principal policy coordinator for all actions on the protection of American IP.
- Provide statutory responsibility and authority to the secretary of commerce to serve as the principal official to manage all aspects of IP protection.
- Strengthen the International Trade Commission's 337 process to sequester goods containing stolen IP.
- Empower the secretary of the treasury, on the recommendation of the secretary of commerce, to deny the use of the American banking system to foreign companies that repeatedly use or benefit from the theft of American IP.
- Increase Department of Justice and Federal Bureau of Investigation resources to investigate and prosecute cases of trade-secret theft, especially those enabled by cyber means.
- Consider the degree of protection afforded to American companies' IP a criterion for approving major foreign

investments in the United States under the Committee on Foreign Investment in the U.S. (CFIUS) process.
- Enforce strict supply-chain accountability for the U.S. government.
- Require the Securities and Exchange Commission to judge whether companies' use of stolen IP is a material condition that ought to be publicly reported.
- Enforce strict supply-chain accountability for acquisitions by U.S. government departments and agencies by June 1, 2014, and work to enhance corporate accountability for the IP integrity of the supply chain.

The Commission made the following medium-term recommendations to build a more sustainable legal framework to protect American IP that Congress and the administration should take:

- *"Amend the Economic Espionage Act (EEA) to provide a federal private right of action for trade-secret theft.*
- *Make the Court of Appeals for the Federal Circuit (CAFC) the appellate court for all actions under the EEA.*
- *Instruct the Federal Trade Commission (FTC) to obtain meaningful sanctions against foreign companies using stolen IP.*
- *Strengthen American diplomatic priorities in the protection of American IP."*

Of particular interest is the mention in the report that an annual survey in late 2012 of member companies of the American Chamber of Commerce in the People's Republic of China "over 40% of respondents reported that the risk of data breach to their operations in China is increasing, and those who indicated that IP infringement has resulted in "material damage" to China operations or global operations increased from 18% in 2010 to 48% in 2012," and that "The longer the supply line, the more vulnerable it is to IP theft."

In conclusion, "The Commission considered three additional ideas for protecting the intellectual property of American companies that it does not recommend at this time." The following one of the three is particularly interesting to me because of the enormous trade deficits we have with China:

> *"Recommend that Congress and the administration impose a tariff on all Chinese-origin imports, designed to raise 150% of all U.S. losses from Chinese IP theft in the previous year,* as estimated by the secretary of commerce. This tariff would be subject to modification by the president on national security grounds."

At that time, the Commission was "not prepared to make such a recommendation now because of the difficulty of estimating the value of stolen IP, the difficulty of identifying the appropriate imports, and the many legal questions raised by such an action under the United States' WTO obligations. If major IP theft continues or increases, however, the proposal should be further refined and considered."

To me, the most important conclusion of the report was "If the United States continues on its current path, with the incentives eroding, innovation will decline and our economy will stagnate. In this fundamental sense, IP theft is now a national security issue."

What is outrageous is that it is obvious that none of the recommendations have been implemented or we would not still have the serious problem of cyber espionage and Intellectual Property Theft five years later.

The risk of Intellectual Property theft is one of the major reasons many companies are returning manufacturing to America through reshoring. This is also why I urge the inventors that are part of the San Diego Inventors Forum to avoid going to China if at all possible. And, if they have to go to China to meet their target Bill of Materials cost, I recommend that they never source all of the parts of their product with one vendor. Otherwise, they are at risk of being victimized by their Chinese vendor stealing their IP and getting a counterfeit version of their product on the market first.

In fact, Chinese theft of American intellectual property has only increased since 2013 when the ITIF Report was published. Two years after this report, on September 24, 2015, Chet Nagle, a former CIA agent and current Vice President of M-CAM, penned an article[23] in the Daily Caller, stating, "At FBI headquarters in July, the head of FBI counterintelligence, Randall Coleman, said there has been a 53 percent increase in the theft of American trade secrets, thefts that have cost hundreds of billions of dollars in the past year. In an FBI survey[24] of 165 private companies, half of them said they were victims of economic espionage or theft of trade secrets — 95 percent of those cases involved individuals associated with the Chinese government."

He blamed the corruption of Chinese government officials for the problem and stated that "President Xi Jinping has instituted a strict anti-corruption campaign[25]. Regrettably, the campaign has focused on "tigers" — senior government officials — at the expense of eliminating the rampant corruption by the "flies" — officials at the provincial and local level. In any event, putting a dollar value on direct corruption does not address the totality of the costs. Business confidence and foreign direct investment in China are already falling because of the absence of the rule of law."

He concluded, "China's disregard of the rule of law should be the underlying driver for all discussions of commercial topics during the coming visit of China's president. Lack of the rule of law is the most difficult challenge American enterprises face in China."

President Trump and Congress need to have the courage to play hardball with China by implementing some of the recommendations of the Commission. Curbing Chinese mercantilism must become a key priority if we want to address this serious threat to American manufacturers and the U. S. economy.

Threat to the American Patent System and Inventors' Rights

On August 11, 2017, a group of inventors went to the United States Patent Office to make a statement and give testimony against new patent laws that promote the theft of our intellectual property instead of protecting it. Afterward, the inventors demonstrated in front of the Patent Office, and several burned their patents. Michael Caputo, Managing Director of Zeppelin Communications, stated, "Patents have become worthless." The C-Span video of the protest can be viewed at https://www.c-span.org/video/?432438-1/patent-trademark-policy-protest.

Why is the American patent system and inventors' rights being threatened? In September 2011, Congress passed and the president signed the Leahy-Smith America Invents Act[26] (AIA) that changed the U.S. patent system to the party "first to file" instead of the "first to invent to bring the U.S. in line with other countries who adopted first to file patent systems years ago, supposedly to simplify the patent process for companies that file applications in multiple countries. Its central provisions went into effect on September 16, 2012 and on March 16, 2013.

At the time, supporters said it would improve patent quality by creating a new process for reviewing patents after they have been issued and allow third parties to provide information on other parties' applications.

Opponents argued that there was no reason to change the U.S. system, and inventors and small businesses complained that switching to a "first to file" system would give large companies an advantage and hurt individual inventors.

To find out what has happened to the American Patent System and Inventors' Rights since 2011, I requested information from Randy Landreneau, Founder Independent Inventors of America, Paul Morinville, Founder US Inventor, and Adrian Pelkus, President of San Diego Inventors Forum.

Randy Landreneau: "America has been the most innovative country on earth from the start. A key reason for this is the revolutionary patent system created by our Founders that provided intellectual property rights to any man or woman, rich or poor. The rest of the world had systems that were for the aristocracy and those favored by the powerful…America maintained a superior system in protecting the intellectual property rights of inventors until …the passage of The America Invents Act in 2011…While it is hard to quantify the effect of changing to First-to-File, this change does place a disadvantage on the independent inventor relative to the large corporation. But another change has had very measurable negative effects.

The America Invents Act created new and easier ways to invalidate an existing patent. Prior to this, to invalidate a patent required going to a judicial court with its various protections offered to the holder of a property right. The America Invents Act created procedures for an administrative court, the PTAB (Patent Trial and Appeals Board), that does not have the same protections. Approximately 70% of the patents that companies try to invalidate using the PTAB get invalidated.

There are efforts underway to get the PTAB procedures ruled unconstitutional or at least reigned in and similar to the procedures of a Judicial court. Certainly, the PTAB procedures are doing great harm to American innovation."

A more recent bill was even worse – The Innovation Act (H.R. 9), which passed the House in December of 2013. But, the Senate version (PATENT Act, S.1137) was fought effectively and did not pass the Senate. However, these bills were reintroduced in subsequent sessions of Congress until the summer of 2016, when it became clear these bills were not moving forward.

Hundreds of millions of dollars have been spent pushing a false narrative that nefarious entities called "patent trolls" are using frivolous litigation to make companies pay them unfairly. More often, in actuality, an inventor has a patent that is being infringed by large corporation that he cannot afford to fight in court. So, he sells his patent to a company that does have the wherewithal to fight in court (a non-practicing entity or NPE), and the infringer loses because he is guilty.

One element of the Innovation Act was 'Loser Pays.' If an inventor sues a corporation for patent infringement and does not win, he could be liable for the infringer's legal costs. This could be more than $5,000,000. This liability would also be a personal liability to an investor with an interest in the patent (piercing the corporate veil and placing personal assets at risk).

There are still efforts underway by multinational corporations to get a similar bill passed in the future. Currently, there is the threat that something similar to the Innovation Act will come back.

But, the more current threat is how the courts have been moving toward not considering a patent as the property right that it has been for 200 years. A three-judge panel actually ruled that a patent is a public right. If the courts start to widely regard patents as not being property rights, as some feel they are already doing, this will greatly harm American innovation. If a court does not respect the rights of an inventor, court procedures end up being applied in ways that work against him. Recently, there have been numerous cases where judges ruled that a patent was too abstract, and the inventor was not given the normal due process of providing witnesses, testimony, or otherwise fighting to retain his intellectual property.

There is an effort underway to get the U. S. Supreme Court to take up this issue and rule in the favor of patents being property rights. If this effort succeeds, we will have, at least temporarily, stopped the erosion of inventor rights that are so important to this great nation. I and others are involved in fighting to maintain the rights of inventors, and to expand them where they have been reduced in recent years."

Paul Morinville wrote his opinion in a paper titled, "We've Been Googled,"[27] when H.R. 9 looked like it would pass in which he stated that "H.R.9 creates a Patent System without Inventors. Over the last decade, Google and others have spent hundreds of millions of dollars to lobby Congress and produce an ingenious 'patent troll' narrative, which distorts the reality of invention in America. In this decade long war on inventors, H.R.9 is the Google lobby's latest accomplishment. Not surprisingly, H.R.9 is not directed to fixing the fictional problem of 'patent trolls.' Instead, H.R.9 mounts its considerable damage on the patent system in general, specifically harming inventors and small patent-based businesses."

Morinville explained, "If this bill becomes law, inventors will not be able to enforce their patent rights against moneyed corporations like Google. However, moneyed corporations like Google will still be able to enforce their patents against small businesses with even more devastating consequences to those small businesses. Patent litigation is about risk and cost versus reward. If risk or cost is too high in relation to reward, a patent cannot be enforced."

Adrian Pelkus: "I'm an inventor named on 14 issued patents and have made my life as a serial entrepreneur doing new product development for over 30 years. Along the way I have created many startups and raised millions of dollars on the back of IP. I have coached inventors and startups every Thursday since 1985 and have run one of the larger inventor clubs in the U. S. since 2005, the San Diego Inventors Forum (www.sdinventors.org.)

He said, "What is most absurd about the America Invents Act to American inventors is the fact that with PTABs we can lose our ISSUED PATENTS... A company challenging a patent wins 90% of the time. The cost to defend is so expensive that inventors give up and are unable to afford achieving their dreams."

Now, issued patents guaranteed as a Property Right in the constitution are being challenged. A business that infringes would just pay a royalty to the inventor if found guilty hence 'efficient infringement.' The biggest incentives to create new ideas and businesses are weakened because the guarantee that an issued patent will protect your IP interests and investments is gone. Patents can now become liabilities. The proposed bills to penalize an inventor with loser pays and threatens to make their investors pay was beyond absurd; it would be economic and intellectual suicide. The end of our rights and hopes as inventors is in plain sight."

Adrian became connected to Randy Landreneau and Paul Morinville when they reached out to other inventor groups, and he was invited to join the fly-in to Washington, D.C. to fight H.R.9 in April 2015. After that fly-in to Washington, D.C. he became focused on fighting against bills that would destroy our patent system and joined the board of US Inventor in August 2016. He was already on the board of the United Inventors Association and had been working to unite the inventor clubs and groups nationwide.

In January, 2017, the Policy Panel of US Inventors authored a USI Policy Section 101 paper and in February, it was determined that they had to *"get as many inventors as possible calling Congress and writing about the threat of a new bill."*

Adrian said, "I sent out my first call to action to all the clubs and sent a second one the next week and every week since. I discussed the plan to unite the groups and clubs with Stephen Key of Invent Right and Louis Foreman of Edison Nation, who asked how they could help. With their help, we have united 24 inventor groups nationwide to fight the threat to our American patent system and protect inventors' rights.

I established a bimonthly phone conference with the heads of the biggest organizations in the inventor community, inventor clubs, and individual inventors in an effort to create a coalition that would support a petition that reflects our concerns about and suggestions to change the America Invents Act. This coalition is a historic cooperation that will unite the inventor community and bring a voice to Washington, D.C. they need to hear!

We now have a petition that we believe will help make America great again by making it a great place for American Inventors again. This petition represents concerned citizens, inventors, entrepreneurs, and businesses from coast to coast. I'm proud to contribute my efforts to help America by restoring its patent system."

I agree with Landreneau, Morinville, and Pelkus that the America Invents Act is gradually destroying the American Patent System. If a bill similar to H. R. 9 becomes law, it would be the final nail in its coffin.

Why is this important? Because most new technologies, especially break-through or disruptive technologies, come from individual inventors who either start a company or license their technology to companies that are more able to take them to the market.

As a mentor for San Diego's CONNECT Springboard accelerator program and fellow director on the board of the San Diego Inventors Forum with Adrian Pelkus, I work with inventors designing new products or break-through technologies. Local inventors have the opportunity to compete in the San Diego Inventors Forum annual invention contest for best new consumer product or best new technology. All contestants must have applied for at least a provisional patent before they can participate. The future success of their product or technology is contingent upon their having a patent they can protect from infringement. Their ability to raise the financial investment they need to bring their product to the marketplace depends upon their being able to protect their patent. No investor will take the risk of investing in a product or technology that cannot be protected.

You can join the American inventors to save American inventors by signing the petition at http://www.usinventor.org/petition.

The Age of Oversupply and Overproduction

I recently became aware of another threat to rebuilding American manufacturing when I attended the July 26, 2017 webinar "The Age of Oversupply and American Employment" presented by Daniel Alpert of Westwood Capital to the Coalition for a Prosperous America members. The webinar was based on his book, *The Age of Oversupply: Overcoming the Greatest Challenge to the Global Economy*, published in 2013.

Mr. Alpert stated, "**The invisible hand of capitalism is broken. Economic and political forces are preventing markets from**

correcting themselves, and we're now living in an unprecedented age of oversupply. The Cold War's end was widely seen as a triumph for liberal free-market democracies, and even as 'the end of history." In fact, in a grand irony, the demise of the socialist experiment set the stage for the greatest threat yet to the economies of the United States and other advanced democracies. The fall of the Bamboo and Iron curtains, along with economic liberalization, quite literally brought the other half of the world on line, more than doubling the global labor force within the space of a couple of decades, and with more yet to come."

He explained that the Advanced Economies of more than one billion people found themselves competing with a newly emerged three billion plus people. There are ten million Chinese entering the workforce every year. This "Age of Oversupply was preceded by disorder in the emerging nations and a productivity boom in the Advanced Economies from 1990 - 1995." When the emerging nations came on line from 1996 – 2001, "it was masked by the IT Productivity Revolution in the Advanced Nations."

Mr. Alpert stated that "The Age of Oversupply" applies to:

- Labor
- Productive Capacity
- Capital (relative to demand for all three)

Expanding, he said, "The oversupply is the mirror image of a demand slump in that it is not caused by a falloff in demand (depression/disaster/war) but, rather, an historically unique and unprecedented, rapid and enormous growth in supply due to lifting of artificial prior constraints on billions of workers.

As a result, "the U.S. suffers a now-17-year-old slump in real median household incomes as labor is devalued," during which time the illusion of prosperity is debt-funded." This has led economists to try to understand the post-crisis collapse in labor force participation," which some attribute to the aging of the Baby Boom generation. However, "there is clearly more to this story than just the larger number of older people because prime aged workers, 25 to 54, have left the labor force, and workers 55 and older are staying in the labor force at record levels.

Labor force participation, the nominal unemployment rate and job formation mask an underlying picture that indicates persistent and sizable labor slack. The U.S. has become increasingly dependent on a subset of Low-wage and Low-hours jobs in the private service sectors for job creation since the Great Recession. Low-wage, low-hours ("LWLH") jobs are concentrated in four service sectors and subsectors, representing 44.5 million positions as of December 2016, or 36% of private sector U.S. jobs. Yet, LWLH (paying less than $20/hour) sectors have accounted for 60% of all net job creation since the end of 2007, the pre-Great Recession peak employment year.

In addition to limiting aggregate incomes of Americans, and thus constraining aggregate demand, we see:

- Much of the recovery in job openings, hires and turnover (taken as a sign of market strength) is occurring within the Low-wage/Low-hours sectors, to a significantly greater degree than prior to the Great Recession.
- Evidence of a correlation between falling productivity growth levels in the U.S. economy and the increase in the proportion of less-productive, low-wage/low-hours jobs.
- High-wage, high hours sectors that are experiencing reported (data-based and anecdotal) evidence of difficulty in filling positions, are often experiencing problems because of unattractive relative wages rather than a shortage of potential workers.

What is even worse is that for production and non-supervisory jobs, which represent 82% of all private sector jobs, 63% of all net positions created since 2007 are in sectors with below $600 in weekly earnings." The result is that "Low-wage/Low-hours jobs are increasing in proportion and paying half as much as high paying, high-hour jobs."

In addition, "the percentage of LWLH jobs, to total jobs, has crept steadily higher for the past 25 years (from 33.5% to 38.2%, and "the aggregate weekly earnings from LWLH jobs, has fallen relative to total earnings from all jobs. Adjusted for inflation, average annual earnings of High-wage/High-hours jobs have risen, while those of Low-wage/Low-hours jobs have declined markedly this century."

He commented, "Many, in the Federal Reserve and elsewhere, have been encouraged by the recovery in Job Openings and Labor Turnover Survey (JOLTS) Data, but they are ignoring that the rotation out of LWLH jobs to better paying jobs, expected in a recovery, has not materialized."
There has been a dramatic fall-off in labor productivity growth since 2005 (except for 2009 and 2010 when increases resulted from job losses exceeding recessionary contraction in GDP). In his opinion, "The increased proportion of LWLH jobs has contributed to the overall decline in overall productivity growth, as such jobs are 30% less productive (as of 2016).

While job openings have recovered sharply (substantially more so than hires and quits, although they have all improved) many are job openings "at a price," with wages less than what workers require to accept such positions and with end-demand still too weak to alter this phenomenon."

Alpert concluded: "There has been a substantial change in the types of jobs available and created in the U.S. during the recovery from the Great Recession (in comparison to prior recoveries) as over 60% of net additional new jobs have been in the Low-wage/Low-hour sectors. The bottom line is that "There is substantial labor slack in the U.S. economy with many workers who would work for higher wages and longer hours not working, or accepting LWLH jobs out of necessity, despite qualifications."

The reason this is a threat to rebuilding manufacturing is that American manufacturers will have to continue to compete with the oversupply of labor in China and the overproduction of goods produced by Chinese manufacturers as long as China continues to be an export-drive economy.

We are in danger of losing our country's assets by letting China buy American companies

We Americans blithely ignore the long-term effects of allowing foreign corporations to purchase the assets of our country in the form of companies, land, and resources. We are selling off our ability to produce wealth by allowing so many American corporations to be purchased by foreign corporations. It is not just foreign companies buying our assets that is the problem — it is the state-owned and massively subsidized companies of China that are dangerous because China uses its state-owned enterprises as a strategic tool of the state. By pretending they are private companies abiding by free-market rules to our detriment makes us the biggest chumps on the planet. As German economist Fredrich List, wrote,[28] "The power of producing wealth is…infinitely more important than wealth itself."

How many Americans paid attention to the news in 2013 that Smithfield Foods was acquired by a Chinese corporation? Shareholders[29] approved the sale of the company to Shuanghui International Holdings Limited, the biggest meat processor in China. Smithfield Foods is the world's largest pork producer, and Americans face the danger of polluted Chinese food since our FDA only inspects 2% of our food imports.

One of the earliest acquisitions by a Chinese corporation was when the Hoover[30] brand was sold to Hong Kong, China-based firm Techtronic Industries after Maytag that owned Hoover was acquired by Whirlpool in 2006.

In January 2014, Motorola Mobility[31] was sold by Google to Chinese corporation, Lenovo, which means that the nation that invented smart phones is just about entirely out of the business of producing smart phones in America. Lenovo is the same company that bought IBM's line of personal computers in 2004. This acquisition will give one of China's most prominent technology companies a broader foothold in the U. S.

Through strategic purchases, China is positioning itself to be our energy supplier as well. Since 2009, Chinese companies have invested[32] billions of dollars acquiring significant percentages of shares of energy companies, such as The AES Corporation, Chesapeake Energy, and Oil & Gas Assets. In 2010, China Communications Construction Company bought 100% of Friede Goldman United, and in 2012, A-Tech Wind Power (Jiangxi) bought 100% of Cirrus Wind Energy.

The acquisition of American companies by foreign corporations isn't something new. Many prominent companies founded in America have been bought by corporations from the United Kingdom, France, Germany, Italy, and other European countries in the latter half of the 20th Century. Most Americans don't realize that such iconic American companies[33] as BF Goodrich and RCA are now owned by French corporations, and that Carnation and Gerber are now owned by Swiss corporations.

Many foreign countries don't allow 100% foreign ownership of their businesses, but sadly, the United States does not exercise the same prudence. We allow sales of U. S. companies to foreign companies unless there are national security issues, and they almost never sell theirs to us. The Chinese government limits foreign ownership to very few selected industry sectors, that can change annually, and requires joint ventures with Chinese corporations for most industry sectors.

What is enabling Chinese companies to go on a buying spree of American assets? Trade deficits - our ever-increasing trade deficit with China over the past 20 years is transferring America's wealth to China and making millionaires out of many Chinese. In 1994, our trade deficit[34] with China was $29.5 billion, and it grew to $83.8 by 2001 when China was granted "Most Favored Nation" status and admitted to the World Trade Organization. By 2004, it had doubled to $162.3 billion. After a slight dip in 2009 during the depths of the

Great Recession, the trade deficit grew to $347 billion in 2016. If you add the annual trade deficits with China alone for the past 20 years, it totals $4.22 trillion. China[35] now has over one billion serious savers and more than a million millionaires whose assets when combined provide billions to spend to buy our assets.

It is our trade deficit with Japan that enabled Japanese corporations to go on a buying spree of American assets during the 1980s when such companies as Columbia[36] Pictures Entertainment was acquired by the Sony Corporation of Japan in 1989, and Bridgestone Corporation of Japan bought Firestone[37] in 1988. However, our highest trade deficit with Japan of $84.3 billion in 2007 was only one fourth of our current trade deficit with China. While we are still transferring wealth to Japan, it is a democracy and doesn't have armed missiles pointed in our direction.

In theory, we have the means to protect ourselves from this. CFIUS, the Committee on Foreign Investment in the United States, has the power to regulate, approve and deny these purchases. However, it is rare for the CFIUS to block deals.

"According to the annual report[38] filed by CFIUS...During the seven-year period 2008-2014 (the latest years for which such data are available), foreign investors sent 782 notices to CFIUS of plans to acquire, take over, or merge with a U.S. firm. In comparison, the Commerce Department reports there were over 1,800 foreign investment transactions in 2015, slightly less than half of which were acquisitions of existing U.S. firms. Acquisitions, however, accounted for 96% of the total annual value of foreign direct investments."

The dangers of these foreign acquisitions were mentioned in the 2013 Annual Report[39] to Congress by the U.S.-China Economic and Security Review Commission, which states, "China presents new challenges for CFIUS, because investment by SOEs can blur the line between national security and economic security. The possibility of government intent or coordinated strategy behind Chinese investments raises national security concerns. For example, Chinese companies' attempts to acquire technology track closely the government's plan to move up the value-added chain. There is also an inherent tension among state and federal agencies in the United States regarding FDI from China. The federal government tends to be concerned with maintaining national security and protecting a rules-based, nondiscriminatory investment regime. The state governments are more concerned with local economic benefits, such as an expanded tax base and increased local employment, rather than a national strategic issue, especially as job growth has stagnated."

This report, continues, "China has amassed the world's largest trove of dollar-denominated assets. Although the true composition of China's foreign exchange reserves, valued at $3.66 trillion, is a state secret, outside observers estimate that about 70 percent is in dollars. In recent years, China has become less risk averse and more willing to invest directly in U.S. land, factories, and businesses."

In the December 15, 2013, *New York Post*, Diane Francis, author of *"Merger of the Century: Why Canada and America Should Become One Country"* wrote[40] "Currently, American authorities only evaluate foreign takeovers on the basis of national-security issues or shareholder rights and securities laws. But these criteria are inadequate. A fairer test in the case of Smithfield, and future buyout attempts by China, should also require reciprocity: Only corporations from countries that allow Americans to buy large companies should be allowed to buy large American companies. That is why Washington must impose new foreign ownership restrictions based on the principle of reciprocity. The rule must be that foreigners can only buy companies if Americans can make similar buyouts in their countries."

In the spring of 2017, the Coalition for a Prosperous America published a flyer on this issue, titled "America Must Modernize its Foreign Investment Rules." It states:

> "A wave of strategic foreign acquisitions of U.S. companies threatens our security and future prosperity. The U.S. liberalized rules on incoming foreign investment believing others would follow our lead. That belief was wrong. freely

invest here while severely restricting U.S. investment there. America's trade deficits result in a tsunami of incoming foreign investment, a change from when the US was the world's sole superpower. The Committee on Foreign Investment in the U.S. (CFIUS) can block incoming investment based upon national security concerns, but not for economic strategy reasons as other countries do."

The Coalition proposed the follow remedies:

- Expand consideration beyond national security to include economic security
- Allow longer review periods, beyond 30 days, for CFIUS to review proposed investments
- Include a "net benefit" test to encompass American economic interests where proposed
- Acquisitions of companies important to future U.S. technology and employment, both civilian and defense related
- Gauge systemic threats to U.S. interests in addition to individual cases
- Require country by country reciprocity to allow foreign investment in U.S. companies and technology only to the extent they allow incoming US investment there
- Prescribe heightened scrutiny of investments by state-influenced enterprises

My question is: Did we let the USSR buy our companies during the Cold War? No, we didn't! We realized that we would be helping our enemy. This was pretty simple, common sense, but we don't seem to have this same common sense when dealing with China.

China has a written plan to become the Super Power of the 21st Century. With regard to China's military buildup, the U.S.-China Commission report states, "PLA modernization is altering the security balance in the Asia Pacific, challenging decades of U.S. military preeminence in the region…The PLA is rapidly expanding and diversifying its ability to strike U.S. bases, ships, and aircraft throughout the Asia Pacific region, including those that it previously could not reach, such as U.S. military facilities on Guam.

It is time to wake up to the real dangers of our relationship with China. The Communist Chinese government is not our friend. They are a geopolitical rival that is striving to replace the United States as the global hegemony. Letting Chinese corporations acquire American companies, especially energy or technology-based companies is the biggest threat to rebuilding American manufacturing. We must not allow this policy to continue if we want to maintain our national sovereignty.

Chapter 3

Have Free Trade Agreements Benefited American Manufacturing?

We all like to get something for free, so free trade sounds good. The question is: do we even *have* free trade? No, we do not. What we call free trade isn't "free," and it isn't "good," at least for most Americans. At best, it benefits large, multinational global corporations that have manufacturing facilities located in other countries. At its worst, it is the primary source of our trade deficit and loss of good paying manufacturing jobs, leading to an escalation of our national debt.

Brian Sullivan,[41] Director of Sales, Marketing and Communications of the Tooling, Manufacturing & Technologies Association says, "We should rename 'free trade' because it isn't free and it isn't fair. Since it's trade that's regulated in favor of multinational special interest groups, why don't we call it for what it is: How about 'rigged market trade' or 'turn your back on your fellow countrymen trade' or 'throw American workers out on the street trade.'"

Businessdictionary.com[42] defines trade as "The interchange of goods and services (but not of capital or labor) unhindered by high tariffs, nontariff barriers (such as quotas), and onerous or unilateral requirements or processes." By this definition, do we really have free trade that is beneficial?

It is only beneficial if the nation benefits from the trade by exporting more than it imports. In 2016,[43] the U. S. imported $ **2.187 trillion** in goods compared to exporting **$1.451 trillion** in goods, resulting in a trade deficit of **$736.7 billion.** Because we have a surplus in exports of services, our total trade deficit was reduced to $505 billion. It seems to me that we are not benefiting from our current trade agreements as we should and that another trade agreement with 11 more countries would only make our trade deficit much worse.

Thomas Donohue, U. S. Chamber of Commerce President, believes free trade agreements create manufacturing jobs. As reported in the May 31, 2010 issue of Manufacturing & Technology news, he blamed labor Unions for blocking the ratification of trade agreements with Colombia, Panama, and South Korea by the U. S. Congress: "Trade agreements 'support' more than 5m US jobs…and for reasons that defy logic or common sense, they vehemently opposed the very policies that could create millions of new jobs for American workers."

I argue that trade agreements create manufacturing jobs, but not necessarily in the United States. They create higher-paying manufacturing jobs in our trading partners and are the foundation of the developing middle class in China, Korea, Mexico, and our other trading partner countries.

The United States has signed only 22 free trade agreements out of a global total of 262. The U. S. Congress ratified the North American Free Trade Agreement (NAFTA) in 1993 and it went into effect in 1994. Supporters of NAFTA point out that during 1993-2007, trade tripled between the trading partners from $297 billion to $1 trillion. Let's consider the question:

For more than the first 150 years of its history, the United States was a protectionist country in order to protect its fledgling manufacturing industries and then gain preeminence as an industrial nation in the 20th century.

After World War II, the U.S. switched from protectionism to free trade in order to rebuild the economies of Europe and Japan through the Marshall Plan and bind the economies of the non-Communist world to the United States for geopolitical reasons.

To accomplish these objectives, the General Agreement on Tariffs and Trade (GATT)[44] was negotiated during the UN Conference on Trade and Employment, reflecting the failure of negotiating governments to create a proposed International Trade Organization. Originally signed by 23 countries at Geneva in 1947, GATT became the most effective instrument in the massive expansion of world trade in the second half of the 20th century.

GATT's most important principle was trade without discrimination, in which member nations opened their markets equally to one another. Once a country and one of its trading partners agreed to reduce a tariff, that tariff cut was automatically extended to all GATT members. GATT also established uniform customs regulations and sought to eliminate import quotas. By 1995, when the World Trade Organization replaced GATT, 125 nations had signed its agreements, governing 90 percent of world trade.

In 1994, GATT was updated to include new obligations upon its signatories. One of the most significant changes was the creation of the World Trade Organization (WTO.) The 75 existing GATT members and the European Community became the founding members of the WTO on January 1, 1995. The other 52 GATT members rejoined the WTO in the following two years, the last being Congo in 1997. Since the founding of the WTO, a number of non-GATT members have joined, and there are now 157 members, including China. The main countries that are not part of GATT are Iran, North Korea, and some nations in Central Asia and North Africa.

A major benefit for GATT and WTO members was the reduction or elimination of tariffs. However, while the U. S. and other member countries complied with this provision, over the years, the other 156 members have replaced their tariffs with Value Added Taxes (VAT), which range from a low of 10% to a high of 24%, averaging 17%. The U. S. is the only member country that doesn't have a VAT.

A VAT is a border adjustable consumption tax on goods and services. This means that virtually all of our trading partners tax our exports with their VATs, when our goods cross into their country, and rebate their VATs when their companies export. VATs are essentially a tariff by another name. Our trade agreements, such as NAFTA, CAFTA, and KORUS do not address VATs, and the WTO rules allow VATs. This means that U. S. companies are at a disadvantage in the global marketplace, so that so-called free trade has become "unfair trade" for U. S. companies.

According to Alan Uke's book, *Buying Back America*, the United States now has a trade deficit with 88 countries. Of course, some deficits are small, but some are enormous, such as China. Our top six trading partners are: China, Mexico, Japan, Germany, and Canada. These five countries represent 71% of our total trade deficit, but China alone represents 38% of the U. S. trade deficit. Our 2016 trade deficit with China[45] was $347 billion, and we are on track to equal that in 2017.

Some may claim that we are still the leader in advanced technology products,[46] but this is no longer true. The U. S. has been running a trade deficit in these products since 2002, which has grown to an astonishing average of $90 billion per year since 2010.

So how do our trade deficits add to the national debt? One way is that many products, especially consumer products, which were previously made in the U. S., are now made in China or other Asian countries, so we are importing these products instead of exporting them to other countries. The offshoring of manufacturing of so many products has resulted in the loss 5.8 million American manufacturing jobs and the closure of over 57,000 of manufacturing firms. These American workers and companies paid taxes that provided revenue to our government, so now we have less tax revenue and pay out benefits to unemployed workers, resulting in an escalating national debt.

Has NAFTA Benefited Americans?

By this question, I mean the American people, not American corporations or even America as a country. There can be diplomatic benefits to trade agreements, such as strengthening our relationships with countries that are allies in the world's political arena. There can be benefits to American global corporations to open doors to new markets in specific countries. These are two of the reasons touted by "free trade" proponents as benefits to negotiating trade agreements.

To discern the answer to the title's question, let us examine whether NAFTA has benefited Americans as a whole. NAFTA was negotiated under President Bill Clinton and went into effect in January 1994. The agreement was supposed to reduce market barriers to trade between the United States, Canada, and Mexico to reduce the cost of goods, increase our surplus trade balance with Mexico, reduce our trade deficit with Canada, and create 170,000 jobs a year. Twenty years later, the fallacy of these supposed benefits is well documented.

According to the report[47] "NAFTA at 20" released in 2014 by Public Citizen's Global Trade Watch, "More than 845,000 specific U.S. workers have been certified for Trade Adjustment Assistance (TAA) as having lost their jobs due to imports from Canada and Mexico or the relocation of factories to those countries."

Major corporations such as General Electric, Caterpillar, and Chrysler announced they would add jobs for increased sales to Mexico; instead they eliminated jobs. For example, General Electric testified before Congress saying: "We are looking at another $7.5 billion in potential sales over the next 10 years. These sales could support 10,000 jobs for General Electric and its suppliers. In reality, "General Electric has eliminated 4,936 U.S. jobs since NAFTA due to rising imports from Canada and Mexico or decisions to offshore production to those countries."

The report also documents the fact that "the small pre-NAFTA U.S. trade surplus with Mexico turned into a massive new trade deficit and the pre-NAFTA U.S. trade deficit with Canada expanded greatly." According to Census Bureau data, in 1993, the non-inflation adjusted U.S. trade surplus with Mexico[48] was $1.6 billion, and in 2016, the U. S. trade deficit had grown to **$64.3 billion.** The non-inflation adjusted U. S. deficit with Canada[49] grew from -$10.7 billion in 1993 to a peak of **$78.3 billion** in 2008 before dropping back down to $10.95 billion in 2016. Together the Mexico and Canada inflation-adjusted trade deficits "have morphed into a combined NAFTA trade deficit of **$143 billion**."

Top 10 Trade Deficit Countries: These countries account for 90% of U.S. 2016 goods trade deficit

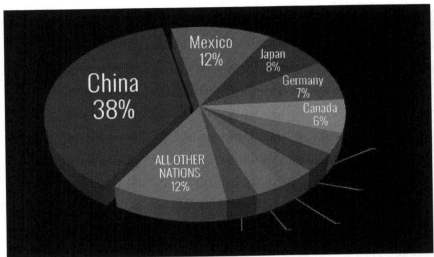

Source: Coalition for a Prosperous America, March 2017

Most people do not understand how trade deficits hurt them. They do not realize that when our country imports more goods than it exports, we go in debt as a country to pay for these goods. We then have to borrow money or increase taxes to have enough money to run our government. This is why we now have a nearly $20 trillion national debt. As individuals, we would soon go bankrupt if we did not earn enough money to pay our bills and had to keep borrowing money, but the government can just keep printing money. The problem with printing more money is that the value of our money keeps going down, so each of us has to work harder to make more money to try to keep our pay equal to what we earned previously.

Our Gross Domestic Product (GDP) equals the sum of Consumption, Investment, Government Procurement, and Net Exports (Exports – Imports). When your Net Exports are a deficit it has a detrimental effect on the economy. According to the Coalition for a Prosperous America (CPA), "the annual trade deficit has reduced each year's GDP by some 3% to 5.5% each year, and these reductions compound over time…Our 41 years of trade deficits have hollowed out our manufacturing and agricultural industries. Since the year 2000, the US has lost 28% of its manufacturing employment."

Source: Coalition for a Prosperous America analysis of Census trade data

Our efforts to keep our wages of equal value have not succeeded because the "NAFTA at 20" report states, "NAFTA has contributed to downward pressure on U.S. wages and growing income inequality." What this means is that as Americans lost their higher paying manufacturing jobs, they had to compete with the glut of other Americans for the non-offshorable, lower paying, low-skill jobs, in retail, hospitality, and food service. "According to the U.S. Bureau of Labor Statistics, two out of every three displaced manufacturing workers who were rehired in 2012 experienced a wage reduction, most of them taking a pay cut of greater than 20 percent." The result is an increasing gap between the rich and the poor and a shrinking middle class.

Manufacturing jobs are the foundation of the middle class; these jobs raised the average daily wage[50] between 1900 and 2000 from $2.50 a day to $96.00 a day. Since the year 2000, U. S. wages have stagnated, and our middle class is diminishing, not growing. If we lose the majority of our manufacturing industry, we will lose our middle class.

We were supposed to realize the benefits of lower prices as consumers, but in contrast, the report states, "Despite a 188 percent rise in food imports from Canada and Mexico under NAFTA, the average nominal price of food in the United States has jumped 65 percent since the deal went into effect."

As a result, our "average annual U.S. agricultural trade deficit with Mexico and Canada under NAFTA stands at $800 million, more than twice the pre-NAFTA level." American ranchers and cattlemen have been hurt by the 130 percent increase of beef imports from Mexico and Canada since NAFTA took effect, "and today U.S. consumption of 'NAFTA' beef tops $1.3 billion annually." U.S. food processors moved to Mexico to take advantage of low wages, resulting in a loss of jobs for Americans at U. S. food processing plants.

The report was a revelation to me about an unintended consequence of NAFTA — the dramatic increase of illegal immigrants to the U. S. in the past 20 years. According to the report, the increased export of subsidized U. S. corn to Mexico resulted in the destruction of "…the livelihoods of more than one million Mexican *campesino* farmers and about 1.4 million additional Mexican workers whose livelihoods depended on agriculture."

The report quotes an exposé, "Trade Secrets," by John Judis in the April 9, 2008 issue of New Republic,[51] which stated. "Wages dropped so precipitously that today the income of a farm laborer is one-third that of what it was before NAFTA. As jobs disappeared and wages sank, many of these rural Mexicans emigrated, swelling the ranks of the 12 million illegal immigrants living incognito and competing for low-wage jobs in the United States."

As a result, "The desperate migration of those displaced from Mexico's rural economy pushed down wages in Mexico's border maquiladora factory zone and contributed to a doubling of Mexican immigration to the United States following NAFTA's implementation."

Prior to NAFTA, jobs at maquiladora factories were responsible for a growing middle class in cities such as Tijuana and Tecate in Baja California, Mexico. The report states that "Real wages in Mexico have fallen significantly below pre-NAFTA levels as price increases for basic consumer goods have exceeded wage increases. A minimum wage earner in Mexico today can buy 38 percent fewer consumer goods as on the day that NAFTA took effect."

The lower wages at Mexican maquiladoras since NAFTA explains why Mexico has been recently benefiting from "near sourcing," which is returning manufacturing from China where wages have risen 15-20% year over year for the past five years. Taking into consideration the other costs and hidden costs of doing business offshore that comprise a Total Cost of Ownership analysis, Mexico is now more competitive than the coastal areas of China's manufacturing industry.

Of course, the influx of illegal immigrants from Mexico is another factor in the downward pressure on wages in the United States. Today,[52] only 1.9 million hourly workers make $20 per hour, which is a marker for jobs that provide a middle-class standard of living, down 60% since 1979, according to the Bureau of Labor Statistics.

I have personal experience with the consequences of NAFTA because I have been selling the fabrication services of American companies to manufacture mechanical parts for Original Equipment Manufacturers (OEMs) for 32 years. My sales territory has included northern Baja California, Mexico as I speak, read, and write Spanish. My husband and I are sole proprietors of a company dba ElectroFab Sales under contract to be independent sales representatives for an average of 10 companies on a commission only basis. We pay our own business expenses and taxes.

Prior to NAFTA, American companies were required to have "twin plants," which could be an office on the U.S. side of the border and an assembly plant on the other side of the border in Baja California, Mexico. After NAFTA, the requirement for an office on this side of the border was eliminated, and engineering and purchasing personnel were moved to the Mexican plant. At first, American workers crossed the border to work at the Mexican plant, but over the years, Mexican engineers and buyers replaced the Americans working at these plants.

The ability to meet with employees at the Mexican plants without an appointment changed to the requirement of having written proof of an appointment with a specific person at a company that one had to show to the Mexican border personnel before one is allowed into Mexico. You also had to purchase a Foreign National (FN) certificate to do business in Mexico ($22 per day). About 10 years ago, a passport also became required to do business in Mexico. It is now not worth my time to sell in Baja California, Mexico when it costs me $22 for a FN certificate for a day and a minimum of $33 for car insurance for one day to see one person. In addition, the wait to get back across the border became so long that one appointment in Mexico took half a day.

This has caused my company a loss of potential business worth thousands of dollars based on the business I once had in Baja California, Mexico.

Opponents of NAFTA and other free trade agreements point out that the "giant sucking sound" predicted by presidential candidate Ross Perot in the 1992 election came true as we've lost more than six million manufacturing jobs since 1994. His prediction came true as we lost about a half a million between 1994 and 1999. However, we have lost another 5.5 million jobs since the year 2000 when China was granted permanent Most Favored Nation status (term changed to Normal Trade Relations in 1998), paving the way for China's accession to the World Trade Organization in December 2000. It hasn't been Mexico or Canada that benefited from the majority of these lost U. S. jobs -- it has been China.

In fact, Mexico has also lost jobs to China over the past ten years. The Mexican shoe industry was the hardest hit by competition from Chinese companies, but many decorative products for the home and garden that were once made in Mexico are now made in China.

Retail stores in Mexico are now just as full of "made in China" products as are retail stores in the United States. Many American companies that set up maquiladoras in Mexico closed them and set up manufacturing in China. Japanese and Korean companies became the major owners of the maquiladoras plants in Baja California, Mexico as companies from these two countries have been the most reluctant to set up manufacturing in China because of wanting to be closer to the U. S. market and wanting to take advantage of the trading benefits of being located in a NAFTA partner country.

NAFTA Renegotiation

Now that the Trump Administration has opened consideration of re-negotiating NAFTA, the Coalition for a Prosperous America (CPA) submitted written and in-person testimony to the U. S. Trade Representative on NAFTA Negotiations on Docket No. USTR 2017-0006 on June 12, 2017, which stated in part: "NAFTA...has caused significant economic harm to the United States. America's trade deficit with both NAFTA signatory countries has mushroomed and US wage growth has stagnated for non-college educated workers. This result shows that mere reciprocal tariff reduction, or even disproportionate tariff reduction by Mexico, does not automatically translate into improved trade performance.

Currency manipulation/misalignment and global consumption tax distortions are more meaningful to US trade deficits and economic health than trade deals and should be addressed first. America's overall objectives for NAFTA renegotiation should include (a) reducing the trade deficit, (b) growing the US goods production base, (c) improving wages and (d) growing our economy...The United States should not be afraid to walk away from and terminate NAFTA if our national economic interests are not achieved."

On September 8, 2017, Daniel DiMicco, Chairman (Chairman Emeritus, Nucor Corp.) Brian O'Shaughnessy, Vice Chairman (Revere Copper Products, Inc.), and Michael Stumo, Chief Executive Office sent a letter[53] to Robert Lighthizer, U.S. Trade Representative, which proposed the following changes to NAFTA

(Recommendations not mentioned in other sections of this book are quoted in full):

"**1.** Reduce Bilateral Imbalances...

2. Effective Currency Manipulation and Misalignment Remedies:

2.1. Market Access Charge in Implementing Legislation...

2.2. Countervailing Currency Intervention in Implementing Legislation...

3. Strengthen Rules of Origin...

4. Reinstate Country of Origin Labeling (COOL)...

5. Eliminate Investor State Dispute Settlement: NAFTA should allow state-to-state dispute resolution. However, it should not give special preference to investor interests through the investor-state dispute settlement process (ISDS). ISDS, which is currently enabled through Chapter 11, Part B of NAFTA, should be eliminated. Domestic courts are sufficient for most disputes and have longstanding rules of evidence, procedure and rights of appeal. Domestic judges are subject to ethics and impartiality rules which do not exist for ISDS tribunals. Foreign investors, among the panoply of stakeholder interests, are not entitled to special treatment in the form of a direct right of action before special tribunals that are unaccountable to any government body.

6. Automaticity of Enforcement: Failure to enforce trade agreements undermines their effectiveness. Trade enforcement should be more automatic and certain. Automaticity is an automatic chain of events that ensues upon the finding of a trade infraction. Reluctance to initiate complaints for fear of foreign policy, economic or business reprisal is common. A new NAFTA should include automaticity in trade enforcement and remedy prescription as much as possible. Remedies should be prescribed to neutralize or punish violations that are economically calculable (ex. tariff, quota, or currency violations) and those that are difficult to calculate (ex. labor or environmental violations or failure to submit notifications).

7. Eliminate Domestic Procurement Chapter: All NAFTA signatories should retain their sovereign right to manage fiscal and economic policy by preferring domestic products and services in government procurement. Fiscal stimulus efforts lose effectiveness when government procurement demand leaks to non-domestic sources. The theory of reciprocity arising from liberalizing government procurement has failed and shows no signs of becoming reality. The US government provides far more access to foreign products than US companies gain elsewhere, in part because the US is the largest consumer in the world. The domestic procurement chapter should be eliminated from NAFTA.

8. Improve Wages and Labor Standards: NAFTA devalued US wages and failed to increase Mexican wage rates. Stubborn wage differentials are a substantial cause of the US bilateral deficit with Mexico and prevent benefits from accruing to any signatory. A new NAFTA should provide a wage floor – sufficient to achieve a decent standard of living - for workers making products exported to NAFTA countries. It should include enforceable labor provisions in the body of the agreement to ensure that low wages and lax labor standards and enforcement by contracting countries do not result in hidden subsidies to the detriment of US-based workers and producers.

9. Food, Product and Highway Safety Standards: Any new NAFTA must ensure full compliance with existing US food and product safety and quality standards and must not inhibit changes to or improvements in US standards. The standards must be effectively enforced at US ports with full inspection. Similarly, the United States must not trade away highway safety, and the cross-border services chapter should exclude long-haul trucking from national treatment and market access coverage.

10. Sunset NAFTA in 10 years: Trade negotiators agree to language based upon expectations and judgment in pursuit of national goals.

However, goals may not be achieved or expectations may not be met. Just as business contracts do not last forever, neither should agreements between countries. Therefore, it is prudent to make such agreements time-limited to ensure that they continue to provide balanced benefits as circumstances change. If a balance does not materialize, the agreement should be renegotiated or discontinued. NAFTA should be sunsetted in 10 years, subject to renegotiation and renewal. Renewal must not occur if the balance of benefits cannot be restored.

11. Perishable and Cyclical Products' Remedies: The WTO and past trade promotion authority statutes recognize that producers of perishable and seasonal agricultural products are particularly susceptible to trade surges arising from over-production, adverse weather or other causes. Short shelf life and/or short selling season characteristics result in producers being unable to store the products until prices rise. NAFTA should provide immediate and automatic relief based upon price and/or quantity measures which are necessary to prevent serious industry harm in these sectors. It should also allow signatory countries to manage supply to preserve industry health to the extent it does not create an undue trade advantage to the domestic industry.

12. Address Border Adjustable Taxes..."

EPI Report Claims U.S.-China Trade Deficit Cost 3.4 Million Jobs

On January 31, 2017, the Economic Policy Institute released a report,[54] "Growth in U.S.–China trade deficit between 2001 and 2015 cost 3.4 million jobs," written by Robert Scott.

Scott explained that when China entered into the World Trade Organization (WTO) in 2001, "it was supposed to bring it into compliance with an enforceable, rules-based regime that would require China to open its markets to imports from the United States and other nations by reducing Chinese tariffs and addressing nontariff barriers to trade."

However, Scott wrote, "China both subsidizes and dumps massive quantities of exports. Specifically, it blocks imports, pirates software and technology from foreign producers, manipulates its currency, invests in massive amounts of excess production capacity in a range of basic industries, often through state owned enterprises (SOEs) (investments that lead to dumping), and operates as a refuse lot for carbon and other industrial pollutants. China has also engaged in extensive and sustained currency manipulation over the past two decades, resulting in persistent currency misalignments."

As a result, "China's trade-distorting practices, aided by China's currency manipulation and misalignment, and its suppression of wages and labor rights, resulted in a flood of dumped and subsidized imports that greatly exceed the growth of U.S. exports to China."

He added, "the WTO agreement spurred foreign direct investment (FDI) in Chinese enterprises and the outsourcing of U.S. manufacturing plants, which has expanded China's manufacturing sector at the expense of the United States, thereby affecting the trade balance between the two countries. Finally, the core of the agreement failed to include any protections to maintain or improve labor or environmental standards or to prohibit currency manipulation."

He explained, "Overall, the U.S. goods trade deficit with China rose from $83.0 billion in 2001 to $367.2 billion in 2015, an increase of $284.1 billion. Put another way, since China entered the WTO in 2001, the U.S. trade deficit with China has increased annually by $20.3 billion, or 11.2 percent, on average.

Between 2008 and 2015, the U.S. goods trade deficit with China increased $100.8 billion. This 37.9 percent increase occurred despite the collapse in world trade between 2008 and 2009 caused by the Great Recession and a decline in the U.S. trade deficit with the rest of the world of 30.2 percent between 2008 and 2015."

Previously, the U. S. had a trade surplus in advanced technology products, but now we have lost that comparative advantage. Scott stated, "Global trade in advanced technology products... is instead dominated by China. This broad category of high-end technology products includes the more advanced elements of the computer and electronic parts industry as well as other sectors such as biotechnology, life sciences, aerospace, and nuclear technology. In 2015, the United States had a $120.7 billion deficit in advanced technology products with China, and this deficit was responsible for 32.9 percent of the total U.S.–China goods trade deficit. In contrast, the United States had a $28.9 billion surplus in advanced technology products with the rest of the world in 2015."

Scott stated, "Due to the trade deficit with China, 3.4 million jobs were lost between 2001 and 2015, including 1.3 million jobs lost since the first year of the Great Recession in 2008. Nearly three-fourths (74.3 percent) of the jobs lost between 2001 and 2015 were in manufacturing (2.6 million manufacturing jobs displaced). After explaining how EPI calculated the loss of jobs due to the U.S.-China trade deficit, he wrote, "U.S. exports to China in 2001 supported 171,900 jobs, but U.S. imports displaced production that would have supported 1,129,600 jobs. Therefore, the $83.0 billion trade deficit in 2001 displaced 957,700 jobs in that year. Net job displacement rose to 3,077,000 jobs in 2008 and 4,401,000 jobs in 2015.

That means that since China's entry into the WTO in 2001 and through 2015, the increase in the U.S.–China trade deficit eliminated or displaced 3,443,300 U.S. jobs...the U.S. trade deficit with China increased by $100.8 billion (or 37.9 percent) between 2008 and 2015. During that period, the number of jobs displaced increased by 43.0 percent."

Scott states, "The growing trade deficit with China has cost jobs in all 50 states and the District of Columbia, and in every congressional district in the United States."

In summarizing the lost wages from the increasing trade deficit with China, Scott stated, "U.S. workers who were directly displaced by trade with China between 2001 and 2011 lost a collective $37.0

billion in wages as a result of accepting lower-paying jobs in nontraded industries or industries that export to China assuming, conservatively, that those workers are re-employed in nontraded goods industries..."

In addition, Scott wrote, "According to the most recent Bureau of Labor Statistics survey covering displaced workers (BLS 2016b), more than one-third (36.7 percent) of manufacturing workers displaced from January 2013 to December 2015 were still not working, including 21.7 percent who were not in the labor force, i.e., no longer even looking for work."

Scott concludes, "The rapid growth of U.S. imports of computer and electronic parts from China also represents a threat to national security because it is connected to the outsourcing of U.S. defense products, as explained by Brigadier General John Adams (2015). The outsourcing of the defense industry makes the United States vulnerable to disruption of supply chains for key missile and communications components. Outsourcing has also reduced the quality of military equipment: a congressional report found nearly 1 million counterfeit components in the supply chain for "critical" defense systems (Senate Armed Services Committee 2012). And outsourcing has eroded the capacity of the defense industrial base for cost innovation, knowledge generation, and support for domestic employment (Alliance for American Manufacturing 2016).

However, the most serious consequences of the U.S.-China trade deficit are:

- The United States net international investment position (NIIP) declined from -$2.3 trillion in 2001, before China joined the WTO, to $-7.2 trillion in 2015 (BEA 2016b).
- Each year that the United States runs a trade deficit is a year that it must borrow from abroad to finance this excess of consumption over domestic production.
- The United States ran a trade surplus in nearly every year between 1946 and 1975, and by 1975 had become the largest net lender in the world.

- The United States has run increasingly large trade deficits in every year since 1976, and has become the world's largest net debtor.

In summary, Scott stated, "The U.S.–China trade relationship needs to undergo a fundamental change. Addressing unfair trade, weak labor, and environmental standards in China, and ending currency manipulation and misalignment should be our top trade and economic priorities with China. It is time for the United States to respond to the growing chorus of calls from economists, workers, businesses, and Congress (Scott 2014b) and take action to stop unfair trade and illegal currency manipulation by China and other countries."

A more recent warning came in an email I received on June 13, 2017 from the American Alliance for Manufacturing by Brigadier General John Adams U.S. Army (Ret.): "There's now just one American smelter that can produce the high-purity aluminum needed for the F-35 fighter jet. There's now just one U.S. steel manufacturer who can make high-end grain-oriented electrical steel, essential for transmission and distribution transformers for all types of energy. Steel and aluminum are vital for America's national defense and critical infrastructure. But a flood of unfairly traded imports has led to dozens of plant closures and tens of thousands of layoffs. We do not want to have to rely on potential adversaries like Russia or China to get the steel and aluminum we need to build our aircraft carriers, battleships, tanks and fighter jets.

American companies operate in a free marketplace. They can't compete against the Russian or Chinese government! Many steel and aluminum makers have closed plants, laid-off workers or gone out of business entirely.

If we don't step up, America's entire steel and aluminum industries could disappear. We'd have to rely on Russia and China for our national defense needs." President Trump and Congress need to protect our steel and aluminum industries with countervailing duties."

Would New Trade Agreements Benefit Americans?

On February 4, 2016, President Obama signed the Trans Pacific Partnership Agreement (TPP) on behalf of the United States. It was waiting for approval from Congress until January 21, 2017 when the first action President Donald Trump took was to withdraw the U. S. from the TPP.

The TPP agreement was between the United States and 11 other countries around the Pacific Rim: Australia, Brunei, Canada, Chile, Japan, Malaysia, Mexico, New Zealand, Peru, Singapore, and Vietnam. But, it was a "docking agreement" so other countries could be added without the approval of Congress. India, China, and Korea have expressed interest in joining the TPP.

The TPP **was** misleadingly called a trade agreement when in fact it was an expansive system of enforceable global government. Only five of its 26 chapters actually covered trade issues, like cutting border taxes ("tariffs") or lifting quotas that limit consumer choice. In reality, most of the Agreement would have imposed one-size-fits all international rules to which U.S. federal, state and local law would have had to conform.

Our Congressional representatives had no involvement in writing the TPP – it was written by the staff of the U. S. Trade Representative office, with over 600 corporate advisors (think corporate lawyers) helping them draft it. It contained more than 5,500 pages, and no member of Congress could view it as it was being negotiated until late 2014.

The major problem with the TPP and any future trade agreement proposed is that according to the rules established by the Trade Promotion Authority (TPA) that passed Congress narrowly in June 2015, Congress would only be allowed 45 days for committee analysis after the bill is introduced, only 15 days after that is completed to bring it up for a floor vote, and only 20 hours of debate in the House and Senate. The TPA does not allow any amendments, filibuster, or cloture. The TPA is in effect until July 1, 2018, but may be extended by Congress to July 1, 2021.

Notice that the TPP is called an "Agreement," as was NAFTA, the CAFTA, the KORUS, and every other trade deal of the past 22 years. The purpose for this term is to get around the requirement of the two-thirds vote of the Senate to approve a Treaty that is required under Article 1, Section 8 of the Treaty clause in the U. S. Constitution. The TPP and any other agreement negotiated under the duration of the Trade Promotion Authority requires only a simple majority vote (50% + one.)

We must make sure that no future trade agreement includes one of the worst provisions of the TPP: ***Investor-State Dispute Settlement (ISDS)***

Lori Wallach of Public Citizen wrote several articles warning about the dangers of the *Investor-State Dispute Settlement (ISDS* chapter of the TPP that is also included in NAFTA, CAFTA, and KORUS). According to her review[55], foreign firms gain the following privileges:

- Risks and costs of offshoring to low wage countries eliminated
- Special guaranteed "minimum standard of treatment" for relocating firms
- Compensation for loss of "expected future profits" from health, labor environmental, laws (indirect or "regulatory" takings compensation)
- Right to move capital without limits
- New rights cover vast definition of investment: intellectual property, permits, derivatives
- Ban performance requirements, domestic content rules. Absolute ban, not only when applied to investors from signatory countries

Ms. Wallach opined that U.S. multinational corporations have the goal of imposing on more countries a set of extreme foreign investor privileges and rights and their private enforcement through the notorious "investor-state" system. "This system elevates individual corporations and investors to equal standing with each TPP signatory country's government- and above all of us citizens." This would enable "foreign investors to skirt domestic courts and laws, and sue governments directly before tribunals of three private sector lawyers operating under World Bank and UN rules to demand **taxpayer compensation** for any domestic law that investors believe will diminish their 'expected future profits.' Over $3 billion has been paid to foreign investors under U.S. trade and investment pacts, while over $14 billion in claims are pending under such deals, primarily targeting environmental, energy, and public health policies."

Trade Agreements Endanger our National Sovereignty

To implement the free trade agreement (FTA), Congress is asked to surrender its responsibility under Section 1, Article 8 of the Constitution to regulate commerce with foreign nations, and grant the president extra-constitutional "Trade Promotion Authority" (TPA) to negotiate final agreements.

Under the TPA fast-track authority, there is no provision for Congress to modify the agreement by submitting amendments. Fast-track authority also treats the FTA as if it were trade legislation being negotiated by the executive branch. The purpose is to assure foreign partners that the FTA, once signed, will not be changed during the legislative process.

United Nations and World Bank Tribunals Would Replace U.S. Courts – the "Investment" chapter would submit the U.S. to the jurisdiction of international tribunals established under the auspices of the United Nations or World Bank. It would shift decisions over the payment of U.S. tax dollars away from Congress and outside of the federal court system established by Article III of the Constitution to the authority of international tribunals. These UN and World Bank tribunals do not apply U.S. law, but rather international law set in the agreement. These tribunals would judge whether foreign investors operating *within* the U.S. are being provided the proper property rights protections. The standard for property rights protection would not be those established by the U.S. Constitution as interpreted by the U.S. Supreme Court, but rather international property rights standards, as interpreted by an international tribunal.

This is why Americans for Limited Government[56] (AFLG) opposed the TPP. AFLG is a lobbying and advocacy organization which describes itself as a non-partisan, nationwide network committed to advancing free-market reforms, private property rights and core American liberties President Bill Wilson states, "This new trade agreement will place domestic U.S. firms that do not do business overseas at a competitive disadvantage. Foreign firms under this trade pact could conceivably appeal federal regulatory and court rulings against them to an international tribunal with the apparent authority to overrule our sovereignty. If foreign companies want to do business in America, they should have to follow the same rules as everyone else. Obama is negotiating a trade pact that would constitute a judicial authority higher than even the U.S. Supreme Court that could overrule federal court rulings applying U.S. law to foreign companies. That is unconstitutional. The U.S. cannot be allowed to enter a treaty that would abrogate our Constitution."

Buy American Act Null and Void

The procurement chapter of the TPP would have made the Buy America Act essentially Null and Void. It would have adversely affected those businesses that sell to the government, whether it be local, state, or federal because the U.S. would have to agree to waive Buy America procurement policies for all companies operating in TPP countries. This means that all companies operating in any country signing the agreement would be provided access equal to domestic firms to bid on government procurement contracts at the local, state, and federal level.

There are many companies that survived the recession and continue in business today because of the Buy American provisions for government procurement, especially defense and military. This procurement provision could be a deathblow for companies that rely on defense and military contracts, such as the U. S. printed circuit board industry. Most of the commercial printed circuit manufacturing was already offshored to China and South Korea years ago. However, it would also affect procurement for infrastructure projects, such as bridges and freeways, as well as construction of local, state, or federal facilities.

Product Labeling could be Made Illegal: If you desire to know if your food is safe, then you won't like the fact that "Country of Origin," "Non-GMO," or "Organic" labeling could be viewed as a "barrier to trade" and thus be deemed illegal.

Many countries are farm-raising seafood in polluted water using chemicals and antibiotics prohibited in the U. S. Farmed seafood from Malaysia, Vietnam, and China is being raised in water quality equivalent to U. S. sewers. Today, the FDA only inspects 2% of seafood, fruits and vegetables, and the USDA only inspects 4-5% of meat & poultry. Increased imports of food from TPP trading partners could swamp FDA and USDA inspections, so that even less is inspected.: Country of Origin Labeling, labeling of GMO products, and "organic" labeling could be made illegal because of being viewed as an "illegal trade barrier." Even the health warnings on tobacco products could be viewed as an "illegal trade barrier."

Bill Bullard, CEO of R-CALF USA (Ranchers-Cattlemen Action Legal Fund, United Stockgrowers of America) stated[57] "that fast food restaurants are not required to disclose the origins of their beef and even when restaurants say the beef is "U.S. Inspected," it is as likely as not to be imported." When we were in Washington, D. C. together last month, Mr. Bullard told me that the increased importation of sheep and lamb from Australia and New Zealand could wipe out the American sheep ranching industry.

Trade Agreements Can Increase Immigration: If you are concerned about jobs for yourself or family members, then you won't like the fact that trade agreements may increase "the number of L1 visas and the number of tourist visas, which can be used for business purposes." For example, under the TPP, any service provider (phone service, security, engineers, lawyers, architects or any company providing a service) could enter into a TPP partner country and provide that service. Companies would not have to hire Americans or pay American wages – they could bring in own workers and pay less than the American minimum wage.

Trade Agreements Increase Job Losses in Key Industries: If the TPP had been approved, The Center for Automotive Research projected[58] a loss of 91,500 U. S. auto jobs to Japan with the reduction of 225,000 automobiles produced in the U. S. And, the National Council of Textile Industries projected[59] a loss of 522,000 jobs in the U. S. textile and related sectors to Vietnam. Future unilateral agreements with Japan or Vietnam could cause this same amount of job loss.

Trade Agreements May Reduce Reshoring: Because trade agreements reduce tariffs in trading partner countries, it could make the Total Cost of Ownership analysis to return manufacturing to America from some countries more difficult to justify. The high U. S. dollar has already diminished reshoring in 2013 – 2015, so Harry Moser, Founder and President of the Reshoring Initiative, told me last year that "The combination of the high USD and TPP will reduce the rate of reshoring by an estimated 20 – 50%."

What is missing from our Trade Agreements

None of our current trade agreements have addressed the "predatory mercantilist" actions that our current trading partners are using that have created the enormous trade deficit. These policies are: currency manipulation, "border adjustable" taxes called Value Added Taxes (VATs), which are a tariff by another name, government subsidies for State-Owned Enterprises, and "product dumping" by manufacturers in one country at below their cost to produce to destroy competition in another country.

"Over[60] 20 countries, representing 1/3 of global GDP, are engaged in currency wars" by undervaluing their currency. These governments work with their central banks to manipulate the currency value in order to provide a competitive advantage to boost exports and impede imports. China's currency is estimated to be 25-40% undervalued. As Paul Volcker, former Secretary of the Treasury, has explained, "In five minutes, exchange rates can wipe out what it took trade negotiators ten years to accomplish." Foreign government intervention in foreign exchange markets is manipulation, not free trade.

Value Added Taxes (VATs) range from a low of 10% to a high of 24%, averaging 17% worldwide. The U. S. is one of a handful of 159 other countries that do not charge a VAT. This means that American products that are exported are an average of 17% more expensive when imported by a country that adds a VAT. In reverse, foreign imports are an average of 17% less expensive because the U. S. does not charge a VAT. Thus, we reduce tariffs through our trade agreements only to have our trading partners add a tariff by another name to the cost of our products that we export. This gives other countries an unfair competitive advantage in the global marketplace.

 We have all read news stories about "product dumping" cases against U. S. industries, such as the tires, steel, and solar panel industries. With regard to government subsidies, the best example is how Foxconn was able to get Apple's business for manufacturing the iPhone, iPad and now the iWatch because the Chinese government gave them the land and built the building for them.

Space doesn't allow me to cover all of the things that are wrong with our current trade agreements with regard to non-trade issues, such as patent and copyright laws, land use, as well as policies concerning natural resources, the environment, labor laws, health care, energy and telecommunications.

Is there a Relationship Between our Trade Deficit and our National Debt?

So how do our trade deficits add to the national debt? One way is that many products, especially consumer products, which were previously made in the U. S., are now made in China or other Asian countries, so we are importing these products instead of exporting them to other countries. The offshoring of manufacturing of so many products has resulted in the loss 5.8 million American manufacturing jobs and the closure of over 57,000 manufacturing firms. These American workers and companies paid taxes that provided revenue to our government, so now we have less tax revenue and pay out benefits to unemployed workers, resulting in an escalating national debt.

As shown by the chart below, we now have a nearly $20 trillion national debt.

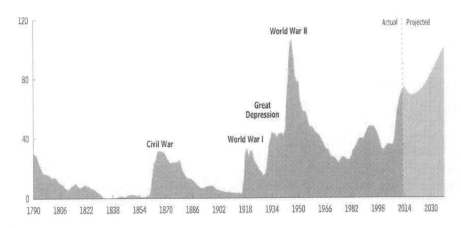

Source: http://en.wikipedia.org/wiki/National_debt_of_the_United_States#mediaviewer/File:Federal_Debt_Held_by_the_Public_1790-2013.png

Notice how it sharply ramps up starting in 2001. The recessions of 2001-2002 and 2008-2009 obviously played a significant factor in the increase in the national debt from $5.8 trillion in 2001[61] to its present level, because during recessions, there is a decrease in tax revenues and an increase in spending for unemployment benefits, food stamps, and other assistance, as well as spending on programs to attempt to stimulate the economy.

However, 2001 also coincides with the first full year of trade with China[62] under the rules of World Trade Organization after "Congress agreed to permanent normal trade relations (PNTR) status," which "President Clinton signed into law on October 10, 2000," paving "the way for China's accession to the WTO in December 2000."

Our balance of payments indebtedness for trade and the additional cost to the government paid by taxpayers for these benefits have resulted in our escalating national debt. The cheaper China price of goods that we import instead of producing here in the U. S. results in a cost to society as a whole. We need to ask ourselves: Is the China price worth the cost to society?

I say a resounding NO! We need to stop shooting ourselves in the foot. We need to stop benefiting the one percent of large multinational corporations to the detriment of the 99% of smaller American companies.

In conclusion, the effect on the United States of this unbalanced trade has been:

- Loss of >600,000 mfg. jobs from NAFTA
- Loss of 3.2 million mfg. jobs between 2000 – 2010 from China's entry into WTO
- Loss of >60,000 mfg. jobs since Korea-US Agreement went into effect in 2012
- Loss of an estimated 3.4 million U. S. service & call center jobs since 2000
- Loss of an estimated 700,000 public sector jobs (2008-2013)
- Racked up cumulative trade deficit of $12 trillion in goods (average $500 billion each year) since 1994

As a result, we now have the worst trade deficit in U. S. history, and we are off to just as high a deficit for 2017.

America is at a crossroads. We can either continue down the path of increasing trade deficits and increasing national debt by allowing anything mined, manufactured, grown, or serviced to be outsourced to countries with predatory trade policies. Or, we can forge a new path by developing and implementing a national strategy to win the international competition for good jobs, sustained economic growth, and strong domestic supply chains.

In conclusion, we can clearly see from the well-documented evidence that trade agreements have not benefited the American people. It may have benefited American corporations that expanded their global sales or moved manufacturing to other countries to increase their profits. However, I am sure that none of the American company owners of the more than 60,000 manufacturing firms that have closed since 1994 or the nearly six million American workers who lost their jobs would say they benefited from these trade agreements.

Chapter 4

Reshoring is the best way to rebuild American Manufacturing

When I first started talking about saving America manufacturing and returning manufacturing to America in 2009 after the first edition of my book, *Can American Manufacturing Be Saved? Why we should and how we can*, came out, I was met with a great deal of skepticism. Some typical comments were: "I don't think we can." "It's too late." "I wish we could." "We need to." Very few thought we actually could return manufacturing to America.

The picture changed in only a few years. At the 2013 Del Mar Electronics and Design Show (DMEDS) in San Diego, CA, a very successful fellow manufacturers' sales rep, stopped me in the parking lot and said, "I used to think you were nuts, but you were right. Manufacturing is returning to America." While this manufacturers' representative sales agency is headquartered in southern California, it has affiliate companies in Mexico, Malaysia, China (Beijing, Shanghai, and Shenzhen) and Taiwan (Taipei and Hsinchu) so I did not take this admission lightly.

What happened to change the picture? Returning manufacturing back to America through "reshoring" has grown increasingly popular in recent years. This ended the wait for government to do something about the offshoring problem and is increasing manufacturing jobs.

In 2009, a survey by Archstone Consulting revealed that 60 percent of manufacturers use rudimentary total cost models and thus ignore 20 percent of their cost of offshoring. But if a manufacturer is not accounting for 20 percent of its cost, offshoring may not actually be its most economical decision. In tough economic times and with stiff global competition, no company can afford this mistake.

The concept of Total Cost of Ownership was originated by the Gartner Group, and there are a number of different methodologies and software tools for calculating TCO for various industries, products, and services. The brief definition of TCO is: an estimate of the direct *and* indirect costs related to the purchase of a part, sub-assembly, assembly, or product. However, a thorough TCO includes much more than the purchase price of the goods paid to the supplier. For the purchase of manufactured goods, it should also include all of the other factors associated with the purchase of the goods, such as:

- Geographical location
- Transportation alternatives
- Inventory costs and control
- Quality control
- Reserve capacity
- Responsiveness
- Technological depth

My definition of TCO also includes the "hidden costs of doing business offshore," such as Intellectual Property theft, danger of counterfeit parts, the risk factors of political instability, natural disasters, riots, strikes, technological depth and reserve capacity of suppliers, and currency fluctuation.

In April 2010, Harry Moser, retired president of GF AgieCharmilles LLC, a leading machine tool supplier in Lincolnshire, Illinois, founded the Reshoring Initiative (www.ReshoreNow.org), providing the right tool at the right time to facilitate returning manufacturing to America with the creation of the Total Cost of Ownership™ worksheet calculator spreadsheet.

Mr. Moser's TCO spreadsheet actually includes calculations for these "hidden costs of doing business offshore, such as Intellectual Property risk, political instability risk, effect on innovation, product liability risk, annual wage inflation, and currency appreciation.

When I wrote an article in August 2010, titled "Why it's important to understand Total Cost of Ownership," Mr. Moser contacted me and told me that I was writing about what he just started. He trained me in his worksheet and authorized me to be his West Coast authorized speaker on behalf of the Reshoring Initiative.

Since then, I've given presentations on returning manufacturing to America to dozens of professional groups and several southern California chapters of APICS, composed of supply chain/logistics people. I learned that in the 13th edition of APICS' dictionary, the definition of Total Cost of Ownership is: "In supply chain management, the total cost of ownership of the supply delivery system is the sum of all the costs associated with every activity of the supply stream." This is a good definition, not as complete as mine or Mr. Moser's, but good. If supply chain personnel had utilized this definition in the past decade, a great deal of offshoring would never have occurred.

To help companies make better sourcing decisions, the Reshoring Initiative provides the Total Cost of Ownership™ spreadsheet for FREE to help manufacturers calculate the real impact offshoring has on their bottom line. The website provides an online library of more than 3,000 articles about cases of successful reshoring. And it provides publicity to promote the reshoring trend. In cooperation with the Reshoring Initiative, the Contract Manufacturing Purchasing Fairs staged by the National Tooling and Machining Association and the Precision Metalforming Association help manufacturers find competitive U.S. sources.

The Reshoring Initiative shows companies how outsourcing within the U.S. can reduce their total cost of ownership (TCO) for parts and tooling and offer a host of other benefits. It documents the benefits of sourcing in the U.S. for large manufacturers and helps suppliers convince their U.S. customers to source locally.

The Reshoring Initiative is supported by major organizations and companies, such as the Association for Manufacturing Excellence, the Association for Manufacturing Technology, Sescoi, GF AgieCharmilles, the National Tooling and Machining Association, the Swiss Machine Tool Society, Mazak, Big Kaiser Precision Tooling, and dozens of other companies.

Reshoring enables manufacturing companies to accomplish a number of things. It reduces product "pipeline" problems and surge inventory impacts on just-in-time operations. It improves the quality and consistency of products. It helps cluster manufacturing near R&D facilities, making innovation easier. And it reduces intellectual-property theft risk and regulatory compliance risk.

In 2011, the Boston Consulting Group's 2011 released a report[63] that there will be a convergence in the total costs between China and the U. S. by 2015. This report was very controversial at the time, and very few thought that their prediction would come true. However, the very next year, the results of February 2012 survey[64] from the Boston Consulting Group (BCG), showed that 37 percent of U.S. manufacturers with sales above $1 billion said they were considering shifting some production from China to the United States, and of the very biggest firms, with sales above $10 billion, 48% were considering reshoring. The factors they pointed to were not only that wages and benefits were rising in China, but the fact that China was also enacting stricter labor laws and experiencing more frequent labor disputes and strikes.

According to BCG, pay and benefits for the average Chinese factory worker rose by 10% a year between 2000 and 2005 and speeded up to 19% a year between 2005 and 2010. Wages were predicted to rise by 60% in 2013 after additional strikes.

Six years later, there is still some debate about how much reshoring is actually taking place, but there is no doubt it is happening, especially in the seven tipping-point industries that the Boston Consulting Group predicted[65] would reshore: transportation goods, appliances and electrical equipment, furniture, plastic and rubber products, machinery, fabricated metal products, and computers and electronics.

For example, we've read[66] about General Electric reshoring appliances such as water heaters, washing machines, and refrigerators to a factory outside of Louisville Kentucky in

Appliance Park and Caterpillar opening a new factory in Texas to make excavators. And, yes, even furniture manufacturing is coming back. Ashley Furniture and Lincolnton Furniture built new factories in North Carolina in 2013.

In 2013, there were numerous articles debating whether "reshoring" was a myth or really happening. For example, the cover article of the April 22, 2013 issue of *Time* magazine was "Made in USA – Manufacturing is Back — But Where are the Jobs?" The first page of the article is full of pictures of products that have returned from offshore, representing an unbelievable cross section of consumer goods, ranging from toys such as the Frisbee, Slinky, Hula Hoop, and Crayola crayons to electric mixers, barbecues, saws, hammers, and many more.

The reason the article posed the questions about how many jobs are being created by the return of manufacturing to America is that the manufacturing plants of the present and future have more machines and fewer workers than in the past. Robotics, automation, and Lean manufacturing are helping companies do more with fewer people, and the rapidly improving technology of additive manufacturing is changing the way parts are being made.

The article featured a glimpse of manufacturing's future in the stories of two companies:

- ExOne, near Pittsburgh, PA, providing Digital Part Materialization (DPM) that transforms engineering design files directly into fully functional objects using 3D printing machines
- GE's highly automated battery factory in Schenectady, NY.

ExOne needs only two workers and a design engineer per shift to support its 12 metal-printing machines. The GE plant produces Durathon sodium batteries that are large and powerful enough to power cell phone towers. Because of being highly automated, the plant employs only 370 high-tech workers in a 200,000-sq. ft. facility.

The article concluded with a quote from GE CEO Jeff Immelt: "Will U.S. manufacturing go from 9% to 30% of all jobs? That's unlikely. But could you see a steady increase in jobs over the next quarters and year? I think that will happen."

On the myth side of the debate, the 2012 Hackett Group's report[67], "Reshoring Global Manufacturing: Myths and Realities" by Michel Janssen, Erik Dorr and David P. Sievers
states, "By next year, China's cost advantage over manufacturers in industrialized nations and competing low-cost destinations will evaporate." However, they conclude that "few of the low-skill Chinese manufacturing jobs will ever return to advanced economies; most will simply move to other low-cost countries."

Using hard data from their 2012 Supply Chain Optimization study, they analyzed the trend in "reshoring" of manufacturing capacity, and their findings debunk the myth that manufacturing capacity is returning in a big way to Western countries as a result of rising costs in China. The report states, "The reality is that the net amount of capacity coming back barely offsets the amount that continues to be sent offshore."

Is Reshoring Increasing or Declining?

In December 2015, two conflicting reports were released, one by A.T. Kearney and one by the Boston Consulting Group. The A. T. Kearney report states that reshoring may be "over before it began," and the Boston Consulting Group report states that it is increasing. Why the difference in opinion and who is right?

This was the second report[68] by A. T. Kearney, in which their "U.S. Reshoring Index shows that, for the fourth consecutive year, reshoring of manufacturing activities to the United States has once again failed to keep up with offshoring. This time the index has dropped to −115, down from −30 in 2014, and it represents the largest year-over-year decrease in the past 10 years."

In fact, they conclude that "the rate of reshoring actually lagged that of offshoring between 2009 and 2013, as the growth of overall domestic U.S. manufacturing activity failed to keep pace with the import of offshore manufactured goods over the five-year period. The one exception was 2011."

The authors of the A. T. Kearney report identify the two main factors contributing to the drop in the reshoring index to be "lackluster domestic manufacturing growth and the resilience of the offshore manufacturing sector."

On the other hand, the Boston Consulting Group survey[69] results showed that "Thirty-one percent of respondents to BCG's fourth annual survey of senior U.S.-based manufacturing executives at companies with at least $1 billion in annual revenues said that their companies are most likely to add production capacity in the U.S. within five years for goods sold in the U.S., while 20% said they are most likely to add capacity in China...The share of executives saying that their companies are actively reshoring production increased by 9% since 2014 and by about 250% since 2012. This suggests that companies that were considering reshoring in the past three years are now taking action. By a two-to-one margin, executives said they believe that reshoring will help create U.S. jobs at their companies rather than lead to a net loss of jobs."

The difference of opinion is based on different data. A. T. Kearney notes that "The manufacturing import ratio is calculated by dividing manufactured goods imports from 14 Asian markets [list of countries] by U. S. domestic gross output of manufactured goods. The U. S. reshoring index is the year-over-year change in the manufacturing ratio."

In contrast, the Boston Consulting Group data is based on "an annual online survey of senior-level, U.S.-based manufacturing executives. This year's survey elicited 263 responses. The responses were limited to one per company...Respondents are decision makers in companies with more than $1 billion in annual revenues, across a wide range of industries."

"These findings underscore how significantly U.S. attitudes toward manufacturing in America seem to have swung in just a few years," said Harold L. Sirkin, a BCG senior partner and a coauthor of the research, which is part of BCG's ongoing series on the shifting economics of global manufacturing,[70] launched in 2011. "The results offer the latest evidence that a revival of American manufacturing is underway."

The BCG survey identified such factors "as logistics, inventory costs, ease of doing business, and the risks of operating extended supply chains" are driving decisions to bring manufacturing back to the U.S. The primary reason for 76% of respondents reshoring production of goods to be sold in the U.S. was to "shorten our supply chain...while 70% cited reduced shipping costs and 64% said "to be closer to customers."

The reasons cited by the BCG survey are consistent with the case studies that the Reshoring Initiative's has captured, but the reshoring trend over the last few years has been driven by a range of factors including rising offshore labor rates, especially in China, as well as the increased use of Total Cost analysis to quantify the hidden costs of doing business offshore. The threat of Intellectual Property theft, cost of inventory (space to store and cost to buy larger size lots to get the "China price," and quality/warranty/rework are also cited frequently. Longer delivery, cost and time of travel to visit offshore vendors, transportation costs, and communication problems also influence the decision to reshore.

In my experience, most companies look only at quoted piece price or landed cost, at best. Because of inaccurate data, many companies make the decision to offshore on the basis of faulty assumptions. The reality is that many companies are saving less than they expected, and in some cases, the hidden costs exceed the anticipated cost savings.

I have been conducting my own informal surveys of manufacturers that I meet at trade shows and conferences. Most of these companies are Tier 2 or 3 suppliers of assemblies, sub-assemblies and component parts. Each year, more and more companies have told me that they are benefitting from reshoring.

At the trade shows I attended in the last two years and conducted my informal survey, I didn't meet a single company that hadn't gotten new business or recaptured an old customer because of reshoring. I believe that there is a great deal more reshoring going on than A. T. Kearney or even the Boston Consulting Group can quantify because it isn't a whole product. It is an assembly, subassembly, or component part, such as metal stamped part, machined parts, sheet metal fabricated parts and assemblies, plastic and rubber molded parts, printed circuit boards, etc.

Harry Moser has provided me with slides for over 300 case studies of companies that have reshored in the last three years to use in my presentations. I can tailor my presentation to include slides for particular industries or geographical location. For example, when I spoke at the Design2Part show in Pasadena in October 2015, I shared case studies for companies that had reshored to California. Whereas when I spoke at the Lean Accounting Summit in San Antonio, Texas in August 2016, I shared case studies of companies that had reshored to the Southeast.

The Reshoring Initiative estimates that "if all companies used Total Cost of Ownership (TCO) analysis, 25% of the offshoring would come back." Their data reveals that about 100,000 manufacturing jobs have already been reshored in the last four years. Harry Moser states, "Excess offshoring represents an economic inefficiency that can be corrected at low cost. It is less expensive to educate companies than to incentivize them."

Mr. Moser's organization promotes and tracks cases of reshoring across the U.S. According to the 2016 Reshoring Report, "The combined reshoring and related FDI trends increased, adding 77,000 jobs in 2016, and a positive adjustment of 13,000 for the years 2010 thru 2015, bringing the total number of manufacturing jobs brought from offshore to over 338,000, since the manufacturing employment low of 2010."

Mr. Moser gave me permission to use the following charts from the report:

Manufacturing Jobs/Year 2016: The Tide Has Turned			
	2000 – 2003 Annual average	2016	~% Change
New Offshoring	~ 240,000*	~50,000*	-80%
New Reshoring & FDI	12,000*	77,000**	+500%
Net Jobs Gained	~ -220,000	~ +25,000	N/A

* Estimated   ** Calculated – Reshoring Library through Dec 31, 2016

Reshoring + FDI Jobs Added
Cumulative 2007-2016

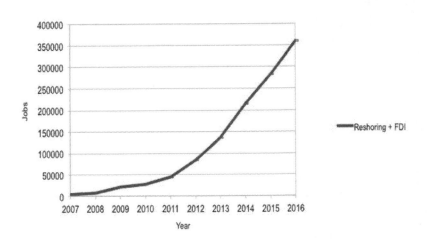

Ranking by job #	Country	Jobs	Companies
1	Asia	138450	1112
2	Western Europe	103879	528
3	North America	35186	235
4	Middle East	5991	34
5	South America	3963	21
6	Australia/Oceania	1398	20
7	Eastern Europe	1045	21
8	Africa	885	7

Table: Reshoring + FDI by International Region From, 2010-2016

U.S. Region	Jobs	Companies	% of Total	Average Jobs/Facility
South	218589	838	67	261
Midwest	57677	430	18	134
Northeast	25025	255	8	98
West	24706	206	8	120
Total	325996	1729	100	189

Table: Reshoring + FDI by U.S. Region, 2010-2016

During a recent conversation with Harry Moser, he said, "The economic bleeding due to increasing offshoring has stopped. The rate of new reshoring is now equal to the rate of new offshoring. From 2010 thru 2016 about 330,000 manufacturing jobs have come back to the U.S. via reshoring by U.S. companies and FDI (Foreign Direct Investment) by foreign companies."

He added, "In the years 2000 thru 2007 we were losing net over 200,000 manufacturing jobs/year to offshoring. In 2016, for the first time in 40 years, we had a net inflow of manufacturing jobs, approximately 25,000. An understanding of the benefits to be gained by reshoring requires a clear understanding of how many jobs were lost to offshoring. One wildly inaccurate study claimed that only 13%, or 750,000, manufacturing jobs were lost to offshoring, and the rest to automation. Research by Bob Scott at EPI, Prof. David Autor of MIT, Adams Nager of ITIF and by the Reshoring Initiative all show that 3 to 4 million manufacturing jobs were lost to offshoring. The challenge is now to reshore the 3 to 4 million manufacturing jobs that are still offshored. About one million could come back now if companies did the math properly. The other 75% require national policies that restore U.S. competitiveness."

Reshoring has Become an Economic Development Strategy

In May 2016, I received information from the International Economic Development Council (IEDC) inviting me to educate my audience on the findings of their research and the tools and resources available when manufacturers are considering reshoring. The IEDC is a non-profit membership organization serving economic developers with more than 4,700 members. Their mission is to "promote economic well-being and quality of life for their communities, by creating, retaining and expanding jobs that facilitate growth, enhance wealth and provide a stable tax base."

In 2015, the IEDC received a grant from the U.S. Economic Development Administration to "examine current reshoring practices and create materials to spread awareness of reshoring trends, tools and resources that are available to ease the process." IEDC has conducted research for 16 months on why companies are choosing to reshore and what resources are available to assist American companies that are considering reshoring. IEDC provided educational training sessions with reshoring experts, such as Harry Moser of the Reshoring Initiative, for economic developers.

IDEC also created the Reshoring American Jobs webpage, a project funded by the U.S. Economic Development Administration (EDA). "It is the go-to place to learn about and find resources to support activities encouraging reshoring in communities. Economic developers will find the latest news, case studies, and in-depth research on reshoring activity to help them stay in-the-know on reshoring trends information." The micro site is divided into three sections:

Understanding Reshoring[71] "discusses the critical role reshoring plays in strengthening the economy, identifies challenges to reshoring, and highlights lessons learned from communities that have worked with reshored companies."

- Defining the Reshoring Discussion" White Paper
- National Assessment of Reshoring Activities
- Webinars: Defining the Reshoring Discussion, Reshoring Tools…They're Out There

Tools for Reshoring[72] "provides resources and best practices in reshoring American jobs to aid economic developers in assisting reshoring companies."

Reshoring in the Media[73] "tracks the latest discussions on trends covered by popular and trade media. The content will help demystify the reshoring movement and serves as a practical reference for economic development professionals."

In March 2016, IEDC published a 30-page white paper on "Defining the Reshoring Discussion[74]," in which the introduction and historical perspective states, "…as foreign countries strengthened their manufacturing competitiveness over the years, American manufacturers struggled to maintain their cost and productivity advantages on a global scale. Some American manufacturers adjusted to foreign competition by shifting their focus to complex, high-value products and industries—and increasing manufacturing investment, output, and employment. Others either closed U.S.-based factories or sought cost savings by offshoring some, or all, of their operations to less expensive foreign locations. Shortly after China joined the World Trade Organization at the end of 2001, a large exodus of U.S. manufacturers occurred."

However, supply chain dynamics have changed, and the report states, "…the cost savings that American firms had enjoyed began to erode around the year 2010. Changing macro-economic factors, such as labor and transportation cost increases, absorbed much of the savings from which manufacturers had previously benefitted. Also, after experiencing offshoring firsthand, many companies found that hidden costs often outweighed the cost benefits of manufacturing overseas. Some of these hidden costs that were not always considered include factors such as increased costs of monitoring and quality control, uncertain protection of intellectual property, and lengthy supply chains."

While the white paper presents a broad overview of the discussion of reshoring, some common themes emerged from their review of resources:

- "The decision to reshore is often described as a response by business to both macroeconomic and internal business-related factors.
- The term reshoring is used to describe a range of activities that occur in numerous industries, not just manufacturing.
- A company's decision to reshore can be encouraged through the creation of favorable business conditions, a skilled workforce, and incentives that encourage innovative manufacturing practices.
- Reshored jobs will likely be different from the jobs that existed before offshoring gained momentum or jobs that currently exist offshore."

The reason economic development agencies have become interested in reshoring is that "The impacts of reshoring extend beyond individual companies and provide benefits for entire regions as the effects multiply through local economies."

From an economic development viewpoint, "it is important to understand that reshoring is fundamentally a location decision. In this sense, a company's decision to stay in the U.S. or relocate will be based on its total operation costs in a given location."

The white paper highlights some of the findings of the data from 25 national economies research studied by the Boston Consulting Group (BCG) from 2004 to 2014. The BCG study found that the following factors significantly impact manufacturing location decisions:

- Increased wages – "China's wages rose 15 to 20 percent per year at the average Chinese factory."
- Fluctuating currency value – "when compared against the U.S. dollar, the Chinese yuan increased in value by 35 percent."
- "Labor productivity, which is measured as the gains in output per manufacturing Worker"
- "Reduction of energy costs from 2004 to 2014, especially in energy-dependent industries such as iron and steel and chemicals industries"

Naturally, the white paper mentions the work of Harry Moser, founder of the Reshoring Initiative, in developing the **Total Cost of Ownership Estimator**™ in an effort "to help decision-makers estimate total costs of outsourced parts or products by aggregating, then quantifying all cost and risk factors into a single cost."

The paper then discusses the different definitions of reshoring from a popular understanding to a more academic definition. The most common definition is "the return of Manufacturing to the U.S." From an economic development perspective, the following definition may be more appropriate: "a manufacturing location decision that is a change in policy from a previous decision to locate manufacturing offshore from the firm's home location." Cottrill divides reshoring into four categories:

In-house reshoring refers to the relocation of manufacturing activities, which were being performed in facilities owned abroad, back to facilities in the U.S."

Relocating in-house manufacturing activities, which were being performed in facilities abroad, back to U.S.-based suppliers, is labeled "reshoring for outsourcing."

Outsourced reshoring describes the process of relocating manufacturing activities from offshore suppliers back to U.S.-based suppliers.

Reshoring for Insourcing is "when a company relocates manufacturing activities being outsourced to offshore suppliers back to its U.S.-based facilities, it is considered reshoring for insourcing."

The authors comment that reshoring applies to industries other than manufacturing, such as the information technology (IT) sector, stating that" challenges such as time zone differences, identity theft, privacy concerns, and issues with utility infrastructure abroad led more companies to return their IT operations to the U.S."

The white paper contains several pages describing what is currently being done to encourage reshoring by government programs such as the Make It in America Challenge and National Network for Manufacturing Innovation (NNMI), which are too lengthy to discuss in this short article. However, I do want to describe the following tools that can be useful to economic development professionals as well as companies in the reshoring process:

Assess Costs Everywhere (ACE)[75] **Tool**: This U.S. Department of Commerce tool was developed within the Economics and Statistics Administration, in partnership with the NIST-MEP, and with support from various agencies within the U.S. Department of Commerce, the United States Patent and Trademark Office, and SelectUSA. "The tool provides a framework for manufacturers to assess total costs by identifying and discussing 10 cost and risk factors. These include: labor wage fluctuations; travel and oversight; shipping time; product quality; inputs such as energy costs; intellectual property protection; regulatory compliance; political and security risks; and trade financing costs." ACE also provides case studies and links to public and private resources.

National Excess Manufacturing Capacity Catalog (NEXCAP)[76]: This resource was developed by the University of Michigan and "provides a catalog of vacant manufacturing facilities as well as critical data on skilled workforce supply, community assets, and other information pertinent to location decision making." It was funded by the Economic Development Administration.

U.S. Cluster Mapping Project[77]: This is another project funded by the EDA and led by Harvard Business School's Institute for Strategy and Competitiveness by "conducting research and publishing data records on industry clusters and regional business environments in the United States…[allows] users to share and discuss best practices in economic development, policy and innovation."

The paper discusses the importance of "industrial commons," a term coined by Harvard Business School's Gary P. Pisano and Willy C. Shih in 2009, which refers" to a foundation of knowledge and capabilities that is shared within an industry sector in a particular geographic area. This includes technical, design, and operational capabilities as well as "R&D know-how, advanced process development and engineering skills, and manufacturing competencies related to a specific technology."

Next, it discusses the impact of innovation and one point particularly worth noting is: "Manufacturing outputs have more than doubled since 1972, in constant dollars, even with a 33 percent reduction in employment…Improved output and efficiency is largely attributed to technological advancements that increase productivity and decrease labor-intensive activities. As gaps between wages in developed and developing economies continue to shrink, U.S. manufacturers will need to focus on innovation, using technology to improve productivity and reserving labor for value-added activities."

While no in-depth studies have been conducted on the potential effect of reshoring on creating jobs, the paper provides the following chart showing estimates under various scenarios (recreated):

Scenario Description	Source	Jobs Reshored	Cumulative Total Jobs
Using TCI analysis	Reshoring Initiative	500,000	1,000,000
If Chinese Wage Trends continue at 18%/year	Boston Consulting Group	1,000,000	2,000,000
Adoption of	Federal	2,000,000	4,000,000

better U. S. training, increased process improvements & competitive tax rates	Government's Advanced Manufacturing Partnership		
End of foreign currency manipulation	Almost all manufacturing groups	3,000,000	6,000,000

Note: Cumulative Total jobs is based on two support jobs created for every manufacturing job reshored

The paper states, "The brightest reshoring prospects involve those that can profit from the current manufacturing environment. This would include manufacturers that depend on natural gas, require minimal labor, and need flexibility in production to meet changing customer needs."
The authors' conclusion is that "there are opportunities for various levels of government, the private sector, and partnerships between the two to create an environment to support the manufacturers who can reshore."

What are the Obstacles to More Companies Reshoring?

There are three main reasons why more companies are not reshoring?

1. Most companies don't conduct a Total Cost of Ownership Analysis when making a decision to outsource manufacturing.
2. The United States has a high overall cost of manufacturing.
3. There are still tax incentives to offshore manufacturing.

Most manufacturing companies that have sourced and are still sourcing parts and products offshore don't do a Total Cost of Ownership (TCO) analysis. They base their decisions largely on low pieces that are based on cheaper foreign-labor rates and government subsidies by the governments of foreign countries to their manufacturers as part of their country's predatory mercantilist practices.

I have asked purchasing agents what prevented them from doing a Total Cost of Ownership analysis. A common answer was: We are not allowed to consider anything but the piece price and sometimes transportation costs in making the decision to select domestic vs. offshore vendors. Another answer was: We have been mandated by upper management to outsource to China to save money. Others thought that their managers were doing what everyone else was doing; i.e., going to China to save money.

In the past, corporate cultures, supply chain reward systems, and investment have been heavily focused on offshoring. Many companies followed each other offshore in following what Mr. Moser and I call "herd behavior." We are endeavoring to change the mindset from offshoring is cheaper to sourcing domestically may be the better choice.

Another problem mentioned was that in the cost accounting systems used by most corporations, transportation costs, travel costs to vendors, rework costs of defective parts, cost of inventory, etc. are in separate accounting categories and there wasn't any software available to do a true Total Cost of Ownership analysis until Harry Moser developed his TCO estimator.

After speaking at the Lean Accounting summit three times, I now believe that Chief Financial Officers (CFOs) are critical in turning the tide towards reshoring vs. offshoring. If more companies would adopt Lean accounting rather than use Standard Cost Accounting, they would be able to do a Total Cost of Ownership Analysis.

Transforming to the value stream method of Lean Accounting would facilitate being able to do a Total Cost of Ownership analysis more than Standard Cost Accounting because all of the costs related to that value stream are put into the category of Conversion costs and not put in the separate accounting categories of standard cost accounting.

Another way would be to change the way buyers/purchasing agents in supply chain groups are being evaluated and compensated. Currently, they are rewarded on the basis of their success in achieving purchase price variance; i.e., selecting sources on the basis of the cheapest price. CFOs need to allow their company's supply chain department to utilize expenses in the other accounting categories that must be taken into consideration to do a Total Cost of Ownership analysis, such as transportation costs, travel and communication costs related to the supply chain, and the cost of quality problems related to rejected parts and reworking of salvageable parts.

It is crucial for American companies that do not have offshore plants to be trained on how to do a true Total Cost of Ownership Analysis using the TCO Estimator as a counter to the continuing trend of offshoring manufacturing jobs by multinational corporations that have facilities all over the world. For multinational corporations, the U. S. market represents a smaller piece of a bigger whole in the global economy. While offshoring may no longer be a relentless search for the lowest wages, many corporations go to Brazil, to China, to India, and other countries because that is where their customers are located.

We can accelerate reshoring if we can expand the reach of our education and training on understanding and using a true Total Cost of Ownership analysis to CFOs and other C level management. Mr. Moser and I are no longer the only persons singing the "reshoring" tune. Consultants at the Manufacturing Extension Programs nationwide, such as California Manufacturing Technology Consulting (CMTC) are being trained in how to use the Reshoring Initiative's Total Cost of Ownership™ Estimator. I have even met former "offshoring" consultants who are rebranding themselves to be reshoring consultants.

In spite of the fact that I have spoken to hundreds and hundreds of people about the importance of doing a Total Cost of Ownership Analysis since my book came out in 2009, and Harry Moser, has spoken to thousands and thousands of people since releasing his free Total Cost of Ownership Estimator™ in 2010, we have reached only a small percentage of the people making the decisions about outsourcing.

While the number of companies bringing products lines back to America is increasing, I have to admit that as manufacturers' sales reps for all American companies; we are still losing business to China for individual parts our principals are quoting, especially rubber and plastic injection molded parts. However, I am sure that the decisions were made based on the lower piece price without doing a TCO analysis because most companies are still set up to do only a "purchase price variance" analysis or a "landed cost" analysis. When the Chief Financial Officer of a company is using Standard Cost Accounting instead of Lean Accounting, it is difficult, if not impossible, to access the data needed to do a Total Cost of Ownership analysis.

After doing a thorough TCO analysis on all of outsourced parts for your products, the next step is to build an integrated team that will periodically refine and refresh the analysis. You can even expand the definition of TCO to include the physical length of the entire supply chain and the lead times associated with the entire process.

If a company chooses not to practice TCO, it will impact their success or failure in the long run. It would be better if more companies would move forward by utilizing the freely available TCO spreadsheets, such as the one developed by Harry Moser that will allow you to quantity even the hidden costs and risk factors of doing business offshore.

With regard to the question of whether the reshoring trend is declining or increasing, the reality is that the Federal government keeps no related data. ATK tried to measure reshoring indirectly by measuring imports. It would be better to measure the actual phenomenon. BCG uses surveys of reshoring plans, but companies' actions often differ from plans. The Reshoring Initiative counts the actual reshoring cases and jobs reported in the media and privately by companies. Readers can help resolve the dispute by reporting their cases of successful or failed reshoring to Harry Moser at harry.moser@reshorenow.org.

High Cost of Manufacturing in America

While the difference in labor rates between the U. S. and Asia is diminishing, the U. S. has the highest corporate tax rates now after Japan reduced their corporate tax rate in 2010. In addition, the U. S. has high health care costs that got worse instead of better under the Affordable Care Act, and the U. S. has the most stringent environment regulations in the world.

In an article titled, "What's Wrong with the U.S. Economy? of July, 7, 2015, Stephen Gold, President and CEO of MAPI, wrote, "It's generally recognized that tax policy is a key tool for stimulating investment; our current corporate tax code is underutilized in this area, to say the least. Two elements are at fault: First, the U.S. has the highest corporate tax rate of all our major trading partners, a distinct disadvantage considering higher tax rates raise the effective cost of capital. Second, of all the major Western countries, the U.S. is the only one that employs a worldwide tax reporting system, taxing the active foreign earnings of its corporations globally. This is a monumental disincentive to repatriating income earned overseas."

According to the third quarter NAM 2016 Manufacturers' Outlook Survey[78] 74.8% of manufacturers are concerned about rising healthcare/insurance costs and 73.6% are concerned about unfavorable business climate (e.g. taxes, regulations).

Tax Incentives for Offshoring

According to an article[79] in the Houston Chronicle, the U.S. tax code provides the following deductions, offsets, tax credits and incentives to corporations to "offshore" their profits overseas: Tax Havens —

"The Organization for Economic Cooperation and Development (OECD) defines a tax haven country as one that imposes no or low taxes, does not exchange information about economic activity and lacks economic transparency." Tax havens are used by a majority of the largest American corporations.

Offshore Deferral — U.S. citizens and corporations are supposed to pay tax on income earned abroad, but "multinational corporations are allowed to "defer" paying income tax on profits made overseas until — or if ever — those profits are repatriated back to the United States." U.S. corporations take advantage of this offshore deferral rule by setting up subsidiaries in lower tax countries. Subsidiaries, even when they are wholly owned by a U.S. parent company, are not subject to U.S. taxation. The deferral clause has been in the tax code for more than half a century and has outlasted numerous reform efforts. A USA Today article states that in April 1961[80], President Kennedy asked Congress to rewrite tax provisions that "consistently favor United States private investment abroad compared with investment in our own economy."

Profit Shifting — A U.S. corporation can also avoid paying taxes on its income by shifting its income to its foreign subsidiary in a practice called profit shifting. "Profit shifting involves an accounting practice of transferring assets, such as intellectual property rights and patents, to subsidiaries in tax haven countries. All royalty income earned from these assets is booked by the foreign subsidiary and so is not subject to U.S. taxation." This practice is particularly prevalent in the pharmaceutical and computer industries; for example, pharmaceutical company Merck made more than $9 billion in profits in 2010 but paid no U.S. taxes.

Earnings Stripping — Earnings stripping is a practice in which a U.S. parent corporation undergoes a corporate inversion so that its foreign subsidiary in a tax haven country becomes the parent company and the U.S. corporation becomes the subsidiary. This "paper inversion" allows all of the corporation's global income to be booked by its new foreign parent. In addition, the new foreign parent can "loan" money to its U.S. subsidiary. Because it is a debt of the subsidiary, the money is not taxable. What's more, the interest on the "loan" that the subsidiary pays to the foreign parent is tax deductible in the United States for the subsidiary.

The same USA Today article[81] states, "Corporate lobbyists say that any move to eliminate deferral would have to be packaged with a significant cut in the 35% corporate tax rate…Otherwise, the largest companies, facing an effective tax increase, would have an incentive to switch their legal residence to another country." Obviously, no one would want large American corporations to move totally out of the U. S. so the only way to address this problem is to eliminate these tax loopholes while significantly reducing the corporate tax rates. We are long overdue for comprehensive tax reform for both personal and corporate taxes.

What can you do?

I believe that as wages continue to rise offshore, especially in China, transportation costs continue to increase, and risk factors such as political instability, intellectual property theft, and counterfeit parts take their toll, more and more companies will see the economic advantage and wisdom of reshoring.

If you are the owner of an existing manufacturing company, then you could do a Total Cost of Ownership analysis for component parts that you are having made offshore to see if you could "reshore" some of all of them to be made in the United States. Check out www.reshorenow.org for a TCO worksheet estimator to conduct your analysis.

Also, you could choose to keep R&D in the United States or bring it back to the United States if you have "offshored" it. Every manufacturing job you keep or bring back to the United States will create an average of two to three support jobs for other Americans.

If you are an inventor ready to get a patent or license agreement for your product or an entrepreneur starting a company to manufacture a product, select American companies to make parts and assemblies for your product as much as possible. There are some electronic components that are no longer made in the U. S., so it may not be possible to source all of the component parts with American companies.

Don't forget about the danger of having your Intellectual Property stolen by a foreign company that will use it to make a copy-cat or counterfeit product, sold at a lower price than your product.

You can help return manufacturing to America by doing the following:

- Use the TCO spreadsheet available for free at www.reshorenow.org.
- Use the archived webinars to inform staff and customers.
- Work with groups being trained on TCO – Manufacturing Extension Program (MEPs) sites around the country.
- Submit your case of reshoring for publication and posting using the Reshoring Initiative's template.
- Sponsor the Reshoring Initiative.

I strongly believe that if more companies would learn to understand and utilize the TCO estimator spreadsheet of the "Reshoring Initiative," they would realize that the best value for their company is to source their parts, assemblies, and products in America. Doing this would help return manufacturing to America to create a far higher percentage of jobs than the 15% that have been brought back to America thus far and help maintain more manufacturing in U. S. If enough manufacturing is "reshored" from China, we would drastically reduce our annual average trade deficit of $500 billion. We could create as many as three million manufacturing jobs, which would, in turn, create 9 – 12 million total jobs.

Chapter 5

Advanced Technology is critical to Rebuilding American Manufacturing

There was a great deal of press about advanced manufacturing after the establishment of the Advanced Manufacturing hubs by the Obama administration. However, most people don't know what this really means. In February 2015, the Brookings Institute released a report[82] that provides the answer: "America's Advanced Industries, what they are, where they are, and why they matter." The report "provides a wide-angle overview of the advanced industry sector that reviews its role in American prosperity, assesses key trends, and maps its metropolitan and global competitive standing before outlining high-level strategies to enhance that."

New technologies such as advanced robotics, 3-D printing, the "digitization of everything" are part of these advanced industries, but "the sector encompasses 50 industries ranging from manufacturing industries such as auto making and aerospace to energy industries such as oil and gas extraction to high-tech services such as computer software and computer system design, including for health applications."

An industry had to meet both of the following criteria used to identify advanced industries:

- "An industry's R&D spending per worker must fall in the 80th percentile of industries or higher, exceeding $450 per worker
- The share of workers in an industry whose occupations require a high degree of STEM knowledge must also be above the national average, or 21 percent of all workers."

Key findings of the overview of this sector are:

1. "Advanced industries represent a sizable economic anchor for the U.S. economy and have led the post-recession employment recovery."
- Sector grew at a rate of 5.4%, 30% faster than economy
- Average earnings increased almost five times as fast as overall economy
- Employs 12.3 million U.S. workers or about 9% of total U.S. employment
- Employs 80 percent of the nation's engineers
- Performs 90 percent of private-sector R&D
- Generates approximately 85 percent of all U.S. patents
- Accounts for 60 percent of U.S. exports

2.. "The advanced industries sector is highly metropolitan and varies considerably in its composition and depth across regions...in nearly every U.S. region..."
- 100 largest metro areas contain 70 percent of all U.S. advanced industries jobs.
- San Jose is the nation's leading advanced industry hub with 30.0% of its workforce employed in the sector; Seattle follows with 16.0% of its local jobs in advanced industries; Wichita (15.5%); Detroit (14.8%), and San Francisco (14.0 %).
- Advanced industries account for more than one in 10 jobs in

  nearly one-quarter of the country's major metro areas.
- Clustering occurs in a variety of configurations.
  - Grand Rapids, MI — automotive
  - Portland, OR — semiconductor
  - Wichita — aerospace manufacturing
  - Bakersfield and Oklahoma City — strong energy specializations.
  - Boston, San Francisco, and Washington — services such as computer systems design, software, and research and development
  - San Jose, Detroit, and Seattle — depth and balance across multiple advanced industry categories.

- Number of extremely dense concentrations of advanced industry has declined
  - In 1980, 59 of the country's 100 largest metropolitan areas had at least 10 percent of their workforce in advanced industries.
  - By 2013, only 23 major metro areas contained such sizable concentrations.

3. "The United States is losing ground to other countries on advanced industry competitiveness...most productive advanced industries in the world, behind only energy-intensive Norway. However, this competitiveness appears to be eroding."
- The sector's employment and output as a share of the total U.S. economy has shrunk since 2000.
- U.S. employment in advanced industries is low by international standards and falling rapidly.
- Since 1999, U.S. has had a trade deficit of $500 - $600 billion in advanced technology.
- U.S. share of global R&D and patenting is falling much faster than its share of global GDP and population.
- Among the nation's most patent-intensive regions, just two— San Diego and the San Jose-San Francisco combined area— rank in the global top 20 and just two more (Boston and Rochester) score in the top 50.
- The sector faces a labor supply challenge as only 15 of the large metropolitan areas are home to more STEM graduates than Finland, the global leader and 33 metropolitan areas rank below Spain at #24 globally.

In the concluding section of the report, Implications: Strategies for Promoting U.S. Advanced Industries, the authors write that their "assessment of the advanced industry sector points to significant opportunity—but also challenges...On the positive side, the combination of intensive technology investment and highly skilled STEM workers in the advanced industry sector represents a potent source of U.S. prosperity—including for workers without a bachelor's degree. Advanced industries power the national economy and their success is a prerequisite for building an opportunity economy in the United States…. America's advanced industries are not national. They are local, and in regions like Austin, Boston, San Diego, Seattle, and Silicon Valley, they are world-class hubs of prosperity."

The authors warn that "The deterioration of the nation's balance of trade in advanced technology products over the last decade raises especially sobering questions, not just about trade policy, but about the long-term vitality of the sector. Likewise, too few regional advanced industry ecosystems now retain the technology inputs, labor pools, and supplier density to generate the synergies that drive global competitiveness. Making matters worse is the gridlock in Washington that continues to preclude national action to strengthen advanced industries through sensible corporate tax reform or strategic trade liberalization and enforcement."

The authors recommend that the nation's private- and public-sectors should:

Commit to innovation — "both the private and public sectors need to radically rethink their technology development strategies…need to ramp up the scale of their innovation efforts and reconsider the formats through which they conduct them. More R&D conducted within new, more open or networked innovation models will be necessary in the coming years."

Recharge the skills pipeline — "both private- and public-sector actors—often in partnership—need to bear down on improving the availability of skilled workers by developing smart, industry-led, sector-specific, regional skills initiatives."

Embrace the ecosystem — "firms, governments, and other relevant actors must work to strengthen the nation's local advanced industry ecosystems—the regional industrial communities within which firms operate…. in too many places America's advanced industry clusters are thin or eroded, after decades of offshoring and disinvestment."

I completely agree with the authors' concluding statement: "America's advanced industries are a critical anchor of national prosperity. Business leaders, government, and the civic sector need to work together in new ways to augment their vitality."

Follow up Brookings Report Identifies New Trends in America's Advanced Industries

On August 4, 2016, The Brookings Institute's Metropolitan Policy Program released an update to their 2015 report referenced above. This report[83] is "America's advanced industries: New trends" by Mark Muro, Siddharth Kulkarni and David M. Hart.

The Metro Program began to focus on this sector after the 2008 economic crisis because of the "importance of these high-value innovation and technology industries to any future shared prosperity..."

The report adds two more years of data to the analysis and "looks beyond the immediate recovery years and into what has been a restive 'new normal' characterized by a U.S. high-tech boom shadowed by a global trade slowdown, an oil and gas glut, and stubbornly high rates of poverty and disaffection."

The authors comment that "Leaders in cities, metropolitan areas, and states across the country continue to seek ways to reenergize the American economy in a way that works better for more people. To support those efforts, this report provides an update on the changing momentum and geography of America's advanced industries sector...worker intensive industries the vitality of which will be essential for supporting any broadly shared prosperity in U.S. regions."

The "analysis takes a fresh look at the changing momentum and geography of 50 industries whose vitality will be essential to any future broadly shared prosperity in U.S. metropolitan areas. Output and employment growth data for the years 2013–2015 are compared to those for 2010–2013 for the 50 advanced industries at the national level, across all 50 states, and in the largest 100 metropolitan areas. New trends are identified across both industries and places."

The three major findings of their analysis are:

1. "The advanced industries sector continued to expand between 2013 and 2015 despite global headwinds, and it now employs 500,000 more workers than before the recession."
    - "The sector added $143 billion to U.S. gross domestic product (GDP) in 2013–2015, and accounted for more than 20 percent of the growth of the economy."
    - "The sector accounted for 11.3 percent of all U.S. job growth in 2013–2015."

2. "Growth in the advanced sector, however, emanated from a narrower set of auto manufacturing and "tech" service industries in the last two years than in the previous three."
    - "Three auto industries and four digital services industries accounted for more than 60 percent of the nation's advanced-sector growth over the time period."
    - "High-tech service industries emerged as the nation's leading source of advanced industries' growth between 2013 and 2015."

3. "U.S. advanced industries' growth trends grew more uneven across the country between 2013 and 2015."
    - "All but seven states saw both output and employment expansions, as did 80 of the largest 100 metropolitan areas.
    - "Northeastern and Western states captured larger shares of the nations' 2013–2015 advanced sector growth than they did in the previous three years."

As a result, the authors state that we now find "the U.S. economy still performing only modestly well. Output growth remains positive but middling, given sluggish labor productivity that limits the possibility for fast gains in standards of living. Employment growth remains steady if unspectacular, but more than one-half of the nation's hiring since 2010 has been concentrated in lower-wage industries with pay levels under $52,000 a year."

Maps, charts, individualized state and metropolitan "trend profiles" for the 100 largest metropolitan areas are available on the report website showing the changing momentum and geography of the sector.

One major revelation of the analysis is that "the advanced industries sector is the portion of the economy that is at once developing and utilizing the nation's most transformative technologies."
While this sector includes a "wide array of industries using a wide variety of technologies…the flow of technology use and business transformation among the advanced industries appears to be erasing conventional industry and sector distinctions and turning the super-sector into the leading focal point of technology convergence in developed economies."

In fact, "the advanced sector can be characterized as the nation's prime site for technology development, application, and hybridization."

- "The physical and digital worlds are converging in these industries as the '**digitization of everything**' pervades all of its fields, transforming nearly all enterprises with software, "big data," and connectivity to the internet
- The related **Internet of Things (IoT)**—the convergence of industrial machines, sensors, data, and the internet—is unleashing new ways to optimize the functionality, efficiency, and reliability of physical systems.
- **Advanced robotics, artificial intelligence, and machine learning** are making it possible to automate more and more worker tasks, opening the possibility of both productivity gains and labor market disruption.
- Applied physics, materials science, and chemistry are interacting to develop **advanced materials** with radically useful attributes, including incredible strength, conductivity or the ability to "remember" previous states.

- **Next-generation genomics** is bringing low-cost genetic analysis and "editing" to bear to improve medical diagnostics, accelerate drug discovery, and develop drought- and pest-resistant crops."

The special value of the advanced industries sector "stems from its inordinate role in generating prosperity." The generative role begins with its defining characteristics of R&D spending and STEM workers. These industries are the nation's main source of industrial innovation and technical skills and generate the following economic benefits:

- The sector is **highly productive**, which makes it competitive and profitable. Its aggregate productivity increased by about 2.7% annually since 1980, far faster than the annual productivity growth of just 1.4% for the rest of the economy.
- The sector generates **60% of U.S. exports** even though it represents less than 10% of U.S. employment.
- The sector **pays well** - average worker earned **$95,000** in total compensation, or nearly double the $53,000 of the average worker in other sectors in 2015.
- Each worker generates approximately **$214,000 worth** of output compared with $108,000 for the average worker outside the sector.
- The sector's substantial **"multiplier effect"** means that every new advanced industry job creates 2.2 additional jobs domestically: 0.8 jobs locally and 1.4 outside the region for some 39 million jobs nationally—one quarter of all private employment.
- Advanced industries purchase some **$236,000** in goods and services per worker from other businesses annually compared with $67,000 spent by other types of businesses.
- The sector is the nation's prime source of the **technology and productivity diffusion,** by which innovations spread through the economy to benefit workers, firms, industries, and regions.

The authors emphasize that the "sector's **innovation** capacity matters because technology advancement represents the most viable way for nations, states, regions, companies, and workers to increase their productivity and continue to improve their standards of living...the advanced sector is critical to U.S. local and national prosperity because it conducts 89 percent of the nation's private-sector R&D and generates more than 80 percent of the nation's patents...'Advanced industries' vitality and growth will be **essential to delivering on the advanced economy aspiration.**"

In conclusion, the authors state, "...the trends reveal both the value and evolving distribution of advanced economic activity and the need for urgent federal as well as state and local efforts to boost their growth and broadening their reach...we hope that city-metropolitan, state, and national leaders will profit from using this report and its interactive website to assess their current progress in assembling a key portion of the industry base they will need to craft an advanced economy that works for all."

Additive Manufacturing is Making Rapid Technological Advances

Additive manufacturing/3D printing is transforming the world of manufacturing. At first, it made it possible to get rapid prototypes of new products, which has helped inventors and entrepreneurs launch their businesses more rapidly and obtain inventors. Now, with the ability to make metal parts using various additive manufacturing processes, it has enabled companies to make complex geometry metal parts in low quantities without having to invest in the expensive tooling.

Additive manufacturing/3-D printing now allows the seamless creation of products using a single machine. This provides a lot more possibilities for how you design a part. For example, for a product where you would normally need six pieces, 3-D printing can achieve the same thing in one piece without additional processes like welding or screwing.

Advances in additive manufacturing and 3D printing are occurring so rapidly that in 2015 a daily newsletter[84] on 3D printing started up. Design News, Industry Week, Manufacturing.net, and many other publications are also publishing frequent articles on additive manufacturing, and most trade shows are now scheduling one or more sessions related to the topic of additive manufacturing/3D printing. The latest machines are incorporating technology that has speeded up the additive manufacturing process to the point that it can be used for low volume production of both plastic and metal parts.

For example, an e Newsline from Manufacturing.net had the headline, "Liquid Printer[85] Turns 3D Manufacturing Upside Down" and describes the new 3D printer introduced by Carbon3D at the TED conference on March 16, 2015. The new "3D printer can print up to 100 times faster than conventional additive manufacturing thanks to its ability to 'grow' materials upward from a pool of liquid," using "their Continuous Liquid Interface Production (CLIP) technology, which builds material upward in a continuous stream." The Carbon3D printer uses UV light to trigger "polymerization, the creation of three-dimensional polymers, while oxygen inhibits the reaction" and "can be used with a broad range of polymeric materials."

Dr. Joseph DeSimone, the CEO and co-founder of Carbon3D, said "Our CLIP technology offers the game-changing speed, consistent mechanical properties and choice of materials required for complex commercial quality parts."

A couple of months later in 2015, I was contacted by Zach Simkin, Co-President of Senvol LLC, a company that does analytics exclusively for the 3D printing industry, letting me know that they recently launched a tool, the Senvol Database,[86] which is the first and only searchable database for industrial 3D printing machines and materials. Simkin said, "Users are able to search the database by over 30 fields, such as machine build size, material type, and material tensile strength. The database is online and free to access.

The database already has thousands of regular users since launch, many of whom are engineers across a variety of verticals."

A few days later, I interviewed Annie Wang, Co-President of Senvol LLC, and she said, "Additive manufacturing is never going to replace 100% of subtractive manufacturing." She emailed me the Video link to their presentation from the RAPID Conference last year — "Determining Cost-Effectiveness of Additive Manufacturing." She also emailed me the write up from the Wohlers report ("Cost-Benefit Analyses for Final Production Parts"), which gives an overview of two case studies that they did for GE and Johnson Controls. She said, "We used the Senvol Algorithm to determine whether or not it's cost-effective to switch from conventional manufacturing to additive manufacturing."

While the results of the analysis are proprietary, Wang and Simkin provide guidelines in the introduction of their study, writing, "However, just because a part *can* be produced using AM does not mean that it *should* be. Prior to implementing the technology, it is essential to conduct a thorough cost-benefit analysis. Generally speaking, it is often stated that AM is economically suitable for parts that have the following features: low volume, complex, and small. Although this can be true, it is not sufficient to only consider features of the part. Rather, when trying to determine whether a particular part can be cost-effectively produced using AM, it is critical to analyze the entire supply chain."

In the report, they provide "… the seven supply chain scenarios that tend to lend themselves well to AM. If a part falls into one or more of these scenarios, then that part may be cost-effective to produce via AM. If a part does not fall into any of these scenarios, then the part almost certainly will not be cost-effective for AM given the current AM technology." They are:

Expensive to Manufacture – If you have parts that are high cost because they have complex geometries, high fixed costs (e.g. tooling), or are produced in low volumes, AM may be more cost-efficient.

Long Lead-Times – Does it take too long to obtain certain parts? Are your downtime costs extremely high? Do you want to increase speed-to-market? Through AM, you can often get parts more quickly.

High Inventory Costs - Do you overstock or understock? Do you struggle with long-tail or obsolete parts? AM can allow for on-demand production, thus reducing the need for inventory. Through AM, you can often get parts more quickly.

Sole-Sourced from Suppliers - Are any of your critical parts sole-sourced? This poses a supply chain risk. By qualifying a part for AM, you will no longer be completely reliant on your current supplier.

High Import/Export Costs - Do you pay substantial import/export costs on parts simply because of the location of your business unit and/or your supplier? On-site production via AM can eliminate these costs.

Remote Locations - Do you operate in remote locations where it is difficult, time consuming, or expensive to ship parts to? AM may allow you to manufacture certain parts on-site.

Improved Functionality - AM can enable a part to be redesigned such that its performance is improved beyond what was previously possible.

Simkin and Wang state, "For parts that fall into one or more of the above scenarios, a detailed, quantitative cost-benefit analysis is warranted. To conduct such analyses, an algorithm, courtesy of Senvol, was used to determine what types of parts can be more cost-effectively manufactured using AM versus the status quo. The algorithm analyzes an array of variables that span the entire product life cycle."

I told Wang that 3D printing is greatly accelerating the development of new products by the inventors that I advise as part of the San Diego Inventors Forum and as a mentor for CONNECT's Springboard Program, but there are many times when a part can be made by 3D printing can't be replicated in a production process. For example, you can produce "chunky" plastic parts using 3D printing that cannot be made in the production process of injection molding.

The use of 3D printing enables inventors to have a sample product to show/demonstrate in person or by means of a video to secure potential investors, but the inventor needs to do a careful analysis of the best manufacturing process to use for production, depending on where it will be used (home, office, or outdoors), product certifications required, and projected life cycle volumes, among other considerations. A 3D printed sample can be the essential ingredient of a video to do a crowdfunding campaign via Kickstarter or Indiegogo.

I told her that I give a presentation each year at our meetings on "How to select the right manufacturing process and sourcing location for your product," which incorporates the Reshoring Initiative's Total Cost of Ownership analysis. We agreed that companies could benefit from doing a cost-benefit analysis of comparing conventional manufacturing to additive manufacture as well as doing the Reshoring Initiative's Total Cost of Ownership analysis when making the decision to manufacture in the U.S. vs. offshore.

How Will Automation/Robotics Affect Manufacturing Jobs

Artificial Intelligence (AI), the Internet of Things (IoT), greatly improved sensors, and vast improvements in machine vision are contributing to the advances in automation and robotics.

Unfortunately, I have seen very little use of automation and robotics in the plants of San Diego manufacturers in my over 35-year career in San Diego's manufacturing industry. This is because in San Diego County where I reside, 97% of manufacturers are under 50 employees. These companies produce low to mid volume niche products, so they don't have the production volume to justify the cost of automation and robotics.

Therefore, I was surprised when I visited R&3D Engineering in March 2017 and interviewed Martin Bouliane, founder and President. He is a mechanical engineer who started his career in 1993 in Canada doing product development. After moving from Quebec, Canada to California in 2007, he worked for two medical

device companies before re-launching R&3D Engineering as a U.S. company in 2012. He said, "The company was originally focused on medical device design, but some of my customers turned to me to help them get into production. I started working with robots that they purchased from Fanuc. A team from Fanuc visited our company and invited me to become an authorized Fanuc robot integrator. We now focus on custom robotic automation design and fabrication for about 75% of our business, and we have grown to a dozen employees."
He explained, "One of the big reasons for advances in automation is that machine vision has become more and more advanced, so we can program the robots to do inline inspection. We also design and build the peripheral systems to surround the robots. The robot might be only 10% of the system, and we can configure the robot to do multiple tasks. More and more companies are benefiting from integrating robotics and automation into their manufacturing operations."

He added, "We have a customer who makes desalination filters, and we started working with them two years ago and have designed a robot system to move the filters, which were heavy for workers to move around. Some of our local customers have been in the biotech and pharmaceutical industry for high volume production of disposables. We are creating a system for one company that dispenses oil, and are building machines to produce the blister pack for the oil."

Since my customer base for the fabrication services I represent doesn't include the biotech and pharmaceutical industry in San Diego, I was unaware of the use of automation and robotics in these industries.

On MFG DAY, October 5, 2016, I had the opportunity to tour Magnaflow, in the City of Oceanside, which produces catalytic converters, manifolds, universal mufflers, and builder's kits for fabricating custom systems. Kevin Wiley, Director of Manufacturing, gave the tour and said that the company moved to Oceanside from Rancho Santa Margarita (in Los Angeles County) four years ago and just moved into its second building.

We toured the building doing the production of the catalytic converters, manifolds and mufflers. Because of their high production volume, they have three robots doing welding and have two automated tube-bending lines for making manifolds, and another automated line for making hangars. They have even computerized their Forklifts to take material/parts off shelves that are 7-8 levels high.

They average 6,000 manifolds per week. Their failure rate went down from 8% to 7%. There are three Kamatsu presses owned and operated by a stamping supplier in their plant, and I saw rolls of steel being automatically fed into the presses for stamping.
They produce about 2,000 – 2,500 per day of finished catalytic converters in-house. The most amazing machine cut steel sheet into the right size for their muffler housings, rolled the steel into a cylindrical shape, laser etched the logo/part number, and welded the mating edge as the end operation. After the muffler tubing was cut and welded, the tubing was wrapped in lava rock and compressed into the housings. End caps were assembled and welded onto the housings, and the muffler assembly was checked for air leaks before being packaged.

Other Examples of Automation/Robotics

In the past two years, I have had the opportunity to visit manufacturing plants in other parts of the country to write articles for my Industry Week column.

My first experience was when I visited Toledo, Ohio as the guest of the Regional Growth Partnership in July 2015. We visited the Rossford plant of Pilkington North America, Pilkington is part of the NSG Group, one of the world's largest manufacturers of glass and glazing products for the architectural, automotive industry and technical glass sectors. Founded in 1918, the company was transformed in 2006 with the acquisition of Pilkington plc, itself a global leader in the glass industry and the inventor of the Float Glass process. The Pilkington name was retained as a brand for the Group's architectural and automotive products.

Pilkington North America has five float glass lines in the U.S. — Rossford, Ohio (2); Laurinburg, North Carolina (2); and Ottawa, Illinois (1). The company has approximately 4,700 employees in North America. The Rossford plant makes float glass for the automotive market and also fabricates glass for specialty transport vehicles, such as farm equipment.

V. P. of Sales and Marketing, Stephen Weidner, conducted the tour for us and told us that the Rossford plant has about 2.5 million sq. ft. of floor space and the glass float production line is as long as a football field. At the beginning of the line, the furnace melts the pure Silica in the form of sand, limestone, and other ingredients into a liquid at 2900° C, which is cooled down to 1,050° C as it floats over the liquid tin and then further cooled down to about 200° C by the end of the line, where robots score the glass, break it into the right size for the end product, stack the glass into "books" until it is cool enough for human handling. This production line was truly an amazing sight to a person who is fascinated by all types of manufacturing processes.

On this same trip, we visited the General Motors Powertrain plant in Toledo where the six and eight-speed transmissions are manufactured. Plant Manager Joseph Choate gave us an overview of the division and a plant tour of both the six and eight-speed transmission production lines. This plant has about two million sq. ft. of floor space and about 2,000 employees (1,844 hourly and 184 salaried). As a sales rep who has sold every kind of metal casting processing, I have never seen such complex, intricate die castings as those supplied to GM. I was also impressed with the integration of robotics and automation with the human production line workers, which essentially made their jobs easier to perform, ergonomically safer, and more varied because every worker is cross-trained for every job in both the six and eight- speed transmission lines.

On a recent trip to North Dakota in April 2017, my host and I visited Giant Snacks, a manufacturer of large sunflower seeds, pumpkin seeds, and pistachios. We met with General Manager Lucy Spikermeir, who told us "The President, Jay Schuler, took over his father's business. We came out on our own to be only the second company to specialize in large seeds. We select sunflower farmers with proven excellence for growing large sunflower seeds. We work with each farmer during the growing process and monitor the seeds as they are processed, cleaned, seasoned, and roasted to perfection. We had the roaster custom built for us. We are using more and more robotics and automation in our plant."

When she gave us a plant tour, I was quite impressed with the size of the tanks for the processing and cleaning of the seeds. They are huge – possibly 10-12 ft. in diameter and 12 – 15 ft. high. Their roaster is nearly as big, and everything from the transfer of seeds from one stage to another as well as the filling of the individual bags is all automated. There were actually only about 15 people working on the shop floor to do everything from processing the incoming seeds to packing the bags into shipping boxes. They design their own boxes so they can be used on their automated line.

How will Automation/Robots Affect Manufacturing Employment?

Contrary to many experts who believe that automation and robotics will eliminate the majority of manufacturing jobs, I believe that the use of automation and robotics by American companies are important factors that are enabling companies to return manufacturing to America through reshoring and still be competitive in the global market place.

Many of these experts are only familiar with the high-volume production of consumer products (Business to Consumer or B to C) and forget about the large market sectors of Business to Business (B to B) and Business to Government (B to G). These latter two sectors have much lower volume production requirements than consumer products. High volume consumer production sometimes occurs around the clock or at least for two of three possible 8-hour shifts. For the low to mid volume production that can be accomplished in one daily shift, it is more difficult to justify the cost of automation and robotics.

I am not alone in my opinion. In an article[87] titled, "Five Trends for The Future of Manufacturing by Francois Barbier on July 31, 2017, he wrote, "While there are still some significant challenges ahead, the outlook is strong despite the obvious concern of robots displacing jobs. The bulk of automation is used for work that would be considered unsafe or impossible for humans. This makes robots a complement to, not a replacement for, human workers. Because of robots, we'll be able to increase our output.
We will still need people who can manage new operations, manage the robotics, program them and maintain them. Just as there was a shift from farm work to factory work in the early 20th century, almost every sector will need new kinds of workers: those who can build hardware, software and firmware; those who can design automation and robotics; and those who can adapt and maintain new equipment…"

The increased efficiency of additive manufacturing/3-D printing, IoT, and automation/robotics could spell a bright future for American manufacturing. The shift to smart manufacturing using these new technologies will save our corporations money and translate into greater profits, more jobs, and more prosperous economies, locally and nationally. As our manufacturing industry moves into a more complex age, so will our workers and products, ushering in a new era of production.

Chapter 6

Becoming a 'Lean" Enterprise is key to rebuilding American manufacturing

When I wrote the chapter on what manufacturers can do to save themselves for my book, *Can American Manufacturing be Saved? Why we should and how we can*, one of my top recommendations was to implement Lean manufacturing. I included the recommendation from Luke Faulstick, then COO of DJO Global, that "any company embarking on the Lean journey should rethink its offshore outsourcing." I have now come to believe that any company that becomes a Lean company will not need to offshore manufacturing to be globally competitive.

What has made me make such a bold statement? I say this partly because in the last nine years, I have benefited from attending dozens of two-to-four-hour workshops offered by the Operations Roundtable, now under the purview of Tech San Diego. Nearly all of these workshops focused on applying Lean methodologies and tools to manufacturing, derived mainly from the Toyota Production System and identified as Lean in the 1990s by James Womack who wrote the book The Machine That Changed the World.

The main reason, however, is that in 2014 I read the book, *Lean Company*, by Luis Socconini, Founder and Director of the Lean Six Sigma Institute (LSSI), as well as taking his Lean Six Sigma Yellow belt class to get my certificate.

LSSI was founded in 1998 by Mr. Socconini in Mexico, expanded into other countries in Latin America and Spain, came to the United States two years ago, and is now headquartered in Chula Vista, California. *Lean Company* is Mr. Socconini's third book. All three are written in Spanish, but *Lean Company* is being translated into English and should be released in the fall of 2017.

Since I have a degree in French and Spanish and have had the opportunity to maintain my Spanish fluency, I was able to easily read his book.

Lean Company is the "everything you ever wanted to know to become a Lean company" guidebook. Most companies are using the Lean methodologies and tools to eliminate waste and improve productivity to become a Lean manufacturer, but Mr. Socconini shows that there are processes in every critical activity within a company that can be made Lean, so that you can become a "Lean company."

In his book, Mr. Socconini presents a holistic approach to becoming a Lean Company through using a collection of strategies, methodologies, and tools that can be applied to any key process within a company to eliminate any type of waste and integrate every process. He also shows that you do not have to be a medium to large-sized company to become a Lean company, even small companies can do so.

He presents an innovative way to use and implement the Lean methodology and tools to improve the following processes:

- Talent Development
- Marketing and sales
- Design (new product development)
- Logistics - planning, purchasing, warehousing, shipping
- Financial - budget, cost accounting, financial accounting
- Manufacturing
- Maintenance
- Service
- Quality
- Information Technology

He writes that all of these processes need to be done in the shortest amount of time and with the best quality data. Good management requires making the good decisions based on your strategic plan and using a simple system to evaluate results on a weekly basis. Traditional companies evaluate their decisions monthly based on financial reports, and then it is too late to make correct decisions. The key points he makes in his book are:

Talent Development requires that all jobs should be learned in the shortest amount of time and performed correctly; otherwise companies are wasting time, money, and efforts trying to fix problems because personnel are not correctly trained.

Marketing and Sales processes need to eliminate waste from complex procedures so that simple and dynamic decisions are driven by the real demand not by forecasts.

The new product design process must be quick and reliable, so that products will have the best quality at the lowest cost, saving millions of dollars in the long run.

The logistics process requires an integrated collaboration between sales, purchasing, inventory management, and shipping to keep the company running smoothly and meet the customer's needs consistently. Lean logistics develops a supply chain concept where all types of waste are eliminated creating a highly reliable value stream.

The manufacturing and service processes must respond with the best quality and when the customer needs it. For these processes, it is necessary to implement continuous flow, quick set-ups, Kanban to synchronize information and material flow, quality control at the source, Total Productive Maintenance, etc.

In the financial processes, companies need to utilize true cost calculations, continuous profit and loss calculations to make better decisions, accurate invoicing, inventory control, and accounts receivable/accounts payable to eliminate all the waste of those transactions.

The quality processes are so complex in traditional companies that sometimes they are designed more for external auditors and certification purposes rather than being simple and easily used internally to improve quality.

Socconini argues that one of the major constraints to the development of a company is its structure, usually organized by functional departments and separated from each other by barriers of command so that employees focus working for their bosses rather than the company's clients.

A unique idea in the book is the recommendation that companies should be organized through the value stream structure, which integrates teams of people with multiple skills to achieve full potential in business and satisfy the needs of all customers. Note: Value Steams are the people, equipment, and activities involved in designing, producing, and providing a specific good or service of a business unit, along which information, materials, and value-added flows.

Socconini also proposes a method to develop highly innovative companies and bring them quickly to their maximum level of development. He presents the following seven-step process for this methodology:

1) Company design – this is where the management team designs the strategic plan, the value stream structure, and the talent development process.
2) Define indicators - there are three levels of indicators:
    a. Company indicators that must be analyzed monthly
    b. Weekly indicators, analyzed by the use of a box score
    c. Process indicators, measured monthly by specific groups within the value streams.
3) Implement Lean Six Sigma basics - housekeeping (5 S), visual management, teamwork methods, and standard work. Those tools will be the foundation to any improvement effort.
4) Measure performance: To be able to understand the real priorities, every company should focus their improvement efforts

on the bottleneck (constraint) by developing their value stream map. Understanding the true costs using Lean accounting methods will be another important activity to cover in this step.

5) Analyze performance: Every company should measure their performance continuously to increase their chances of making better decisions. In this step, it will be necessary to spend at least 45 min. every week in a box score meeting to evaluate any type of waste, variability, and overburden. Results may be evaluated using Pareto analysis, trend graphs, cause and effect diagrams, and brainstorming ideas to improve.

6) Preventive and corrective actions: If the performance analysis shows that a key performance indicator presents an opportunity to solve a problem or prevent one, then the methodology of using a problem-solving technique or a failure mode and effect analysis (FMEA) is required.

7) Improve: when the performance analysis shows that the team hasn't reached the goal for any specific key indicator, then the improvement tool box must be opened to implement what is needed, such as continuous flow, Kanban, quick set ups, TPM, etc.

Lean Company provides an innovative model for integrating everyone in the company to participate in a dynamic movement towards improving the company, working collaboratively, understanding the company as a whole, and finally presents a way to measure processes, not people.

In conclusion, Mr. Socconini writes, "Lean Company is a system that requires a team that is integrated, prepared, and disposed to think in a different manner respecting the form in which the company functions and is ready to change the old paradigm through simple and powerful formulas that significantly improve the functioning and results of the company." (My translation of Spanish approved by Mr. Socconini)

Adopting Lean Accounting is Critical to Sustainability

During my Yellow Belt class, I heard a testimonial from a small San Diego company, Apollo Sprayers International, by CEO John Darroch. He stated that in 2012 his company was in such bad shape that they were in danger of going out of business. They had 15-day lead times for delivery, were so disorganized that they only produced 15-20 units per day, and had no standard operating procedures in their production department.

After receiving training by the Lean Six Sigma Institute, he said, "We are consistently delivering product in 2 to 3 days that once took 3 weeks; we increased capacity by 100%, and our inventory is substantially lower. Apollo Sprayers is once again a thriving company with productive and motivated employees. I thank Lean Six Sigma Institute for leading us back to success."

By implementing continuous improvement, the company was producing 60-70 units per day in 2014, which is a capacity improvement of about 300%. Apollo Sprayers was also featured as an example of a company that had adopted Lean accounting, and the benefits to the company were impressive.

After I read the above-mentioned book and got my Yellow Belt Certificate in Lan Six Sigma, I arranged a follow-up interview with Mr. Socconini to find out more about the benefits of Lean accounting. Here are the highlights of the interview:

When and where did you learn about Lean accounting?
"I learned about the basics of Lean accounting when I received certification in "Throughput" accounting directly from Dr. Eli Goldratt back in 1998, where I found it very interesting to be able to calculate the real cost. 'Throughput' calculates the profit/minute, but it doesn't include the quality, only the speed.

In 2005, I took certification training in Lean accounting at Monterrey Tech in Monterrey, Mexico. Lean accounting is the next step of 'Throughput' accounting as it adds conversion costs to the profit/unit calculation. After implementing Lean accounting in more than 35 projects, I learned that one of the most important objectives was to know the real cost of every individual product or service."

When did you start to teach and/or utilize Lean accounting in working with clients?

"I started in 2005 in a large textile company where the high mix and low and high volume was hiding the real cost because they were using standard cost and therefore losing a lot of money in several contracts. We found the root cause of that problem was in the cost system where standard cost was giving a complete different result. I also taught a "Theory of Constraints" class at Monterrey Tech for seven years, which covered the basics of Lean accounting. My company now has an agreement with 26 universities to teach this course in Mexico, Bolivia, Colombia, Ecuador, Costa Rica, Peru, and Spain, as well as Southwestern College in Chula Vista."

How has your view of Lean accounting changed since you first started using it?

"I changed my perception from it being a really complex system, difficult to understand and difficult to explain, to a very simple methodology to make it easy to calculate the real cost every week, every day, and even every hour. This makes it possible to make better decisions in real time and enables all the value stream leaders to understand if they are losing or wining."

What does a company need to start measuring to get started on using Lean accounting?

"First, they need to select Lean accounting as one of the most important strategies for their business. Second, they need to implement calculating their "box score," which is a tool to evaluate the financial results every week. Third, by using the box score, they will be able to calculate direct cost of products (normal material) and conversion cost (all the rest of the costs like energy, salaries, utilities, rent, etc. (everything but material or direct cost). With the conversion cost by hour, any company from any size or industry will be able to calculate real cost every day regardless of the mix or complexity. Real cost equals Conversion cost per unit plus material (direct cost)."

What are the benefits of using Lean accounting compared to cost accounting?

"A company is able to know what is the real cost and with this knowledge, they really know if the company is making money or losing money in real time. They are able to define correct prices for their products or services, decide which products or services are contributing profits and which of them are losers, prepare quotes with realistic information increasing the possibility of making better deals, and be able to define a target cost and compare it constantly with the real cost to drive the most important kaizen events."

With regard to the future of Lean accounting in five to ten years, Mr. Socconini believes that only the companies that use Lean accounting will be able to understand their critical numbers and therefore will be the companies that can remain in the marketplace. He added that within five years, the top management teams will adopt Lean accounting in all accounting processes — Lean budgets (S&OP) and transform their financial processes of accounts receivable, accounts payable, credit, payroll, financial statements, inventory valuation, etc.

I concluded the interview by asking why he thinks companies are so slow to switch over from traditional cost accounting to Lean accounting. He replied, "There are two main reasons: Accountants normally don't participate in the Lean training or implementation; they only validate results with traditional calculations. Lean Accounting is not something that is being offered in traditional training at colleges and universities, so accountants don't understand what Lean Six Sigma is as a philosophy and they don't apply Lean Six Sigma principals and tools in their processes."

He added, "Another possible reason is that they think that Lean accounting is going to affect the generally accepted accounting practices, but the truth is that the accounting procedures for calculating and paying taxes are not affected at all."

He said, "I am very optimistic that in the near future accountants will one of the most important professionals to create a real change when they understand and participate in the Lean transformation as a systematic approach and when they are trained and invited to participate in the company transformation."

I believe that it is critical for accountants to be trained in Lean accounting and participate in the company transformation in order to have a sustainable company in the increasingly competitive global marketplace.

Lean Principles Must Expand Beyond Shop Floor

I had the pleasure of attending the 2014 Lean Accounting Summit on October 21-22 in Savannah, GA, produced by Lean Frontiers, headed up by founder and President, Jim Huntzinger. It was two days of information-packed presentations and workshops that included case studies showing Lean principles in action. I was honored to be part of such an illustrious group of Lean experts to give a presentation on "Returning Manufacturing to American Using Total Cost of Analysis." I attended all five of the keynote presentations during the two-day summit and selected one of the four sessions in each breakout period between the keynotes.

The summit began with a keynote presentation on "The Future of Lean Leadership, How Leaders Build Sustainable Cultures of Excellence Based on Principles," by Robert Miller, now President of Arches Leadership and former Executive Director of the Shingo Prize.

Miller outlined how we got to the present concept of Lean starting with the quality circles of the 1960s, leading to the Kepner-Tregoe methodology of work simplification in the 1970s, the Just-in-Time and Statistical Process Control programs of the 1980s, the Total Quality Management (TQM) philosophy of the 1990s, and now the Lean Six Sigma culture of the 21st Century.

As a sales rep for Tier 2 and 3 suppliers to Original Equipment Manufacturers starting in the mid-1980s, I remember how difficult it was for the companies I represented to comply with the JIT and SPC requirements of our customers. I took an intensive 100-hour class in 1993 to get my certificate in Total Quality Management to be prepared for the future, but saw TQM fizzle out as the decade ended because it wasn't embraced by the top management of companies.

Miller affirmed my opinion by saying, "We keep reinventing new versions of known practices, tools, and programs, using a few key principles that are timeless, universal, natural laws that govern consequences in our businesses... Tools and systems are necessary, but are insufficient. Sustainability requires culture. Culture is the sum of all learned and socially demonstrated behavior patterns that exist at many levels: civilizations, regions, countries, communities, organizations, families, etc."

He explained that "individual acts or behaviors are visible, observable, recordable, and measurable. You can't improve unless you measure, but measuring requires a standard or principle... Culture is influenced by a leader, reinforced by rules, embedded by routine, validated by recognition, and guided by beliefs. Beliefs are deeply personal."

He then outlined the six strategies for leaders based on the 10 universally accepted Guiding Principles of The Shingo Model™:

1. Leaders understand principles and know what behaviors flow from principles
2. Leaders have to be honest with themselves and others
3. Leaders are humble
4. Leaders value potential of everyone
5. Leaders ensure systems align with principles
6. Leaders balance Scorecard (results and behaviors)

He concluded, "Sustainability requires changes in thinking ...attempting to implement practices without understanding the reasons behind them leads to failure," This is what we saw happen with the philosophy of Total Quality Management because company leaders didn't learn to understand the principles and didn't practice the strategies necessary to embrace and embed the philosophy into the culture of their companies. Lean Six Sigma will only be sustainable for the next ten years and beyond if company leaders follow these six recommended strategies so that Lean becomes embedded into the culture of their companies and embraced by all employees.

The next keynote speaker, Tom Hood, CEO of the Maryland Association of CPAs and Business Learning Institute, spoke on "What's the Future of Accounting?" He caught everyone's attention by showing the list of jobs that are most likely to being disrupted by technology, and accountants were the second most likely at 94%, just after telemarketers at 96%. He said, "We are in a race with machines, and we can't beat them."

He continued, "We are experiencing the largest shift change in history in: leadership, learning, technology, generation, and workplace...For every two Baby Boomers, there is only one Gen Xer, while Millennials (Gen Ys) are equal or greater than Baby Boomers in numbers."

He questioned whether the" leadership of accounting is changing in collaboration, cultural awareness, technology and transparency." He explained that "incumbent practices, resources, and institutions are in decline, and new business models, practices, and technologies are emerging...The challenge and opportunity is to make the shift from the first curve to the second at the right time and with the right strategy."

He stated that the MACPA CPA Vision for 2025 is: "CPAs are trusted advisors who, combining insight and integrity, deliver value by:

- Communicating the total picture with clarity and objectivity
- Translating complex information into critical knowledge
- Anticipating and creating opportunities

- Turning insights into action to transform vision into reality

He briefly highlighted the five ways to thrive in a shift change:

1. Power of vision, purpose, and alignment
2. People – strengths and positivity
3. Collaboration and engagement
4. Learning and Development
5. Technology (RONI = Risk of Not Investing)

In conclusion, he stated, "In a period of rapid change and increasing complexity, the winners are going to be the people who can learn faster than the rate of change and faster than their competitors." Next, I attended an interesting breakout session by Bill Waddell, author of *Simple Excellence* and *Rebirth of American Industry*, on "How to Create and Transition into Value Streams." From my Lean Six Sigma Yellow Belt class, I learned how manufacturers can organize based on their product value streams, but I still didn't understand how other types of companies could transition into value streams.

Waddell stated, "How we construct value streams should be different for each unique value proposition we have to optimize in order to achieve the objective." He briefly outlined the following steps a company can take to "pursue the things that have the greatest impact on results:"

- "Nail down the markets you serve and separate them by the different value propositions/necessary cost structures they require.
- Identify critical key performance indicators (KPIs) that define how to achieve strategic objectives.
- Select your value stream managers.
- Determine initial scope of the value streams by function.
- Assign the human and physical resources.
- Restructure core managements systems, ERP systems, accounting, budgeting, and supply chain systems to match value streams"

Waddell featured Wahl Clipper Corporation as an example of a company that has been successful in transitioning to value streams. Wahl has been manufacturing professional styling products, home styling products and animal grooming products since 1919. As an advocate for manufacturing in America, I was delighted to hear that "Wahl has captured 80% of the consumer market in clippers" while manufacturing in the U. S.

On the second day of the Lean Accounting summit Cheryl Jekiel, author of *Lean HR*, gave the keynote presentation on "The Future of the Horizontal Lean Enterprise, Rev Up Your Engines." Ms. Jekiel led off by comparing the support functions of a company (Accounting/Finance, Information Technology, Human Resources, Quality, etc.) as "potentially the engine of the organization" in "driving strong performance."

She outlined six ways to power up support functions to create a different attitude in the whole team:

1. "Gain clarity on how your work impacts your external customers.
2. Shift attitudes beyond current expectations.
3. Focus on highest priorities — what is the #1 problem in your business?
4. Develop a service attitude – how do you measure service? Does it meet the needs of your customers? Survey internal customers (other departments).
5. Synthesize skills of Finance, IT, etc. and combine various items into a cohesive whole.
6. Leverage diversity of skills — you are better together"

In summary, she recommended that companies "identify ways that support staff impact external customers, expect more of team members in support functions, and prioritize work based on ability to achieve objectives."

At the summit, a comment made by retiring American Manufacturing Excellence President, Paul Kucharis kept running through my mind, "What got you here, won't get you there." We have come a long way in the last 25 years since Lean concepts, principles and tools diffused out of the Toyota Production System, but it is a never-ending road of continuous improvement to reach an ever-changing target.

The underlying discussion during breaks and meals among speakers and attendees seemed to be questioning whether enough progress had been made. The consensus from discussion was that we now have many companies that have become Lean on the shop floor, but how many have become Lean companies? And, of particular importance to the theme, how many are using Lean accounting rather than standard cost accounting?

This is why I selected the breakout session on Accellent Corporation's "Solving the Standard Costing Problem," presented by Jeremy Friedman, President and COO of the Cardio & Vascular Division. Accellent is a medical device manufacturer with 17 factories, 5,000 employees, and 20,000 SKUs.

He said, "Standard cost accounting is incomprehensible; we didn't know where the numbers came from...Our prices were as high as three times competition. Standard costing didn't work for our 20,000 SKUs...There were too many assumptions, too many variances." When he was the Executive V. P. and CFO, he researched the subject, read several books, and spoke to some of the experts, such as Jerry Solomon, Brian Maskell and Nick Katco, whom I met at the conference.

The decision was made to eliminate standard cost accounting, and they made the switch to "plain English P & Ls on October 1, 2012." He said, "We began with value stream management and focused on cutting costs...We eliminated variance analysis and changed from using standard costs and adding a markup...We had to teach that pricing isn't a function of cost. Besides the benefits at the operations level, we are no longer pricing products at two to three times higher than competition. We changed to a new paradigm — Lean cash flow." The old model was "What is the lowest price we can charge based on standard costs and markup." The new is "What is the highest price we can charge and still win the business."

The companies I represent sometimes lose orders for being two to four times higher than the competition, so I have a very good reason for encouraging a transition from standard cost accounting to Lean accounting. I firmly believe that if more companies would make this transition, we would be losing less business to China and other offshore suppliers.

Next, I attended the session on "Lean Product and Process Development — Creating the Future" by Dr. James Morgan, President of Emc Network and a Sr. Advisor for the Lean Enterprise Institute. Dr. Morgan shared his experiences as the Director of Global Body Exterior, Safety and SBU Engineering at Ford Motor Company from 2006 to early 2013 when he left the company. He said, "Every time you develop a new product, you have the opportunity to create/change the future...Apple and Google changed the future."

"In many companies," he commented, "new product development is a nightmare: design and quality problems, late launches, [etc.] ...Great products drive enterprise growth and require interdepartmental collaboration...Lean product development requires that you develop the people and product simultaneously." Morgan said that at the time of the economic crash in 2008 "Ford had $17 billion in losses over the previous three years and a 20-year market share decline...Ford's recovery was a product driven recovery based on a new product portfolio and new global development process.

The Body department was organized around the value stream and developing engineers was made a priority following the Technical Maturity Model (TMM), Technical Independent Development Process (TIPD), using mentoring and targeted assignments, and design reviews to demonstrate efficient design. They included the extended enterprise of the UAW and suppliers and used the Matched

Pair Process for engineering and purchasing to shape processes, tools, and objectives. They spoke as one voice."

In summary, he said, "They tightly synchronized activities to create effective concurrency and increase probability of success. The process they followed was:

- Study - to create the right product
- Execution - to deliver the right product
- Reflection/learning

He recommended that "you use A3 forms for business planning and align your organization with the right tools and stretch your team." In between, the keynotes and one-hour workshops, I attended two of the 20-minute "scrambles." The first was "Kata, Coaching and TWI" by Jim Huntzinger and Dwayne Butcher, the principals of Lean Frontiers. I was familiar with TWI (Training within Industry) from my Lean Six Sigma Yellow Belt class. It was briefly described as the program implemented during WWII to train women and non-military qualified men to replace men in industry who had been drafted. It contained three "J" programs: Job Relations, Job Instruction, and Job Methods.

They explained that the objective of Coaching Kata is: "Create an organization that solves every problem every time...Coaching Kata shows how to develop problem solving skills one-on-one using PDCA [Plan Do Check Act] in coaching/mentoring on actual projects." Huntzinger said, "You will not become Lean by doing TWI, but you will not become Lean without doing TWI."

To me, the last "scramble" of the day came full circle from the first keynote by Robert Miller on the future of Lean leadership and put everything into perspective — Orry Fiume's discussion of "Executive Leadership." He stated that whether or not your company has built a sustainable culture of excellence based on Lean principles can be easily determined by using the following simple comparison Mr. Fiume presented:

Traditional	Lean
Functional form	Business form
Managers direct	Managers teach
Management delegates	Management supports
Blame people	Root cause analysis
Us vs. Them	Real teams
Results focused	Process focused
Internal focus	Customer focus
Managers control	Workers control
Hierarchy	Flattened organization
Employee is a cost	Employee is an asset
Rewards individual	Rewards group sharing
Standard Cost Accounting	Lean Accounting

Less than half the attendees and speakers were present for the final panel discussion on "Your Organization in 10 years." The consensus of comments by panelists and members of the audience seemed to be that while the "Lean movement" has come a long way, many companies, still have a long way to go.

Within the San Diego region, I see many companies that participate in the Operations Roundtable workshops apply Lean principles and tools on the shop floor. They seem to have transformed from traditional companies to Lean companies in about half to two thirds of the above matrix. However, I don't know of any company that utilizes Lean accounting.

Very few companies under 50 employees have begun to adopt Lean principles and tools, and in San Diego, 97% of all manufacturers have less than 50 employees. Only two of the small companies I have represented in the past 20 years since Lean became in vogue have gone through Lean training.

The first was Pacific Metal Stampings with less than 40 employees. They obtained the training through one of the California Centers for Applied Competitive Technologies offsetting the cost with some funding from the Employment Training Panel. As a result, average throughput was reduced from five weeks to five days, on-time delivery improved by 70% and work-in-process was reduced by 40%. They did not adopt Lean Accounting and still had a problem with prices being higher than competition.

The other was Century Rubber Company with only 15 employees, and they received their training through the southern California Manufacturing Extension Partnership, California Manufacturing Technology Consulting. Their biggest benefit was eliminating wasted movement and time by implementing 5S and rearranging equipment. The cost of their training was also reduced by Employment Training Panel funding. Century utilizes a modified version of calculating conversion costs like Lean Accounting does, and their pricing is very competitive.

Small companies have the advantage of not having much of a hierarchy to flatten, and the president has to be fully committed to becoming Lean to even initiate the training. This makes it easier for Lean to become integral to the culture of the company.
Utilizing Lean tools is not enough to become a Lean company. Lean concepts and principles must become part of the culture. Lean will not be sustainable in the long run unless it does.

Leadership is Key to Becoming a Lean Enterprise

I attended my second Lean Accounting Summit October 8-9, 2015 in Jacksonville, Florida, produced by Lean Frontiers. Again, it was two days of information-packed presentations and workshops that included case studies showing Lean principles in action. I was honored to be invited back to give a presentation on "How to Return Manufacturing to America Using Total Cost of Analysis." I attended all five of the keynote presentations during the two-day summit and as many of the different breakout sessions as I could between the keynotes.
The First keynote, "Lead with Respect," was given by Michael Bole', author, speaker and associate researcher at Telecom Aristech. He first challenged the audience with questions, such as "What is the meaning of leadership? How do you get people to follow you? What

do they know how to do? " He stated, "Lean has a focus — reduce waste and do more with less. The world is moved by ideas and words. To lead people, you need to take into account their experience, skills, and opinions to help them develop their autonomy. You need to create experiences for them so you can see at what level they are." Then, he asked, "How do you teach? You show them by means of problem based learning: Express the problem, look for the cause, and confirm the corrective measure." He then outlined his seven-step model of Lean leadership.

The first breakout session I attended was "The Lean Management System: an Engine for Continuous Improvement" (CI) by Dean Locher, a four-time author and faculty member of the Lean Enterprise Institute. Dean said, "Lean creates a culture of continuous improvement you can actually see." He asked, "What is it to be a Lean enterprise? It is an organization where all members continually strive to do better and to develop a culture of continuous improvement. What is needed? Purpose, direction, CI methodologies and tools, processes, and engagement."

He briefly described the methodologies and tools: Hoshin Kanri (policy deployment process), value stream mapping, Gemba walks, daily management process, 5S, Kaizen events, 7-step DMAIC, Andon (visual management), Kata, Leader Standard Work, and Voice of the Customer.

The next breakout I attended was "First Steps to Lean Accounting Statement" by Jean Cunningham, President of Cunningham Consulting, co-author of *Real Numbers*, and one of the original thought leaders for the Lean Accounting summit. She showed how to restructure financial statements to provide a Lean accounting statement presentation in addition to the traditional presentation of standard cost when a company hasn't gotten rid of their standards cost system yet. She said it was necessary to:
- "Separate variable from non-variable costs,
- Separate direct from shared between value streams,
- Separate accounting transactions for labor and overhead,
- Use easy to understand language

- Organize by groupings meaningful to the business."

She emphasized that "money is language of business so it is really important to have an understandable language. Operations and finance have to come together."

In the afternoon, I attended the breakout session in which Eldad Coppens, CFO, and Anna Berkner, Director of Finance/Controller of QFix shared their company's story about converting to Lean Accounting. QFix is a world leader in radiotherapy patient positioning and immobilization products. They are vertically integrated as an innovator, manufacturer, distributor, and marketer and have 100 employees. They have an extensive product portfolio with over 6,000 SKUs. They aim to be a one-stop solution, so they distribute what they don't make.

Eldad said, "You can't do Lean accounting without doing Lean operations. We did Value Stream Mapping and a spaghetti diagram, and then reorganized by value streams: composites and devices, thermoplastics, and resale of other people's products. The value streams are supported by marketing, sales, and customer service, and technical support. The challenges were: high SKU/BOM, Box Score Analysis, new product development, profitability by product, target costing, and tracking and reducing inventory. The benefits of Lean accounting have been: financial x-ray of company, timely reporting, consistency with GAAP, insight into economics, insight into traditional accounting, internal diffusion of financial results, and a baseline for incentive programs and the QFix Performance Bonus for employees.

On day two, the morning keynote speaker was Jamie Flinchbaugh, co-founder of the Lean Learning Center, and co-author of *The Hitchhiker's Guide to Lean*, who spoke on "Leading Lean." He said, "Leading is a verb whereas leadership is a noun…What is the adoption rate of Lean? Good intentions are not a good solution to the problem…An operating system is how everything fits together: (1) process, (2) skills and tools, (3) evaluation, and (4) behaviors. All four need to work together and be consistent. An operating system may be good, but doesn't work because of behaviors. You need to be relentless on the path, but need to be patient with those who just got on the path. Evaluation starts with a hypothesis of if I do ____, I expect to see____. It includes Total Shareholder Return (TSR), strategy, culture, and behaviors." He gave suggestions of how to hook a CFO into adopting Lean accounting: "Start with why you are doing it. What is your purpose? Define your own personal reason for the Lean journey." He also recommended that CFOs talk to other CFOs.

The final keynote session featured Bill Waddell and Jim Huntzinger discussing "The Lean Economy: The Importance of Tying Micro and Macro." One of the most important truths Bill said was, "Individual people are the source of all productivity." He described how companies following the Lean business model are the micro part of the economy, and in turn, they are part of the macro economy of a city, state, or country. He said, "Reducing waste equals increased capital (both human and capital.) He commented that "retail stores are going by the wayside to Amazon to direct buying from manufacturers…you need to eliminate the non-value added. If you don't know where you are adding value and your customer doesn't know where they are adding value, then you are doomed."

Practicing Lean is Theme

I was honored to be invited to speak for the third time as a representative of the Reshoring Initiative on "How to return manufacturing to America" at the Lean Accounting Summit held in San Antonio, TX August 25-26, 2016.

The conference started Thursday morning with a keynote presentation by Mark Graban on "Practicing Lean." Mark is an internationally recognized expert in the field of "Lean Healthcare" as a consultant, author, keynote speaker, and blogger, whose new book is *Practicing Lean,* reflecting on more than 20 years of trying to get better at Lean in manufacturing and healthcare.

Mark's first point for the audience to ponder was, "Are we practicing Lean? He answered his rhetorical question, saying, "Lean is a learning process. It is a learning experience that develops skills and knowledge. We need to try to stop using the word "implement" because it implies being done. "Practicing" implies continuous learning. Learning by doing — with a qualified coach. I've been learning Lean — I didn't learn Lean."

A few other points he made that I noted were: "We are all human so we make mistakes, but we need to stop repeating the same mistakes. Are we doing Lean or LAME (Lean as Mistakenly Explained)? We all start somewhere. We need help to do better. Don't ask what tools should I start with — start with the need. Talk about the current state to find the need. You don't have to always start the same way — 5S isn't always the best tool to start with. Learn but don't just copy what someone else has done. In healthcare, it's important to get it right the first time — mistakes can cost lives."

During each breakout session, there were four tracks. I chose "Bridging the gap between accounting and operations" presented by Jerry Solomon, who is a founding thought leader and subject matter expert in Lean Accounting, author of three Lean books, and a three-decade teacher and Lean practitioner.

He told the story of MarquipWardUnited, a division of Barry-Wehmiller, Inc. in Hunt Valley when he was V. P. of Operations from 2003 to 2014. The highlights from his presentation were: "Lean focuses on safety, quality, delivery, cost, elimination of waste, and respect for people. How is it typically implemented vs. how should it be implemented? It should mean no layoffs. Lean requires a C-level champion, organization by value streams, recognition, empowerment, coaching, training, inspiring leadership, and Lean accounting. Lean accounting is applying Lean tools to eliminate waste and frustration in accounting — "plain English" financial reports. Accounting is often one of the biggest roadblocks to a successful Lean transformation. In a Lean journey, the greater the initial success with Lean, the more likely earnings will be negatively impacted. Lean is not a cost reduction program — it is a cash flow generator, a capacity generator, and most of all, a people system. The benefits of Lean are based on how these improvements are utilized!" Here is how the company changed from 2003 to 2014:

2003	2014
Orders	Up 110%
Revenues	Up 90%
Operating Income	Up 400%
Investment in R & D	Up 550%
Team Members	Up 20%
Inventory Turns	Up 100%
Working capital investment	Negative working capital
Functional/silo organization	Value stream organization
Standard cost system	Lean accounting

He provided examples of value stream costing, and "plain English" financial statements and asked, "How accurate are your costs at the SKU level?" He said, "The average is 70% accurate." Value stream costing: direct and fixed costs = conversions costs + material. He concluded, "As we physically change processes during the Lean journey, manufacturing and accounting must work together to transition to Lean accounting."

Next, I attended "Attack on Traditional Accounting," presented by Bob Hahn, who has been a partner at Hahn & Houle LLP Chartered Accountants since 2004. He shared details from his CPA firm and those of his clients about how to identify the eight deadly wastes, eliminate them, and measure the solution's ROI. He said, "Broaden your horizons and identify each of the wastes." In conclusion, he shared his thoughts concerning the measurement of the waste and the role of the accounting department.

On Friday, I attended "The Lean Management System" presented by Joe Murli, president of The Murli Group LLC. His career includes extensive coaching by retired Toyota executives when he was at Pratt & Whitney (P & W), being General Mgr. at Chengdu Aerotech (joint venture of UTC and a Chinese company), Director of N.A.

operations at Ensign Bickford, and president of Manufacturing at Kaman Corporation before founding his company in 2003.

He said, "Lean management is about unlocking the human potential. Why do it? Always start with a need. In 1990, Pratt &Whitney went from 30,000 employees to 20,000 in 18 months because of the end of the Cold War and cut in defense spending. Toyota people came to visit P&W, and Joe was responsible for showing them around for a week. After that P&W hired Lean consultants to go Lean.

We did a Kaizen event every other week at every plant around the world. We changed into cell manufacturing, but when we returned later, it hadn't been sustained. Why? The team members hadn't bought into the change. Nothing is more important than every member of the team seeing the problem.

Later, I did an extensive overview of different management systems. The distinguishing factor in Lean is continuous improvement. It is a system of continual improvement. True North inspires and nurtures the human spirit with a vision, mission, and purpose. True North is Standard Work, Visual Management, 5S, etc. In Standard Work, you find a problem, solve it, and then establish one best way as the one agreed upon."

He explained that Lean is a people system and Human Resources needs to be part of the transformation from the start: from recruitment, how you promote, how you compensate, etc. To establish Leader Standard Work and behaviors, you need to be humble, appreciative, ask open-ended questions, etc. Accountability comes through: transparency, facts, fast identification of problems, overt problem solving, team learning, and continually improving." He asked to whom are we accountable and answered: "our customers, our investors, our employees, and society."

The third presentation I attended was "Why Lean requires moving beyond budgeting" by Steve Player, Director of Beyond EPS Advisors, a business consulting firm, and founder of Live Future

Ready – a member-based community of practice that implements more effective ways to plan and control operations.

Steve said, "Stop doing dumb stuff! Monthly close of statements is dumb. Live Future Ready's ambition is the help people plan for the future. Traditional budgets block your efforts to become Lean. There is waste in budgeting: rework, overproduction, defects, unnecessary processing, waiting, and design doesn't meet needs. $DVF > R$, where D = Dissatisfaction, V= Vision, F= Known first steps, R = Resistance to change. The problems with budgets are: take too long, based on inaccurate assumptions, triggers unnecessary spending, gives the illusion of control, causes gaming that erodes ethics, it brings out the most unproductive behaviors, and it costs too much." The Beyond Budgeting principles are:

1. Values - bind people to a common cause
2. Governance - govern through shared values and sound judgment
3. Transparency - make information open and transparent
4. Teams - organize around seamless network of accountable teams
5. Trust- trust teams to regulate and improve performance
6. Accountability - base on holistic criteria and peer reviews
7. Goals - set ambitious medium goals
8. Rewards - base rewards on relative performance
9. Planning -make it continuous and inclusive

Steve added, "Planning is changing from the ship you are to the ship you want to be. Need to transform while delivering on a day to day. Target rolls with the market. Command and control vs. adaptive. Revolutionary approach - change is very fast 12 to 18 months. Evolutionary -more gradual, 2 to 5 yrs. Check, plan, act. Forecast vs. target - rolling forecast.

The next session I attended was "Moving Beyond Budgets at Holt Cat" presented by Gretchen Stepke, Director of Business Systems, and Susan Nufer, Controller-Dealership Operations. Holt Cat is family owned business, founded in 1983 and is a Caterpillar dealership. They acquired another dealer in 2002 and created teams to evaluate their systems. They began searching for a budgeting system and selected Clarity Systems in 2004 to get more reliable data than what was available using Excel spreadsheets.

They shared that they had 23 years of growth until 2009 when they hit the trough. They assembled a leadership team and a new plan was made. They worked with Steve Player and switched to rolling forecasts and declared budgeting dead. Forecasting became a better tool. Seven keys to better forecasting are:

1. Your job of influencing is never done
2. Use language that helps people to change
3. Try to eliminate "budget" from vocabulary
4. Desire to grow helps move to forecasting
5. Change takes time
6. Processes are getting formalized to drive the organization.
7. You never stop learning

They went back to basics: how many people do we need what resources do we need, etc. They applied the 12 Beyond Budgeting principles. Goals and rewards are the most difficult. They are a member of the Beyond Budgeting Roundtable.

CAT dealers have a benchmarking system (DFRS) to use to compare themselves to other CAT dealers. They developed Ace and Pulse reports and worked to break down silos. In 2010, they had a 33% percent increase in sales and reduced expenses by 1%. Using forecasts, they are achieving target goals. Now they are powering for the future: new locations, focus on excellence, and growing the "core." They have added lines, such as Link Belt, in order to grow. They have outgrown Clarity and are looking at new tools.

It's very difficult to get stories of the application of Lean accounting, but at this same conference, I attended a presentation by Steve Brenneman, President, and Duane Yoder, Production Manager, of Aluminum Trailer Company, titled "The ATC Story."

Mr. Brenneman titled his presentation, "It's a lean life!" His definition of lean is "using the scientific method to continuously improve the business and other related parts of the entire value stream. Also, it is a complete change of the way that we work as human beings. We go from individual heroes to strong teams."

ATC is a privately held company with eleven owners, 9 of whom "are involved in and manage every aspect of the company…Each owner contributes to the company in almost every phase of the business by doubling their duties as both Owner and CEO, CFO, Production Manager, Engineering Manager, Sales/Marketing Director." The company was founded in 1999 and is located in Nappanee, IN, within Elkhart County, which is touted to be the Trailer Capital of the U. S. for RVs and Cargo Trailers.

"ATC is one of the only manufacturers who can build all models and custom trailers in, both, steel and aluminum…This can range from a barebones 5' x 8' trailer up to a mobile command center fully fit up with dual slide outs, custom finishes and 60 KW power generation. ATC produces a wide array of trailers to meet every customer request."

ATC is very vertically integrated in their manufacturing processes, so the website states, " By fabricating and building components on site, we eliminate the overhead costs that come from outsourcing. Every hour spent and piece of material used is transparent and reflected in the pricing you are quoted."

ATC has come a long way since the economic crash of 2008 that led to a near collapse of the trailer and RV industry in 2009. ATC owned a window manufacturing company, Nappanee Window, which they had to shut down in 2009 and sell off its assets.

Brenneman said, "We had built ATC up from scratch in 1999 to $26 million business in 2006, but from 2007 to 2009, sales dropped 60%." This dire situation led to a serious examination of where they were headed. Steve said, "We had only dabbled with lean previously. After reading *Lean Thinking*, we saw all of our mistakes at

Nappenee Window and saw many of the same issues at ATC, but now we saw them through lean eyes."

Brenneman said, "We had relied heavily on tribal knowledge, and as a result our average vendor was paid 25 days late. We had negative equity, and we only did five raw material inventory turns/year. We started practicing Lean and changed to building a standard line of trailers.

Duane took over as presenter and explained that they separated into three product lines based on work content and complexity of the trailers. He said, "We set up three Value Stream teams, composed of Trailer Design, Inside Sales, Value Stream Leader, and the Value Stream team members. We created a lean office for each value stream. Steve and I became leaders for two of the value streams. We now have five value streams and are trying to change the mindset of everyone."

As a result, Steve said, "We were profitable the first year after starting to practice lean. Our sales went from $10 million in 2009 to $42 million in 2015, and our net income has grown dramatically as well. Our inventory turns tripled from 2010 to 2014. Our long-term debt has dropped by over 50%."

Steve said, "After seven years of hard work, we have:

1. Improved flow - went to one building from two
2. Cleaned up the mess
3. Did 5S for maintenance department
4. Established a supermarket/material supply system
5. Use a Materials/Kanban to all lines
6. Changed to Value Stream Management since 2012

"We use visual controls on the shop floor. Standard Work was the most difficult to do. We developed a Leader Standard Work Bus schedule.

From January 2015 to February 2016, we reduced labor time from 181 minutes down to 84 minutes for our simplest trailer (Line 1). On our Open Utility line, we reduced labor minutes from 360 minutes in January 2015 to 248 minutes by mid-April 2016. We use "kitting" and improved cell arrangement to eliminate as much walking as possible.

The change took nine months — three months longer than we had planned. It took four years to gradually switch over to Lean accounting. It is simple and just makes sense to Lean organizations. Now we get P & L weekly."

In an interview after the summit, Steve said, "Lean just seemed like a better way to think about operational excellence. It was more of a method rather than just trying harder or doing what everyone else was already doing. It felt right for some reason. Our biggest stumbling block was that we tried to do too much too fast before allowing people to start to understand these new concepts with us. We tried to just be the experts and do the thinking for everyone."

In answer to my inquiry about how becoming a Lean company changed the culture of the company, he replied, "Lean has really helped us to have a unified concept that everyone could get behind. It provided a common framework that we could point out to people as to where we were headed and why. The biggest benefit of becoming a Lean company is that we get to involve everyone in the process of making things better. Then, we all get to share in the proceeds. I like that a lot. It seems to fit within my view of how the world should work."

This story is an example of how transforming into a Lean Company can make the difference between success and failure as a company.

I can't stress enough the importance of your company beginning the Lean journey. I am certain that becoming a Lean Enterprise is one of the most important actions American manufacturers can take to be globally competitive and is one of the keys to rebuilding American manufacturing to create jobs and prosperity.

Chapter 7

How some American companies are succeeding against global competition

Since my last book was published in 2012, I have had the opportunity to interview numerous American companies around the country that perform all or the majority of their manufacturing in the U. S. to find out what they are doing to successfully compete in the global marketplace. I have so many good stories that I had to select the companies that had used innovative strategies to survive the Great Recession, started their Lean journey, or reshored at least some manufacturing from offshore.

At the 2013 FABTECH Expo in Las Vegas, I had the opportunity to interview several companies. The first company was Laserstar Technologies, located in Riverside, RI, and I interviewed Peter Tkocz, Regional Sales Manager, southwestern states. Laserstar makes laser welding and marking equipment using the "free-moving" concept they developed, enabling users to eliminate costly fixturing devices, benefiting from pin-point accuracy, increasing the range of assembly and repair applications, and minimizing the potential hazards of heat damage.

When I met Mr. Tkocz at the FABTECH expo, he told me that the company was 55 years old and only made jewelry for many years. He said, "When jewelry making went overseas in the 1990s, the company had to reinvent itself and get into new markets to survive. We set a goal to enhance the quality, performance, and innovation of our products, programs, and services on a continuing basis and became a Lean manufacturing company." Since then, they have developed a diverse customer base of six major markets:

Medical - cardiac pacemakers, defibrillators, guide wires, catheters, hearing aids, orthodontic appliances, prosthetics and surgical tools
Dental - crowns and bridges, partial and implant fabrication and repair.

Electronics - a wide variety of different materials, component parts or final assemblies
Micro technology - wide range of complex applications for laser welding and marking
Tool and die repair – ideal for modifications and repairs on molds, tools and dies as the process is quick, precise and will not damage surrounding surfaces.
Jewelry - a fast fix to repair jewelry and eyeglasses, and their new Fiberstar machine can weld down to 12 microns, which is critical for high-end gem stones

Laserstar's Research & Development laboratory is focused on inventing new technologies that change markets and create business opportunities, utilizing input from customers. Laserstar sells through learning centers vs. distributors, and the three learning centers are located at their Rhode Island headquarters, California, and Florida. Their laser education courses provide a solid foundation of fundamental laser welding and laser marking skill sets to immediately gain a revenue impact for the new or existing iWeld, Laserstar or Fiberstar laser welding or laser engraving system.

At the same show, I interviewed Mike Albrecht, National Sales Manager, at the Scotchman Industries booth. Scotchman Industries, Inc. has been a leading manufacturer of metal fabrication equipment, accessories, and custom tools, such as ironworkers, cold saws, band saws, tube and pipe notchers, and measuring systems for nearly half a century.

Mr. Albrecht said, "Art Kroetch founded Scotchman Industries, located in Philip, SD, in the early 1960s to make and sell farm-related products, such as pickup stock racks, corral panels, gates and chutes. In 1966, the company purchased the patent for a hydraulic ironworker, the first machine of its kind in the world, and began manufacturing ironworkers. This machine, using hydraulic pressure, created up to a 35-ton force that could punch, bend and shear metal."

He added, "In 1978, Scotchman purchased Excel Manufacturing Ltd. of Winnipeg, Manitoba, Canada, and was able to provide a line of ironworkers that ranged from 30-ton to 90-ton capacities for the world market. Today, we have a complete line of thirteen different ironworkers, ranging in capacities from 45 to 150 tons, with component tool design, and a fully integrated European style. We have successfully acquired and maintained a large portion of the ironworker market. We are proud to be an American manufacturer who has always been export-minded. Our company was given the President's "E" Certificate for Exports in 1981 by the Secretary of Commerce, for excellence in its increased exporting of products. Today, we continue to export our products to many countries around the world. All of our products are manufactured in the USA, and we have donated equipment to the Workshops for Warriors located in San Diego, CA."

Finally, I interviewed Heather Gaynor, Marketing Communications Manager, at Swagelok, located in Solon, OH. Swagelok is a privately-held company that designs, manufactures, and delivers an expanding range of the highest quality fluid system products and solutions, such as tube fittings, valves, regulators, hoses and other products that are vital to fluid system solutions in industries such as power generation, oil and gas production, chemical processing, biopharmaceutical research, semi-conductor manufacturing and more.

Ms. Gaynor said, "We manufacture everything in the U. S. and are very vertically integrated. Swagelok products and services are delivered locally through a network of more than 200 authorized sales and service centers that support customers in 57 countries on six continents."

While the products and services of the companies I interviewed at the FABTECH Expo are quite different, there are common threads:

- All of the products are sold to other businesses (referred to as B to B) instead of directly to consumers (B to C).
- The products fill specific needs and requirements of other manufacturers.
- All of the companies manufacture their products in America.

- The companies export their products to other countries.

These companies demonstrate that American manufacturers with unique products that satisfy customers' needs can compete successfully in business-to-business global markets where the predatory mercantilist countries of China, Korea and India haven't targeted to take over the market and destroy their American competition.

Successful Indiana Manufacturers

In 2014, I had the opportunity to interview three companies in Northern Indiana, where many were hit hard by the recession and the dramatic downturn in the auto industry. Indiana ranks as the top state where manufacturing contributes the most to the nation's total economic output. These companies shared the stories of how they were able to weather the storm, recover rapidly, and resume good growth well before the rest of the country.

Micropulse Incorporated - I interviewed Brian Emerick, CEO, who founded Micropulse in 1988 and is the sole owner of the company. The company now manufactures from a state-of-the-art 100,000 square foot facility with over 200 employees next to the farmhouse where the company was originally started.

Mr. Emerick said, "Micropulse prototypes and manufactures the most demanding instruments and implants in the medical device industry. We don't have our own product line and make custom parts for Original Equipment Manufacturers (OEMs). We are a contract manufacturer selling to the orthopedic industry. About 50% of our business is spine related, and the rest is a mix of hip, knee, and other joint implants.

Our employees have been trained in Lean manufacturing principles and tools using the local Manufacturing Extension Program and courses at the regional community colleges. We have several Black Belts now on staff, and they do regular Kaizen events and utilize Six

Sigma practices and tools. Our quality system is certified to ISO 13485."

Mr. Emerick explained, "We started being impacted by competition from offshore, especially China about 10 years ago, but business is coming back. Some of our bigger customers like Johnson & Johnson and Zimmer set up plants in China. We do more work with smaller companies that don't have their own plants in China because the quality requirements for implants are too stringent to use Chinese contract manufacturers.

We were flat in 2009 during the recession, but the orthopedic industry as a whole was down about 25%. We have great customers and started growing again in 2010. Our growth since has been about 10% per year. We recovered by not buying much and cutting expenses. We spend about $2 million per year buying new equipment and updating software systems. We are considering adding another 60,000-sq. ft. within the next 18 months."

Mr. Emerick concluded, "The secret to our success is the employees that make up our team. We have a solid workforce with very low turnover and have quality customers."

C&A Tool - Richard Conrow founded C&A Tool in 1969 in a garage in Churubusco, Indiana as a tool and die operation with 10 employees. C&A Tool is a poster child for the manufacturing revival in the U.S. As a privately held company, C&A Tool has continued to add jobs, machinery and square footage each year. Having sustained 44 years of economic ups and downs, the company has grown to employ more than 530 people with 750,000 square feet of manufacturing space.

I interviewed Rob Marr, V. P., who said, "Our services are contract machining and high precision grinding. We don't have our own products, but do a lot of prototype and development for our customers. We bought Direct Laser Sintering equipment to be able to do Additive Manufacturing [also known as 3D printing] that utilizes 3D CAD data to produce a part. The parts we make are metal, not plastic, made by Direct Laser Sintering. This technology produces metal prototypes and production parts in a matter of hours."

Their main markets are: orthopedics for instruments and implants, automotive, electric motors, fuel systems, and aerospace. The company currently has four facilities and has invested in new capabilities, adding new equipment to support jet engines, power generation, and industrial markets. This market mix means that they are ISO 9001:2008 certified, as well as TS949, AS 9100, and ISO 13485 certified.

Mr. Mahr said, "Training the next generation of manufacturers is critical for the future. We are passionate about educating the manufacturing workforce, the general public, and our local community that manufacturing is not the dark and dingy days of our forefathers. For the past 36 years, our company has partnered with the local high schools to offer part time jobs to more than 60 students during the school day that allow them to have on the job training and transition from the classroom to the workplace more seamlessly. In addition to training high school students, we bring in math teachers to show them the real world of manufacturing."

When I asked if they have been impacted by competition from offshore, he said, "We were impacted by China, but have been getting business back for a couple of years. We compete more with Europe than China because of their high precision machining and grinding."

With regard to the impact of the recession, he said, "Our automotive business was particularly impacted. During part of 2009, our business was down by 40%. New development was down, but we didn't lay off anyone and even bought another facility in 2009. We did not do anything special to recover, just continued our business culture. We focus on investing heavily in capital equipment and software every year, even during the recession. We buy new equipment as our motto is 'to maintain an excess capacity of square footage and equipment, even if it doesn't have the customer base to support the investment at the moment to be able to take advantage of new opportunities."

Mr. Mahr concluded, "The secret to our success is that our founder laid a foundation for the company with the right people and equipment. We have evolved over the years. It really comes down to the people and allowing them to succeed and learn from their mistakes. We do what's right by investing in people and equipment so our employees can take pride in their work, and we elevate the industry."

Forest River Inc. - Peter Liegl founded Forest River in 1996 to be a RV company dedicated to helping people experience the joy of the outdoors by building better recreational vehicles. After purchasing certain assets of Cobra Industries, the company started manufacturing pop-up tent campers, travel trailers, fifth wheels, and park model trailers.

Forest River now operates multiple manufacturing facilities throughout the Midwest and West Coast producing motorized Class A, B, and C vehicles, travel trailers, fifth wheels, pop-up tent campers, park model trailers, destination trailers, cargo trailers, commercial vehicles, buses, pontoons, restroom trailers, and mobile offices.

In 2005, the company was acquired by Berkshire Hathaway, but Mr. Liegl has remained the CEO. Forest River shares 80-81% of the industry with two other companies, leading with a 35% market share.

Doug Baeddert, GM of 14 operating units, said "We don't sell direct to the public; we sell through dealers focused on their main markets of recreation, commercial businesses for vehicles, pontoons, and mobile offices, and municipalities for buses and restroom trailers.

Our plants are non-union, and 85% of all production occurs in Indiana. The industry is an assembly-based industry not a vertical industry. We rely on our suppliers and are basically an "assembler" of parts, components, and assemblies that are manufactured by our vendors. For example, many of our wood assemblies are made by small Amish wood shops that are located in Northern Indiana."

Mr. Baeddert said, "In 2008-2009, there was a 33-34% reduction of manufacturing of RVs industry-wide. The consolidation of companies has been healthy and good for the financial stability of our industry. There has also been a consolidation of dealers so there are about one-third fewer dealers than prior to the recession.

We don't have a formal budget for investing, but we are continually doing new product design and improving our existing products. Each division is autonomous in product development and is very entrepreneurial, innovative, creative, and visionary in their design work for new products. They can make minor changes from concept to prototype in as little as three days. However, a major technology change, particularly vehicles, can take up to a year."

Mr. Baeddert concluded, "The secret to our success is the right leadership of our founder, Pete, our people, our products, and our processes. We give enough rope to our people to succeed or fail and have a very low turnover."

Notice that the answer to my question about their secret to the success of these Indiana companies was consistent: They all said their core competency as a company is the talent and expertise of their people from management on down the line, not just their equipment or facilities. My own experience in business has convinced me that it is a company's team of people that is the key to its success or failure.

Miller Ingenuity Combines Innovation and Lean to Create a Unique Culture

In 2015, I had the pleasure of interviewing Steve Blue, President of Miller Ingenuity, located in Winona, Minnesota. Mr. Miller said, "'Rudy' Miller founded the company more than 60 years ago after inventing the wick lubricator, a maintenance free lubricating system for locomotives. Miller's inventiveness enabled the company to develop into a successful company by means of the ability to design, produce and deliver innovative railroad parts that meet the needs of the industry. "

Miller Ingenuity currently has 50 employees at their 70, 000 sq. ft. plant, but has 18 sales people around the world selling to 100 countries, including Asia. The company remained a privately held enterprise of the Miller family after Mr. Miller's death in 1997 when Mr. Blue became president in 2000.

Mr. Blue is carrying on the innovation legacy of Mr. Miller: "Our continued innovations are driven by three core motivations: to take on customer challenges, to think more creatively about solutions, and, humbly, to be everyday heroes to our customers. We put these beliefs into action based on deep and "factory floor" relationships with our customers and on our ability to invent, engineer, and deliver ingenious solutions."

Mr. Blue told me that the company started on their Lean journey in 2005, and every employee went through the training. Two of their employees are Black Belts from training they had received when they worked for General Electric. The company has expanded Lean out of the shop floor into "lean office," but not into "lean accounting" as yet.

Mr. Blue added, "We do continuous training as part of our Lean program. We have self-directed work teams and utilize peer interviewing and reviews. We have a "bounty" program with a $5,000 cash award for the most innovative ideas. For example, six production workers reduced a stamping die set up from four hours to 16 minutes."

Since I saw a wide variety of products on their website utilizing many different fabrication processes, I asked if they were vertically integrated to do sheet metal fab, machining, rubber and plastic molding, wire forming, electronics assembly in-house or if they subcontracted some of these fabrication services. Mr. Blue said, "We do metal stamping, compression rubber molding, and injection molding of plastics in-house, and subcontract out the other fabrication processes."

Naturally, I asked if he outsourced any manufacturing offshore to China or other Asian countries, and he responded, "We have some electronic subassemblies and surface mount printed circuit boards sourced overseas, along with some over molded rubber parts because our competition was selling products at our U. S. cost."

Mr. Blue said, "We acquired the Larry McGee Company in March 2015. They were our third acquisition since 2005. They had a great product line of radio-controlled interface devices, but no sales force. It was a low risk opportunity to enter into a different technology. We moved their operations into our plant from their Chicago facility."

Mr. Blue explained that one of their secrets to success was fostering creativity and innovation, saying, "We started the Creation Station because our ability to innovate was slowing down and needed to be accelerated. We hired the ex-Chief Creativity Officer from QVC to teach us innovation principles. We started by having an innovation session every Tuesday, but wanted innovation to be more spontaneous and not wait until Tuesdays. This led to creating a space away from employees' working space in the middle of the manufacturing area. Glass panels provide natural light. Smart boards are scattered about the room, and there is a pool table in the middle of the room. But, the magic is in the people, not the room."

He added, "Creation Station is a big investment in creativity and entrepreneurialism in manufacturing at a level where it needs a shot in the arm. It's truly a breakthrough moment for our company, the town of Winona, the region, and small and mid-sized manufacturers in this country. Creation Station offers a flexible workspace designed for both large and more intimate presentations, trainings and meetings. Creation Station will also be made available during off-business-hours for regional organizations and companies looking for a high-tech "think tank" space."

In answer to my final question as to what does he attribute the company's ability to prosper after 60 years in business, he answered, "Our culture by design, not default, has enabled us to prosper. We have a cohesive, collaborative, and creative culture."

Northwest Ohio's Advantages as a Manufacturing Location

In July 2015, I was provided the opportunity to be hosted to tour manufacturing plants in the Toledo, Ohio region by the Regional Growth Partnership (RGP), a privately held economic development corporation covering three counties in northeast Ohio and two in southern Michigan. John Gibney, V. P., Communications and Marketing, was the tour host for the five companies we visited. I was very impressed by the diversity and use of advanced technology, automation, and robots at these companies. These were no "rust belt" companies.

We first visited Plastic Technologies, Inc. (PTI), located in Holland, where Chairman and founder Thomas Brady, Ph.D., and President and COO Scott Steele gave us a thorough company overview and tour of their facility. PTI is the leading industrial source for preform and package design, package development, rapid prototyping, pre-production and material evaluation engineering of PET bottles and containers. PTI manufacturing capabilities include injection molding of preforms and blow molding utilizing their injection molded performs.

Dr. Brady told me that when he worked for Owens-Illinois, Inc. from 1971-1984, he had become the VP and Director of Technology and led the development of the first PET plastic (polyester) soft container and directed the technical activities for O-I's plastic product lines.

He said, "In late 1985, I had a unique opportunity to start the company. Coca-Cola bottlers were seeking to expand their successful PET bottle manufacturing and develop new and innovative PET plastic soft drink packaging products. The four Coca-Cola cooperatives agreed to jointly sponsor and fund product development and engineering projects, and they approached me to manage these project development efforts. I made a counter offer to the Coca-Cola cooperatives to establish a separate independent company for the purpose of managing these projects. I left O-I and started Plastic Technologies, Inc. after signing long term contracts with the four Coca-Cola cooperatives."

Dr. Brady said, "Because of my industry experience, I was quickly able to identify additional customers that were non-competitive to Coca-Cola and hired a small, but highly experienced professional staff, to do the technical development for the Coca-Cola Cooperatives and other customers. Because of our professionalism, we were able to establish a reputation in the industry as a high-quality PET R&D and technical support company. As our technical staff expanded and our revenue grew at compound annual rates of 35%, we moved to a larger facility in 1989 and set up both analytical testing and process development laboratories, with the capability of prototyping and testing PET containers and preforms.

We supply preforms to use for blow molding to customers needing specific quantities or unusual designs. We have learned how to work with competitive customers and have become recognized for our excellence in protecting customer intellectual property and confidentiality.

We founded Phoenix Technologies in 1991 in nearby Bowling Green and expanded the plant three times to do production volume of recycled PET containers. We broadened our customer base and became involved in developing several different products, including health care products, plastic recycling, specialty compound development, and leisure products."

I asked if they were affected by the recession of 2008-2009 and if so, what did they do to survive it. Dr. Brady said, "It had a big effect on business, but it wasn't really the recession per se. The Recession just added to the challenge of change. We had to do some things differently during the recession. We had to get more professional and organic about sales. Sales has changed — there are many more companies selling the same technology and service now. More business is handled by professional purchasing agents, so you have to be more price competitive than previously.

We also went through formal training in Lean, which has been beneficial to our manufacturing business. You have to be more efficient to be competitive. Becoming Lean didn't affect our testing lab. Becoming ISO certified had more of an impact on the lab There are a lot of changes coming to the world and the changes are happening more rapidly... What we do is not as different and special as it was. The challenge is to find where are the "gaps" in the market in the future that we can fill. Our growth hasn't been about becoming a bigger and bigger company.

Our growth is through entrepreneurism and ownership, growing as a family of companies... PTI employees are in a position where they can truly feel it's their company. Any employee can be considered by the management team for an opportunity to buy an equity stake, and 40% of PTI employees are owners today. We have more than 200 employees worldwide and many of the products you buy every day are sold in plastic containers designed by one of our companies."

Southwest Florida Attracts Manufacturers, not just Retirees

In September 2015, I was the guest of the Lee County Economic Development agency, and my tour host, Shane Farnsworth, Manager of Business Development, told me that in recent years, there has been an increasing number of business owners that have been regularly vacationing in the area who decided to either move their business or set up a business where they like to play.

Lee County is on the Gulf of Mexico side of Florida about 125 miles south of Tampa and about 50 miles north of the Everglades National Park. There are five incorporated cities in the country: Cape Coral, Ft. Myers, Bonita Springs, Ft. Myers Beach, and Sanibel.

My first interview was with Bill Daubmann, founder and Senior V. P. of KDD, Inc. dba My Shower Door and a member of D3 Glass LLC. Bill originally established a closet organization business in

Springfield, MA in 1986 and obtained a license agreement with Mr. Shower Door in 1989. After visiting the Lee County region for several years on vacation, he decided to move to Naples in 2001 and opened a showroom in 2003. His son, Doug, moved also and joined the company. He took the Fast track entrepreneur course by the Kaufman Foundation with one son in 2007 to "hone" their management skills, and took it again in 2011 with his other son.

Mr. Daubmann said, "It was a tough struggle from 2008 – 2010 due to the Great Recession, as southwest Florida was "ground zero" for the decline in the new home building market. We survived by mostly doing home remodeling."

In 2011, they were informed that their Mr. Shower Door license would not be renewed for 2012, so they explored setting up their own manufacturing plant to make the tempered and glazed glass needed for shower doors. After analyzing how much glass they were buying out of the state and the problems they had with breakage and defective glass, they set up D3 Glass LLC in 2012 when new home building started coming back in a building they had bought during the recession. Mr. Daubmann's oldest son, Keith, became President of KDD, Inc. dba My Shower Door. Mr. Daubmann said. "The ovens for tempering the glass cost one million and everything else cost another million. We also had to buy two custom-outfitted trucks to deliver the glass to our showrooms and customers."

Since Florida requires a license for the glass and glazing business, Mr. Daubmann and his sons took the test and got their licenses. Mr. Daubmann said, "We hired a consultant to do a "SWOT" analysis for our shower door business to make sure that our business model worked in all parts of the country. We wrote a business plan and did a beta test site. We are now selling our business model to others and running an academy on how to run a shower door business. We have four affiliate stores: Oklahoma City, OK, Grand Rapids, MI, St. Paul, MN, and York, PA. We also sell the specialized hardware for shower doors to our affiliates and other shower door companies."

In the last two years, they expanded from just doing shower doors into other markets for tempered glass and recently finished providing all of the tempered glass for the new Hertz headquarters building that will open next month. Mr. Daubmann said, "We went from 22 to 50 employees in 18 months and are now up to 64 employees. We just made the INC magazine list of 5,000 companies at #2,085 and will be going to the big event next month."

After I told him that I am part of the Reshoring Initiative to promote bringing back manufacturing to America, he said, "We were buying aluminum extrusions from China, but just switched to a vendor in the United States."

In answer to my question about the advantages of being located in the region, he responded, "It is easy to deal with the people in the local government agencies, there is good transportation available on I-75 and Rt. 41, the new airport has flights going to our markets, and there are good local colleges for preparing the future workers we will need."

My second interview was with Brian Rist, President and CEO of Smart Companies, of which Storm Smart is the largest subsidiary. Storm Smart is Florida's largest manufacturer and installer of hurricane protection products and is the ninth largest manufacturer across all industries in Lee County.

Mr. Rist is the inventor of the innovative Storm Catcher Wind Abatement Screens. He also moved from the northeast to southwest Florida to run his business. Mr. Rist said, "I started out with a couple of partners in a general contracting business and wound up as the sole owner. The first three years were a struggle to find a niche. The building codes were changing and I became the expert in the new codes, even teaching architects.

After Hurricane Ambrose came in 1994, I tried to find a fabric that would replace plywood for covering windows. We talked with people in energy management and got everyone's opinion. I founded

Storm Smart in 1996 to manufacture fabric window protection. We became known as who to talk to about window protection."

Mr. Rist explained that the building codes changed in Florida for developing sites in 1997 requiring window protection to be part of building a home. In 2001 new codes came out and insurance regulations changed also. Everyone has to have separate hurricane insurance. Insurance companies offered special rates for homes that had protection, and the State of Florida offered a rebate program.

"We started making polypropylene window protection by hand cutting the material, but we needed to ramp up to higher production. Getting a sales tax credit helped us to be able to buy a laser cutting machine in 2013, and it eliminated the bottleneck in our business helping us develop new products."

They work with the biggest companies in the world that use fabric for hurricane protection. While their products protect homes from hurricanes, they also reduce energy costs. Brian said, "You can build a business based on a known market of saving energy and not just protection from hurricanes. Impact-rated windows are a fast-growing part of our business. Most new homes come with impact rated windows."

He added, "The building codes changed again and now are much more about retaining heat rather than saving heat. International codes are also changing. We watch what percentage of our business is with builders. We went to Cancun and set up small operation in Mexico during the recession. We are currently doing work in Los Cabos, Mexico also. We sell to Caribbean countries like Bermuda, Jamaica, and wherever else there are resorts.

We have experienced fast growth and have been picked by Inc. magazine four times as one of the 5,000 fastest growing companies. We went from 26 employees to 100 employees after Hurricane Charlie. We went from five to six jobs per month to about 100 jobs per month.

We looked at all of our jobs and decided to really go back into the customer service business to be a sustainable business. We started to invest in our people and getting to know who they were. We had to make sure they were doing things right. We have to 'walk the talk.'"

In answer to my inquiry about Lean training, he said, "We have been very involved with lean manufacturing and are working with the Florida Manufacturing Program. We are going through a program for an ERP system in order to continue to grow. We have a plan to develop the company over the next three years. Part of it will involve having licensed dealers."

We also visited Shaw Development, which is a family-owned company with the third generation now involved. The company specializes in the design, development and manufacturing of custom fluid management solutions, including Diesel Emissions Fluid (DEF) systems (headers, reservoirs, caps, adapters, strainers, etc.) for heavy-duty vehicles and machinery, such as trucks, buses, construction, mining, military vehicles, as well as agriculture and forestry equipment, power generation, and locomotive equipment.

Stephen Schock, Director of Manufacturing, gave us a plant tour first, and then we met with Lane Morlock, Chief Operations Officer. Lane told me that Frank Shaw founded the first Shaw company, Shaw Metal Products, in 1944 Buffalo, New York as a machine shop to support the military and developing the aerospace market.

Shaw Aero Devices, Inc. was founded in 1954 to add engineering to their core capability and develop products with proprietary intellectual property. Frank's son, Jim Shaw, headed up this company, and it became the industry standard for a variety of fuel, oil, water, and waste components and systems. Shaw Aero Devices moved to Naples, Florida (Collier County) in the early 1980s and moved to Fort Myers in Lee County 1993. The company relocated back to Naples in 2001 after it outgrew its Lee County location.

Mr. Morlock, said, "Shaw Development, LLC was formed in 1959 to transfer Shaw Aero Devices technology to ground vehicle markets particularly the lift and turn technology for fuel caps. We moved into our current 50,000 sq. ft. plant in Bonita Springs in 2008. Shaw entered into the DEF system business early on, and DEF business has grown dramatically in the last 6 to 7 years."

When I asked how much they outsource, he said, "We have a fair amount of capability in-house — machining, stamping, forming, welding, painting, assembly and test capabilities. In 2009, we vertically integrated plastic injection molding by acquiring Gulf Coast Mold to bring back our molding from China. We bought a robot for welding that saves us a great deal of time. We buy some machining and sensors outside. In 2014, we added 17,000 sq. ft. to our production space in the plant and expanded our injection molding operation by 6,500 sq. ft. We added 75 employees over the past 3 years and our revenue has been increasing 25% YOY in this time period. We are now up to about 200 employees, so we are the second largest manufacturer in the region."

With regard to my inquiry about being a lean company, he said that he had spent two years at NUMMI (Toyota Joint Venture) gaining an in-depth understanding of the Toyota Production System prior to spending seven years in a leadership role at General Motor's corporate Lean Office. He added, "We have a full time Lean black belt to train our employees. We have gone from 43-day material turnaround to an average of 27 days in the past two years. Our model for business planning is Hoshin Kanri, and we have a five-year business plan and an annual business plan tied into it. Our on-time delivery is 98.8% year to date, and our quality PPM has improved by 60% in the past two years. We use a two-bin KanBan system and one-piece flow for our assembly line operations. Our employees are cross trained, and we review our manufacturing cell metrics at weekly meetings."

The stories of these companies are good examples of innovation to develop new products, becoming a lean company, creating a new business model, and expanding into new markets.

Louisville Knocks Manufacturing out of the Park

In mid-November 2015, I had the pleasure of touring manufacturing plants in the Louisville, Kentucky region as the guest of the marketing consortium of the Greater Louisville Inc. Initiative. Well-known as the home of the Louisville Slugger baseball bat and the start of the "Bourbon Road" tours of bourbon and rye whiskey distilleries, Louisville has a much more diverse manufacturing base than I expected. My hostesses for the plant visits were Eileen Pickett and Ceci Conway, members of the marketing consortium.

We visited D. D. Williamson (DDW), the world leader in caramel color and a leading provider of natural colors for major food and beverage companies. DDW's natural colorings are used in everything from beer, malt ale, soft drinks, sauces, baked goods, cheese, ice cream, and confectionery products.

I was frankly astonished when Chairman and CEO Ted Nixon told me that the company had been founded in 1865 by Dutch immigrant Douw Ditmars Williamson in New York to manufacture burnt sugars for the brewing industry. He said that the company was well positioned to provide caramel color when the cola soft drink industry started and then expanded into colors for other products in the latter part of the 1900s. The company set up a plant in Louisville in 1948, and then moved its headquarters to Louisville in 1970.

Nixon said, "We set up our first plant outside of the U. S. in Ireland in 1978 to produce caramel for the European cola industry. Then, we set up a plant in Shanghai to manufacture caramel color for customers in Asia. In 1999, we began producing in Swaziland to supply customers in Africa, the Middle East and South Asia. In 2001, we opened a plant in Manaus, Brazil to service the South American market and acquired a company in Manchester, England in 2004. Now we have nine plants on five continents."

He added, "About ten years ago, we launched the first certified organic caramel colors in North America and added annatto extract, turmeric, paprika, and red beet to our natural color portfolio. Our lab is continually working on new natural flavors to keep us as the leading producer of natural colors."

The next day, we visited Amatrol, located across the river from Louisville in a 120,000 sq. ft. headquarters plant in Jeffersonville, Indiana. President Paul Perkins said that his parents, Don and Roberta Perkins, founded the original parent company, Dynafluid, Inc. in 1964. He said the company started as a manufacturer of industrial automation systems for many Fortune 500 companies including Coca Cola, General Electric, Alcoa, Ford, Chrysler, and others.

Perkins said, "Many of our customers wanted help in training their employees to use and maintain the automation systems and other equipment we built, so Amatrol was created as the educational division of Dynafluid in 1978 and was formally incorporated as a separate company in 1981. Amatrol, short for Automated Machine Controls, first provided training equipment to industrial and educational clients for new technologies like those being implemented in Dynafluid's systems."

Perkins said, "Amatrol was in a unique position to effectively develop training programs for these technologies because its engineers and technicians were thoroughly familiar with the design, application and maintenance of them. Since that time, Amatrol has grown significantly, becoming the leading company in our primary market segments."

Over the years, Amatrol focused its business model by providing training equipment and highly engaging interactive multimedia online training software in the following areas for high schools, colleges, and private industry: Advanced Manufacturing, Biotech, Certified Production Technician, CNC Machine Operator, Construction Technology, Engineering Technology, Green Energy Technology, HVAC, Industrial Maintenance, Iron and Steel, Mechanical Maintenance, Mechatronics, Mining, Oil and Gas, Packaging, Power and Energy, Solar Technology, and Wind Turbine Technology.

Perkins said, "A key factor to our success is that we have a group of people who have developed a very close connection and understanding of the needs of our customers and a realization that satisfying the needs of our customers to make them successful makes our company successful."

The last company I visited on my trip was Dant Clayton that manufacturers bleachers and stadium grandstand structures. Founded in 1979 by Bruce Merrick, the company started out making bleachers for Little League ball fields and has grown to providing everything needed for up to 60,000 seat stadiums.

We toured the two production plants built next to the corporate headquarters of the Dant Clayton campus, consisting of 350,000 sq. ft. of production space, spanning 25 acres. The company has a full range of material finish capabilities in-house, including powder coating of steel and aluminum and blasted slip-resistant deck. It was astonishing to see 3 ft. X 12 ft. steel beams attached to hooks moving down the 600-ft. robotic powder coating line before entering the oven to cure. I have never seen such a large supply of aluminum extrusions anywhere. I am sure that having these capabilities and equipment internally allows for greater quality control and continuous improvement.

Merrick said, "For the first few years, we experienced 20% growth before flattening for a while. Thereafter, we would experience growth spurts for two or three years, and during the growth spurts, we doubled the seating capacity of our bleachers from 500 to 1,000, to 2,000, to 5,000, to 10,000, to 25,000 and then 50,000." Merrick explained that they are the most competitive when they get involved at the design stage and provide engineering, construction management, and installation services."

When I asked what are the key factors that have led to his company's success, he said, "A culture of continuous improvement that goes beyond lean manufacturing to include product development, R&D efforts, and discovering latent customer needs, as well as rigorous

hiring practices, and a culture of personal development and
accountability by all employees."

The examples of commitment to excellence and continuous
improvement displayed by the companies I visited in Louisville are
what make America great. And, yes, I did get to visit the home of the
Louisville slugger between appointments. The company was wooed
back from Indiana to set up their manufacturing plant right on the
main street of downtown Louisville, and you can watch the bats
being made through windows on two sides of the building and visit
the museum that houses the model bats for all of the famous baseball
sluggers.

Cutting Edge Technologies Fuel Cincinnati Industries

The first week of November 2016, I visited Cincinnati, Ohio as the
guest of Source Cincinnati, an independent, multi-year national
social and media relations initiative that works to enhance
perceptions of Cincinnati as a world-class Midwestern region. Mr.
Paul Fox, VP of Strategic Initiatives at Proctor & Gamble and
"Executive on Loan" to Source Cincinnati for a year was gracious
host and tour guide.

While there, we met with Tony Canonaco, CEO, and Tom
Rosenberg, Director of Marketing, at Balluff's North American
headquarters based in Florence, Kentucky.

Mr. Canonaco said, "With over 50 years of sensor experience,
Balluff is a leading global sensor specialist with its own line of
connectivity products for every area of factory automation. Our
global headquarters is based in Germany, and our North American
headquarters was established in Florence, KY in the early 1980s.
Our products include a wide variety of sensors, mechanical limit
switches, rotary and linear measurement transducers, machine
vision and RFID systems, and distributed modular I/O network
solutions. Our products are involved in making the Industrial
Internet of Things (IIoT) work."

As we toured the plant, I saw their sensors being used right on their own production and packaging lines, as well as for inventory control of finished goods. With IIoT's promise of total visibility, we saw a great example right on their plant floor. IO-Link technology, an advanced point-to-point connection technology, was integrated into all their automated systems providing operators and management a continuous view of the process. With faster response to workload variations, Balluff now has a much leaner operation. Lean examples were also evident in their single-piece flow work cells. Products were produced in a surprisingly small footprint with high efficiency.

Mr. Canonaco said, "Many of our internal transitions towards Lean began during the recession in 2009. It was during this time, we realized that in order to better compete in the future, we needed to eliminate all types of waste and raise the level of productivity of the company. In addition to the change in their own mindset, we accelerated our New Product releases that focused on Automation and Sensing Solutions to help our customers shrink the size of their control panels, reduce their engineering time, and speed up troubleshooting on their machines.

We started our journey to become "Leaner" and our customers were provided with new products to help them realize performance and productivity machine enhancements as a result of the recession. Nearly a decade later, this path has proven to be a win-win for us and our customers.

We have our own accredited laboratory and a quality management system certified according to ISO 9001:2015 to form a secure foundation for optimized added value for our lab customers. Our products increase performance, quality and productivity around the world every day. They satisfy prerequisites for meeting demands for greater performance and cost reductions on the global market. We deliver state-of-the-art solutions no matter how stringent the requirements may be."

An additional customer-focused effect of their Lean journey is their most watched metric — On Time and In-Full Delivery to the customer. They consistently plan to achieve greater than 97%.

We also visited TSS Technologies, located in West Chester, Ohio where we met with CEO, Marc Drapp, followed by a tour of the facility. TSS Technologies provides complex electro-mechanical assemblies and turnkey contract manufacturing solutions to the aerospace, life sciences, energy, semiconductor, solar, sports, consumer, automotive, as well as food and beverage sectors. TSS also builds automation equipment for themselves and other companies.

Mr. Drapp said, "TSS Technologies has been in business for over 65 years and is family owned and operated. We have a machining facility totaling 110,000 square feet and an assembly facility totaling 210,000 square feet. We have approximately 225 employees. We are ISO 9001:2008 and 13485:2003 Certified, as well as AS9100C Certified and won the GE Healthcare Excellence award."

As we toured the plant, we saw examples of many of the above products being assembled or being staged for assembly for a couple new products coming online. Contrary to most contract manufacturers, Mr. Drapp likes to get involved with early stage companies to help them get into batch production and ramp up to full production. We saw a complete "bakery" producing shelf-stable pretzels that is an example of working with a start-up company to ramp up into full production within his facility.

When I asked Mr. Drapp how the Great Recession had affected them and what they did to recover, he said, "The recession was tough on our company, especially our machine shop. We lost a lot of contract machining work to our customers that brought the work back inside their plants. On the other hand, it really allowed for us to right size our operation and allow for us to be more nimble in the coming years.

We capitalized on the tough times by reorganizing our structure and tightening our manufacturing processes. This allowed us to become more Lean and efficient. Ultimately allowing us to come out of the recession quicker and better able to respond to customer needs. The recession really allowed for us to take a look at TSS and what we wanted to be. It allowed us to focus on the right customers for our business. It also allowed us to focus on the right areas for growth. From a Lean perspective, we have always practiced Lean manufacturing. The recession didn't really change that."

North Dakota Companies Capitalize on Industry Diversity

In April 2017, I was the guest of the North Dakota Department of Commerce Economic Development & Finance Division, which is charged with coordinating the state's economic development resources to attract, retain and expand wealth. My host was Paul Lucy, former director of the Economic Development & Finance Division. During my visit, we met with executives of several companies.

In Fargo, we met with Appareo President and CEO Barry Batcheller and Brenda Wyland, Director of Marketing. Appareo designs, develops and manufactures innovative electronic and software solutions for original equipment manufacturers, as well as direct-to-market. Appareo has established itself as a recognized leader in the custom design, development and manufacture of innovative electronic and software solutions within the industries of aerospace and agriculture.

Batcheller said, "I founded Appareo in 2003 and moved into the NDSU Technology Incubator when it opened in 2007. We started designing and manufacturing flight data recorders for airplanes and helicopters. Once we employed 50 people, we built our current building near the incubator in the Research Park and moved into it 2009. In 2013, we expanded our manufacturing facility to accommodate a second production line, but we quickly outgrew our space and purchased the adjacent manufacturing facility in 2014.

Our company surpassed the 200-employee mark in 2016 with NDSU graduates making up over 50% of our employees."

He said, "Appareo's proximity to the NDSU campus played an important role in the company's growth. We have access to the product of NDSU, which is really some of the finest minds in the nation. That is something we consume every day."

He explained. "Through the creative application of cutting-edge technologies, we create complex end-to-end solutions that include both mobile and cloud-based components. We are an accredited FAA Parts Manufacturing facility and are ISO 9001:2008 certified. All of our products are designed, developed, built, and supported in the USA. While our manufacturing expansion takes place in Fargo, we continue to expand our engineering capabilities with teams based in Tempe, Arizona and Paris, France. Having Appareo offices in Paris and Tempe is critical for building upon our global presence, but we have an unwavering commitment to Fargo as our home base. We're fortunate to have access to a rare talent pool here; some of the most passionate, brightest high-tech engineering minds in the nation."

He added, "Contributing to the growth of our agricultural business is a joint venture with AGCO Corporation, the world's largest OEM dedicated solely to agriculture. Under the joint venture, called Intelligent Ag Solutions, we develop innovative electromechanical devices and systems, as well as technology for advanced machine control systems. We are the only company controlling agricultural products by WIFI and GPS, which is good for active RFID tags. We work with agricultural equipment manufacturers to infuse these technologies into their equipment.

We have developed another new family of products under the Stratus name to meet the aviation needs to comply with the FAA mandate that requires all aircraft flying in current Mode-C airspace be equipped with ADS-B Out before 2020. We developed a portable receiver, transponder, antenna, and power charging port to provide real-time weather and traffic information directly to pilots in the cockpit."

His concluding remarks after we toured the shop floor were: "We have established a trajectory of rapid growth, averaging a compounded annual growth rate of more than 45%."

In the nearby city of Wahpeton, we visited ComDel Innovation, where we met with President Jim Albrecht, CFO Bruce Weeda, and General Manager Art Nelson. ComDel Innovation is a precision manufacturer that integrates all aspects of product development. ComDel's contract manufacturing services include precision component fabrication, molding, tooling and stamping dies, injection molding, metal stamping, assembly operations and metal finishing.

Jim said, "Our company was a captive shop for 3M, and Bruce and I had worked for 3M for many years. About four years ago, we decided to spin out on our own as an ESOP (Employee Stock Ownership Plan). We have two buildings totaling 260,000 sq. ft. Our name ComDel represents our commitment to deliver high quality parts and components to meet and deliver innovation and results for our customers. We succeed by utilizing rapid product development and stay ahead of the cost curve. We run 24 hours a day and 360 days a year. We started with 60 people and currently have 275 employees. We are experiencing companies' reshoring products from Asia to the U. S."

I asked if they are a Lean manufacturer, and Jim said. "We had become a Lean manufacturer under 3M and use all of the continuous improvement tools of Lean. We utilize a Total Quality Management Program to manage the quality of materials we purchase. We use computer-aided engineering to design custom assembly equipment, molds, tooling, and fixtures. We use CAD/CAM for our precision machining and grinding.

During the plant tour, I could see why ComDel is being successful in capturing business that is being reshored from Asia to the U. S. I saw considerable automation being used in their machining, stamping, and plastic injection molding departments. They have a Materials Laboratory to perform metallurgic tests, and utilize assembly cells for low to high volume production. They use robots for removing parts from molding machines in the machining, injection molding, and stamping departments. They have invested a considerable amount of money in utilizing state-of-the art equipment and systems. This is the path that American manufacturers need to take to be competitive in the global marketplace.

From these stories, we can see that innovation, cutting-edge technologies, unique capabilities, and Lean transformation have been critical to surviving the Great Recession, achieving good growth and profitability to become successful companies.

Remember, there are only three main ways to create wealth: Grow it, mine it, or make it. The spirit of American inventiveness and entrepreneurism are essential ingredients to rebuilding American manufacturing to create prosperity and jobs.

Chapter 8

How do we foster and develop the next generation of manufacturing workers?

Why do we have estimates of 600,000 to one million jobs going unfilled because of the lack of skilled workers when we have only gained about 600,000 manufacturing jobs since the depths of the recession in February 2010 and have nearly 95 million Americans that have dropped out of the workforce? The main reasons are:

- Unemployed workers are mainly from industries that have been decimated by trade deficits with China.
- American manufacturers chose to outsource manufacturing offshore.
- Fewer young people are choosing manufacturing as a career choice because of poor image.
- Attrition from retirement that is increasing as baby boomers retire.

First, a large percentage of the people who lost their jobs came out of industries that were decimated by Chinese product dumping and the offshoring of manufacturing – textiles, furniture, tires, sporting goods, and the garment industry, to name just a few.

Most of these industries were dominated by large manufacturers employing hundreds to thousands of workers in plants located in the northeast, Midwest, and south. These workers either worked on assembly lines or utilized specific skills suited to their industries. In some cases, a textile plant, furniture plant, or automotive plant was the only large employer in a town. When the plant closed, workers either had to take whatever other job they could find or relocate to another area. In most cases, these workers didn't have the specific skills needed in high-tech manufacturing industries.

An added blow was the decimation of the automobile and auto parts industry during the Great Recession when North American auto production dropped from a high of 17 million vehicles per year down to below 10 million vehicles in 2008 before climbing back up to about 13 million in 2012.[88]

Second, manufacturing's tarnished image has led young people entering the workforce to choose other career paths. In an article[89] titled, "What the shortage in skilled manufacturing workers means to a hungry industry" of the e-newsletter Smart Business, Kika Young, human resources director at Forest City Gear Co. Inc. of Rockford, IL, said "Most people in Gen Y out of high school don't think of manufacturing as a career or as a good option. They don't think of it as glamorous; they think of it as dark and dingy and dirty and aren't interested in going into that."

Emily Stover DeRocco, president of The Manufacturing Institute of Washington, D.C., said,[90] "It's absolutely true that the image and the definition of manufacturing in this country has not kept up with the industry." She added, "Companies need to invest more in employee training and make workforce skills a top strategic priority. Our education system must also do a better job aligning education and training to the needs of employers and job seekers. In the face of a global recession and intense international competition, American manufacturers must differentiate themselves through innovation and a highly skilled workforce."

Third, the attrition of skilled workers through retirement, death, and disability year after year is compounding the problem. Harry Moser, retired president of GF AgieCharmilles and founder of the Reshoring Initiative, estimates that "about 8 percent of the manufacturing workforce is lost each year due to retirement, promotion, career changes, disability, and mortality." In the machining industry, this means a loss of "about 20,000 to 25,000 skilled machinists per year...In contrast, only about 8,000 per year receive sufficient machining training in high school, community college and apprentice programs to be considered good recruits."

In 2011, the U.S. Bureau of Labor statistics estimated that 2.8 million, nearly a quarter of all U.S. manufacturing workers, were 55 or older. While manufacturing has led the United States out of the recession, the improvement has been a mixed blessing because as more skilled workers are needed, the supply is limited because baby boomers are retiring or getting close to retirement. What makes the situation worse is that there are not enough new ones to replace them because the subsequent generations were smaller and fewer chose manufacturing as a career.

The convergence of all of these factors has resulted in an insufficient number of workers trained for advanced manufacturing jobs. It is more of a skills gap in the specific skills needed by today's manufacturers than a shortage of skilled workers. In the past 15 years, the manufacturing industry has evolved from needing low-skilled production-type assembly workers to being highly technology-infused.

The 2016 ManpowerGroup annual Talent Shortage Survey[91] revealed that "the percentage of U.S. employers reporting difficulty filling jobs increased to 46% in 2016. This means nearly half of employers are experiencing difficulty filling positions...Across the United States, employers report that skilled trade vacancies remain the hardest to fill, as was the case in each of the previous six years. Skilled trades have been on the top 10 list nine times in the past 11 years and have maintained the number one position from 2010 to 2016."

Training to Address Skills Shortage:

The last U.S. Government Accountability Office study[92] of federally-funded training programs was done in 2011, based on fiscal year 2009. According to the report, the federal government had 47 programs run by nine different agencies. The GAO noted that more information is needed to measure the true effectiveness of the programs. "Almost all of the 47 programs tracked multiple outcome measures related to employment and training, and the most frequently tracked outcome measure was 'entered employment,' the agency stated. "However, little is known about the effectiveness of employment and training programs because, since 2004, only five reported conducting an impact study, and about half of all the remaining programs have not had a performance review of any kind."

Obviously, we could make government work better and save money in the process by consolidating some of these programs and giving some of the money to the states for programs that work best for their workers. However, it doesn't necessarily mean programs can be combined. It might not make sense, for example, to combine the "Disabled Veterans' Outreach Program" with the "Migrant and Seasonal Farmworkers Program," or the "Native American Employment and Training Program" with the "National Guard Youth Challenge Program." In addition, the programs are not equal in size or scope. The GAO reported that "seven programs accounted for 75 percent of the $18 billion spent on job training" in 2011, while two programs ("Wagner-Peyser funded Employment Service" and "Workforce Investment Act Adult") served about 77 percent of all participants.

However, we don't need to rely solely on government-funded training for manufacturing jobs. A great deal has already been done industry, trade and professional organizations, colleges, and universities to train and retrain today's workers and prepare the next generation of manufacturing workers.

In the last 20 years, the training process has become much more sophisticated. Training is no longer "one size fits all." Organizations are looking at employees individually and building customized training programs to specifically fit their strengths and weaknesses.

Professional and technical certifications provide objective confirmation and assurance of skill achievement in various areas of technical expertise. Certification validates a level of expertise and provides employees with advancement opportunities that motivate them to continue learning.

Certification organizations, such as the National Institute of Metalworking Skills (NIMS), Manufacturing Skills Standards Council (MSSC), SME, and American Welding Society (AWS), require manufacturers to show that employees have applied and retained the knowledge and skills they received through training.

The National Institute for Metalworking Skills (NIMS) was formed in 1995 by the metalworking trade associations to develop and maintain a globally competitive American workforce. NIMS sets skills standards for the industry, certifies individual skills against the standards, and accredits training programs that meet NIMS quality requirements. NIMS operates under rigorous and highly disciplined processes as the only developer of American National Standards for the nation's metalworking industry accredited by the American National Standards Institute (ANSI).

NIMS has a stakeholder base of over 6,000 metalworking companies and major trade associations in the industry. The Association for Manufacturing Technology, the American Machine Tool Distributors' Association, the National Tooling & Machining Association, the Precision Machine Products Association, the Precision Metalforming Association, and the Tooling and Manufacturing Association have invested over $7.5 million in private funds for the development of the NIMS standards and its credentials. The associations also contribute annually to sustain NIMS operations and are committed to the upgrading and maintenance of the standards.

NIMS has developed skills standards in 24 operational areas covering the breadth of metalworking operations, and there are 52 distinct NIMS skill certifications. The Standards range from entry to master level. All NIMS standards are industry-written and industry-validated, and are subject to regular, periodic reviews under the procedures accredited and audited by ANSI. NIMS certifies individual skills against the national standards and requires that the candidate meets both performance and theory requirements that are industry-designed and industry-piloted.

NIMS accredits training programs that meet its quality requirements. The NIMS accreditation requirements include an on-site audit and evaluation by a NIMS industry team that reviews and conducts on-site inspections of all aspects of the training programs, including administrative support, curriculum, plant, equipment and tooling, student and trainee progress, industry involvement, instructor qualifications and safety. Officials governing NIMS accredited programs report annually on progress and are subject to re-accreditation on a five-year cycle.

The SME (formerly the Society of Manufacturing Engineers), the world's leading professional society advancing manufacturing knowledge, also provides the following professional certifications: Manufacturing Technologist, Manufacturing Engineering, Engineering Manager, Lean Certification (Bronze, Silver, and Gold), and Six Sigma. SME's Certified Manufacturing Technologist program is utilized as an outcome assessment by numerous colleges and universities with Manufacturing, Manufacturing Engineering or Engineering Technology programs.

In 2010, the SME acquired Tooling University LLC (Tooling U) based in Cleveland, Ohio to provide online, onsite, and webinar training for manufacturing companies and educational institutions. With more than 400 unique titles, Tooling U offers a full range of content to train machine operators, welders, assemblers, inspectors, and maintenance professionals. These classes are delivered through a custom learning management system (LMS), which provides extensive tracking and reporting capabilities. The competencies tie the online curriculum to matching hands-on tasks that put the theory to practice.

On September 8, 2016, ToolingU-SME, released a report[93] that showed the progress towards achieving the goal of the Mission Critical: Workforce 2021. Based on five years of insights from the Workforce 2021 Assessment tool, the report states, "the results are not encouraging. Responses show there has been little advancement. While it's not too late, companies must take action now to ensure a healthier next decade." The report quotes from report, "The Skills

Gap in US Manufacturing: 2015 and Beyond" by Deloitte and The Manufacturing Institute, which states, "Over the next decade, nearly 3.5 million manufacturing jobs will likely need to be filled. The skills gap is expected to result in 2 million of those jobs remaining unfilled."

ToolingU-SME Vice President Jeannine Kunz wrote in the cover letter, "only a very small number of world-class organizations are prepared for the extreme talent gap predicted by the year 2021. Some of these companies started planning years ago to address the coming labor shortage. Others were forced to take reactionary steps when faced with a shrinking employee pool. Regardless, they started formal training programs, introduced apprenticeships, built relationships with educators and more...At Tooling U-SME, we are concerned that more manufacturers aren't taking action since this has a big impact on the long-term health and competitiveness of the industry as a whole. There is a false sense of security among many manufacturers who are not recognizing these future challenges or investing in the development of their workforce today."

The companies that responded to the survey fall into four categories: procrastinator, strategist, role model, and visionary. The procrastinators nearly make up the majority of the respondents because 49% said that "their company has not begun assessing their manufacturing employee's current skills against skills they will require in the future." In fact, only "1 out of 20 (5%) acknowledge conducting a complete assessment of all staff." Since "nearly 9 out of 10 respondents (88%) said their company is having problems finding skilled works in manufacturing," you would think there would be more urgency to address this problem. This problem will only get worse because "14% of respondents say they will lose a full quarter (25%) or more of their workforce to retirements in the next five years."

The key findings were:

- "Less than one-third (29%) of respondents would characterize their company's talent development as good or excellent"

- "30% say their company has no community involvement (internships, co-op, etc.) to help develop the proper skills of their incoming workers."
- "54% don't budget for employee development"
- "33% say their job-related training options are minimal"
- "88% say their company is below average when it comes to offering outside resources to upgrade the skill sets of employees"

SME contrasts "competency" with a "Competency Model." Competency is defined as the capability to apply a set of related knowledge, skills, and abilities (KSA) to successfully perform functions or tasks in a defined work setting. They serve as the basis for skill standards that specify the KSAs needed for success and measurement criteria for assessing competency attainment. A competency framework is used to design a plan specific to a particular manufacturing environment or organization or when there are no manufacturing certifications tied to desired job roles.

 A competency model is defined as a collection of competencies that together define successful performance in a particular work setting. Competency models are the foundation for functions such as recruitment and hiring, training and development, and performance management. Competency models can be developed for specific jobs, job groups, organizations, occupations, or industries.

Competency models allow companies to combat the increasing talent shortage and achieve stronger performance from their workforce while providing clear development pathways and career growth opportunities for their employees.

Good training requires both knowledge and skills that may not come from informal knowledge transfer or tribal learning. It requires understanding the concepts of what and why a job is done a certain way, and then requires on-the-job training to validate that the worker can fulfill the needs of that job.

The key is commitment from top management down to individual employees. It is important to communicate to all employees that the focus is on knowledge and skill requirements of the job and align training designed to help each person perform his or her job more efficiently, while providing new growth opportunities. An effective training program will include a validation process that not only tests a new skill but provides employees with the opportunity to gain new skills, apply them on the job, and then have their new skill sets validated through assessments, testing, and certifications.

A well-designed competency model can become the foundation for performance management, talent acquisition and leadership development for manufacturing companies. To combat the current and future talent gap and build a high-performance team, it is critical for companies to have a system in place to codify knowledge and skills required for specific job roles aligned with the appropriate training.

The Fabricators and Manufacturers Association International (FMA) champions the success of the metal processing, forming, and fabricating industry. FMA educates the industry through the following programs:

FabCast – FMA's webinar platform utilizes internet connection and telephone to deliver live, interactive technical education programs directly to manufacturers on such topics as laser cutting, roll forming, metal stamping, etc. Companies can train their whole team at once, even from multiple locations. Companies can break up full days of instruction into modules and spread out over a period of time (i.e. two hours four days a week, four hours once a week for a month, etc.).

FMA also offers on-site, live training conducted at companies on their equipment as well as on-line training (e-Fab) that allows a company to get the training that they need, when they need it. E-Fab courses combine a full day's worth of instruction by FMA's leading subject matter experts with the flexibility of online delivery, available 24/7, 365 days a year.

FMA provides a Precision Sheet Metal Operator (PSMO) Certification – the metal fabricating industry's only comprehensive exam designed to assess a candidate's knowledge of fundamental precision sheet metal operations. Fabrication processes covered in the exam include shearing, sawing, press brake, turret punch press, laser cutting, and mechanical finishing.

Workshop for Warriors Trains Veterans in Manufacturing Skills

I first toured Workshops for Warriors during the first Manufacturing Day on October 5, 2012 and met retired naval officer Hernán Luis y Prado, founder and president of Workshops for Warriors (WFW). Hernán and his wife Rachel self-financed the training they began providing in their own garage after he ran into one of his buddies from his service in Iraq confined to a wheel chair after losing both his legs from an IED while Hernán was still in the service. He said that he was heartsick at seeing too many veterans unable to transition successfully into civilian life and even commit suicide. He founded WFW in late 2007 and received non-profit 501(c) 3 designation in April 2008. He and his wife decided to invest all of their assets to expand into their first small building in early 2011. Goodrich Aerostructures, in Chula Vista, California started to donate in 2010 and donated their first mobile classroom when they moved into a building twice the size in October 2011. WFW teaches:

- Computer-Aided Design
- Computer-Aided Manufacturing
- Machinery Repair and Maintenance
- CNC and manual Machining and Turning
- Welding and Fabrication

When I attended a graduation ceremony in December 2016, Hernán said that students are now able to earn nationally recognized portable credentials from The American Welding Society (AWS), the National Institute for Metalworking Skills (NIMS), Mastercam University, SolidWorks, Immerse2Learn, and the National Coalition of Certification Centers (NC3).

He said, "Workshops for Warriors has become a nationally viable advanced manufacturing training pipeline that is ready to be scaled and replicated across America. Once the GI Bill is accepted at WFW, we will be self-sustaining and ready for expansion."

He explained that they have begun a two-year Capital Campaign to raise $21 million to expand nationally. He said, "We have raised 18% of our goal. Phase 1 of building our first of three buildings is scheduled to be completed by fall 2017. Our current San Diego headquarters will become a Train-the-Trainer and Veteran Incubator facility. Our plan is to create 103 WFW facilities across the USA located in areas with high military transition populations and advanced manufacturing training nodes." The formal Capital Campaign was launched at a special gala on April 20, 2017 on the U.S.S. Midway aircraft carrier museum.

At the gala, Hernán said, "Our program is called Rebuilding America's Advanced Manufacturing Force. The purpose is to eliminate Veteran unemployment and underemployment, replenish the lack of talent pipeline for the manufacturing industry, and make a social and economic impact -individual to family to community to the Nation."

The national program will include:

- Train-the-Trainer Blueprint
- Sustainable Model Development (internal efforts)
- Strategic Partnership for National Footprint (external efforts)
- Tuition/Scholarships
- Staff & Top-Tier Teachers
- Job Counseling & Placement
- Land acquisition
- Equipment, furniture & fixtures
- New and renovated construction

Hernán announced that they have graduated 388 veterans, wounded warriors, and transitioning service members who earned over 1,500 national recognized certifications." Hernán said, "Many of you understand our Double Funnel dilemma...a waiting list of over 500 students but over 2,500 jobs available nationwide for each one of our graduates...The Challenge? There is only funding for 50 students every semester."

In the closing remarks, Special Guest Speaker Donald "Doc" Ballard, Metal of Honor Recipient, said, "...only 1% has served our country...Not everyone can serve in the military, but we do have an obligation to this country to thank veterans for the freedom they fought for...We thank a teacher for our ability to read, but we can thank a veteran that we can read and write in English. We can thank veterans by supporting Workshops for Warriors so they can expand to other states. Everyone can serve the military by taking care of the people who are doing the job they can do or won't do for whatever reason..."

Vocademy - An industry driven solution to the skills gap
In the summer of 2016, I had the opportunity to visit Vocademy in Riverside, CA, which is a combination of the "best parts of makerspaces, school shop classes, trade schools, R&D labs, and dream garages, all in one place. Vocademy is the fulfillment of the dream of Gene Sherman "to solve the skills gap for the manufacturing industry." His goal is to replicate Vocademy facilities all over the country and help eliminate the skills gap in just a few years.

When I asked why he started Vocademy, he said, "Over the past 20 years, I witnessed the demise of hands-on skills teaching in this country. Schools have done away with these critical classes that taught practical life skills like woodworking and metal shop. These were the classes where people learned how to use tools and technology and develop the mindsets necessary to create new and amazing things.

Companies used to have apprenticeship programs or offered to hire people and train them. But most of these programs have gone away due to budget constraints or changing technology. Most companies do not have the time or resources to train people in fundamental hands-on skills. So, there is a vast divide between the companies that need skilled people and opportunities for people to obtain those skills. Today, manufacturing is not just hammers and screwdrivers. It's advanced textiles, robotics, automation, composites, and other high-tech hands-on skills. The Skills Gap problem exists, but with very few solutions.

Vocademy is an idea that I had for many years. When I saw 'makerspaces' springing up, I wanted to combine that type space with teaching the kinds of skills that were previously taught in 'shop' classes. I wanted to create a place for those who want to use their hands, in addition to their minds — makers, inventors, and dreamers. I believe that if our country loses its ability to make and build things, we will have lost what made America great.

I wanted to provide access to these tools, but with proper and practical instruction on how to use them correctly and safely. I wanted a place that teaches the most state-of-the-art manufacturing techniques, not just traditional shop skills. I wanted to teach these important skills without the bureaucracy of academia because many more Americans should have the same opportunity to innovate, collaborate, learn, and create their dreams."

He started what has become the Vocademy program in the shop he had built behind his house and started teaching machining skills evenings and on weekends. In 2012, he moved into an office building with the equipment he had and funded Vocademy with his own life savings. Since then, he has been able to increase their equipment by forming partnerships with equipment manufacturers to get equipment at low or no cost. Several companies, such as ProtoTRAK CNC, Weller APEX, Full Spectrum Laser, VPro 3D Printers, Mark Forged 3D Printers, and others have come on board as OEM partners. They see the value in helping create a workforce and the brand exposure Vocademy provides.

When I asked Gene how the "Makerspace" and classes are combined, he said, "From Monday-Friday, it is a place of learning for schools and companies, and then it becomes a 'makerspace' nights and weekends, open to everyone, ages 14+, 7-days a week on a membership basis. We have all the amazing tools you would want in your own dream garage, workshop, or inventor's lab. We make it accessible to all those in the community who want to learn, build, create, and become makers. We have classes that can take anyone from absolute beginner, all the way to expert, and anywhere in between. We provide the best combination of tools, equipment, instructors, access, and education. We offer hands-on skills training for kids, employees, teachers, students, organizations, and companies. We're not a replacement for trade schools or colleges; we're the place where someone discovers that they are makers and gets a solid set of foundational skills — enough skills to get a good entry level job, pursue a higher education, continue on to trade school, or become an entrepreneur."

With regard to his future plans. he said, "Going forward, we plan on replicating this model all over the country. Our second Vocademy will be in Orange County, number three in Pasadena/Burbank area, and number four in San Diego. My long-range goal is to have more than 1,000 facilities nationwide. It only costs about $2,000,000 to set up a 30,000-sq. ft. facility in southern California, so it would be cheaper in other parts of the country. If we could get more corporate sponsors or partners to provide some or all of the equipment, the costs could be reduced. The other big part of our business is helping others set up makerspaces in schools, colleges, communities, and companies. These smaller turnkey makerspaces can be the place where the maker passion is ignited and a career path is found."

I told him that I hope he realizes his dream because it is critical that we get back to being a nation of "makers" as manufacturing is the foundation of the middle class, and our middle class has been shrinking for the last 30 years as we moved more and more manufacturing offshore.

Attracting the Next Generation of Manufacturing Workers:

If we want to attract today's youth to manufacturing careers, we need to change their perceptions about what the manufacturing industry is like and show them what great career opportunities exist in the industry. We need to make manufacturing "cool," so they will choose to be part of the modern advanced manufacturing.

One reason for the shortage is that public misperceptions of advanced manufacturing has led young people entering the workforce to choose other career paths. In an article[94] titled, "What the shortage in skilled manufacturing workers means to a hungry industry" of the e-newsletter Smart Business, Kika Young, human resources director at Forest City Gear Co. Inc. of Rockford, IL, said "Most people in Gen Y out of high school don't think of manufacturing as a career or as a good option. They don't think of it as glamorous; they think of it as dark and dingy and dirty and aren't interested in going into that."

We need to show young people what great career opportunities exist in the industry and expose them to the variety of career opportunities in manufacturing. We need to expose them to the variety of career opportunities in manufacturing, so they will choose to be part of modern manufacturing. Most outsiders have no idea of the variety of management jobs available at manufacturing companies. Besides the usual executive jobs, other management jobs available at medium and large manufacturers are in these areas: operations, plant and facilities, manufacturing and production, purchasing and procurement, sales and marketing, quality, supply chain, lean manufacturing and continuous improvement, human resources, R&D and product development, and safety and regulatory compliance.

We need to help our youth realize that manufacturing careers, and particularly the advanced manufacturing that now dominates the U.S. industrial sector, creates more wealth than any other industry. Moreover, manufacturing pays higher wages and provides greater benefits, on average, than other industries. According to the National Association of Manufacturers (NAM), "In 2015,[95] the average manufacturing worker in the United States earned $81,289 annually, including pay and benefits. The average worker in all nonfarm industries earned $63,830."

We need to reacquaint youth with the process of designing and building products from an early age and provide them with the opportunities to learn in both traditional and non-traditional ways. Here are some suggestions:

Conduct manufacturing summer camps
Restore shop classes to our high schools
Improve the image of manufacturing careers
Establish Apprenticeship Programs

The National Tooling and Machining Association (NTMA) is another trade association that has a program to encourage youth to consider manufacturing as a career. NTMA is the Founding Sponsor of an exciting educational program that provides unlimited career awareness experiences in advanced manufacturing technology for students from middle school through college age. The approach has three components: a robotics curriculum based on national standards, teacher training workshops, and competitive events where students showcase their custom-built machines and compete for top honors. NTMA has six active regional leagues in their National Robotics League, a competition of battling robots that generates huge excitement among high school students.

In 2011, the National Institute for Metalworking Skills (NIMS) launched a new Competency-based Apprenticeship System for the nation's metalworking industry. Employers are able to customize training to meet their own needs while maintaining the national integrity of apprenticeship training. Developed in partnership with the United States Department of Labor, the new system is the result of two years of work. Over 300 companies participated in the deliberations and design. The new National Guideline Standards for NIMS Competency-based Apprenticeship have been approved by the Department of Labor. NIMS has trained Department of Labor apprenticeship staff at the national and state level in the new system.

The National Association of Manufacturers (NAM) heard from its members that they were having trouble attracting employees with the right mix of skills in certain job functions despite layoffs. To learn more, NAM and Deloitte & Touche conducted extensive quantitative and qualitative research across the U.S. They found that an estimated 80 percent of manufacturers reported a moderate-to-serious shortage of qualified job applicants during the recent recession, a problem growing increasingly urgent with the increase in global competition and retirement of Baby Boomers. They also found that manufacturing has an outdated image, filled with stereotypes of assembly line jobs, that has kept young people from pursuing careers in it.

The Manufacturing Institute launched the Dream It. Do It™ network in 2005 to change the perception of the industry and inspire next-generation workers to pursue manufacturing careers. "Members of the Dream It. Do It. program gain access to national support and resources to aid their pro-manufacturing efforts and join a network of industry leaders that implement activities to meet local, regional and statewide workforce needs.

The initiative offers local manufacturers, schools, community-based organizations and other stakeholders the opportunity to partner with a respected national platform to promote manufacturing as a top tier career choice in the United States. Dream It. Do It. promotes manufacturing to three distinct target markets: student, parents and educators. The "campaign was created because these perceptions are out-of-step with manufacturing's broad range of interesting and financially rewarding careers."

The program formed strong and committed coalitions with local civic, political, education, and business entities and formed local partnerships with community colleges, technical schools and universities for students pursuing manufacturing careers.

Since 2005, NAM's "Dream It. Do It ™" program has expanded to 37 states. In 2016, the network successfully engaged:

- 384,952 students
- 68,971 parents
- 19,489 educators

- 4,994 employers

In 2011, the SME Education Foundation initiated PRIME® (Partnership Response in Manufacturing Education) as a major national initiative to take a community-based approach to advanced manufacturing education and create strong partnerships between exemplary schools, businesses and organizations. Through its advanced manufacturing education program, SME is re-tooling and building the pipeline with technically skilled workers as business, industry and academia form partnerships and accelerate their collaborative efforts to provide funding, equipment, mentoring, teacher training and co-op programs for high school students to begin manufacturing products in the classroom. The manufacturing sector is on the upswing and public perception of manufacturing as a career is more positive as students see first-hand the kinds of things they are capable of making.

PRIME® is a collaborative model that engages regional manufacturers, local schools and other community representatives to establish a tailored advanced manufacturing/STEM education that provides high school students with relevant, hands-on knowledge and skills. PRIME® gives manufacturers a voice in education, builds student awareness of manufacturing career pathways, and provides youth with 21st century manufacturing skills, which can lead to industry credentials. Students graduating from the PRIME® program are often capable of successfully transitioning to the manufacturing workforce immediately upon high school graduation.

Established in 2011, PRIME® has grown to 41 schools[96] in 22 states, impacting more than 6,500 students annually with 70 percent of graduating PRIME® seniors pursuing a postsecondary education in manufacturing or engineering. SME Education Foundation has also supported 144 PRIME® students with nearly $400,000 in scholarship awards.

In my home state of California, there are six PRIME® schools: Esperanza High School, Hawthorne High School, John Glenn High

School, Petaluma High School, Rocklin High School, and San
Pasqual High School.

SME Education Foundation is working to expand its network by
working with corporate partners to sponsor the development of new
PRIME® sites at high schools throughout the country. "PRIME® is
forging a path to revitalize manufacturing education and fostering
the development of a highly skilled, STEM-capable workforce," said
Brian Glowiak, director of the SME Education Foundation.
"Through the support of visionary corporate partners, like Alcoa and
Honda, we are helping to create the next generation of
manufacturing engineers and technologists and championing one of
the most critical elements for innovation success."

SME Education Foundation and PRIME® provide a winning
solution for students by offering them opportunities to:

- Collaborate with local SME Chapters and industry partners to
  co-host events
- Engage with other students and educators in the PRIME®
  network to share their experiences and creative lesson plans
  as well as participate in student competitions
- Participate in Advanced Manufacturing/STEM camps with
  younger students and other extracurricular activities
- Receive post-secondary educational scholarships
- Engage with SME members who can share their technical
  knowledge and experience by mentoring PRIME students,
  offering internships and providing job-shadowing
  opportunities.
- Attend student summits at SME's national manufacturing
  events. These summits allow students, parents and educators
  to interact face-to-face with representatives of companies that
  provide revolutionary technologies and business-changing
  innovations.
- Implement training materials and curriculum from Tooling
  U-SME, the industry leader in manufacturing learning and
  development.

- Receive SME's Advanced Manufacturing Media, which produces digital and print publications that cover relevant manufacturing news, technology and advances.

In early 2017, the "SME Education Foundation[27] announced a new partnership with NASA's agency-wide HUNCH (High School Students United with NASA to Create Hardware) program, to get more youth engaged in advanced manufacturing and ultimately encourage them to consider and pursue long-term careers in the industry." This collaboration between HUNCH and the Foundation's Partnership Response In Manufacturing Education (PRIME) initiative will give high school students an opportunity to build actual hardware that NASA astronauts, scientists, and engineers would use in their training programs and at the International Space Station (ISS).

By combining our PRIME network with NASA's HUNCH program and working together to further expand the number of schools in the combined network, we can provide more students with access to a STEM and manufacturing focused education using hands-on learning experiences," said Brian Glowiak, vice president of the SME Education Foundation. "Through this partnership we are motivating youth to consider careers in manufacturing and preparing them with the skill sets and knowledge to succeed."

He explained, "Through the HUNCH program, PRIME students will have the opportunity to design and build actual hardware for in-flight astronaut training or for use aboard the International Space Station, bringing real-world project based learning experiences to the classroom. Alternately, HUNCH schools will now be part of the PRIME network, having access to SME student memberships, mentoring programs, and additional technical resources."

The HUNCH website states, "the idea of HUNCH started when Stacy Hale, the JSC HUNCH project manager, had the innovative idea that maybe high school students could build cost-effective hardware that was needed to help train the ISS astronauts. Bob Zeek at MSFC [Marshall Space Flight Center] and Hale decided to test the feasibility of this idea. Many were skeptical about this idea, but because of the hard work and dedication of Hale and Zeek, HUNCH quickly expanded from 3 schools to numerous schools, in various states; the unique idea of HUNCH was quickly producing extremely positive results to all involved."

Blake Ratcliff, NASA's HUNCH Program Manager, said, "It is a project based program. We give schools real NASA projects that meet the needs and provide them the materials and instructions they need to complete the work. Quality is the most important aspect of the work, and the schools have done an outstanding job. Every year in April and May, we have Recognition Ceremonies for all the students and teachers that have participated in HUNCH at MSFC and JSC. The students present their projects during the HUNCH Ceremony where some projects are selected to be used in NASA systems and on board the ISS. Every year the number of participants continues to grow as well as the quality, quantity, and diversity of the products that students fabricate."

Both the SME PRIME initiative and NASA's HUNCH program are promoting student interest in STEM (Science, Technology, Engineering, and Mathematics.) Another benefit is that while students are building hardware and doing other projects for NASA, they are also building their interest as engineers, researchers, scientists and maybe even astronauts, as well as their self-esteem. HUNCH is a win-win innovative solution for inspiring the next generation of researchers, scientists, engineers, and manufacturing workers while providing cost-effective hardware for NASA.

On a nationwide basis, the non-profit organization Project Lead The Way®[98] (PLTW) has been working since 1997 to promote pre-engineering courses for middle and high school students. PLTW forms partnerships with public schools, higher education institutions, and the private sector to increase the quantity and quality of engineers and engineering technologists graduating from our educational system. The PLTW curriculum was first introduced to 12 New York State high schools in the 1997-98 school years. A year later, PLTW field-tested its four-unit Middle School Program in three middle schools. Today, there are over 400,000 students enrolled in programs in all 50 states and the District of Columbia.

PLTW has developed innovative and mutually beneficial partnerships with more than 100 prestigious colleges and universities, called University Affiliates, to facilitate the delivery of the PLTW programs. They provide and coordinate activities such as professional development, college-level recognition, program quality initiatives, and statewide/regional support and communication.

PLTW has nearly 100 leading corporate sponsors, including 3M, BAE Systems, Boeing, Caterpillar, Chevron, Intel, Lockheed Martin, Northrop Grumman, Qualcomm, Rockwell Automation, Solar Turbines, and Sprint. Some of non-profit sponsors are the Kauffman Foundation and the Society of Manufacturing Engineers Education Foundation. Corporations and philanthropic organizations generously provide PLTW with:

- capital resources which it allocates to schools so that they may deliver leading-edge STEM curriculum, technology, materials and equipment to students;
- access to experienced and talented employees who assist teachers in PLTW classrooms.

PLTW has expanded into several complimentary programs:

- PLTW Launch taps into their exploratory nature of K – 5th grade students, engages them in learning that feels like play, and encourages them to keep discovering – now and for years to come.

- PLTW Computer Science empowers students in grades 9-12 to become creators, instead of merely consumers, of the technology all around them.

- PLTW Engineering empowers students to step into the role of an engineer, adopt a problem-solving mindset, and make the leap from dreamers to doers.

- PLTW Gateway Academy program, sponsored by the SME Education Foundation and other organizations, is a one- or two-week day camp for 6th - 8th graders that is a project based, hands-on curriculum designed by PLTW to introduce middle school students to the fundamentals of science, technology, engineering and math (STEM) learning.
- PLTW Gateway Professional Development is a dynamic learning experience for teachers focused on robust and flexible instructional support, on-demand resources, and a close-knit community of collaboration with fellow educators.

If all 50 states would establish career technical education in their high schools based on the successful PLTW curriculum, we could eliminate the skills shortage of manufacturing workers within the next five to six years and prepare the next generation of manufacturing and biotech workers to ensure that we have enough skilled workers for manufacturers to employ as more and more companies return manufacturing to America from outsourcing offshore and replace the "baby boomers" as they retire over the next 20 years.

Innovative Programs Provide Career and Technical Education in High Schools

There are already a number of innovative high schools across the country that are pioneering a model for career and technical education that has little to do with the narrow vocational classes of yesteryear, like wood shop and auto shop. Instead, at Linked Learning schools in California, at the MET schools in Rhode Island, and at Tech Valley High outside Albany, high school students complete internships in real workplaces, exploring fields as diverse as baking, engineering, and biotechnology. Students have the opportunity to check out more than one profession so they can see how adults use their education in the workplace. This helps students stay motivated to earn a degree and introduces them to the behaviors and practices specific to the working world.

California is one of the states that put vocational training back into the curriculum at high schools and community colleges. During his terms as California's governor from 2003-2010, Arnold Schwarzenegger identified workforce skills, referred to as Career Technical Education[99] (CTE), as a priority for California. The State plan specifies learning goals in 58 career pathways organized around 15 industry sectors. The CTE is delivered primarily through K-12/adult education programs and community college programs.

As a result, California developed "Linked Learning,[100]" an approach that is transforming education for California students by integrating rigorous academics with career-based learning and real-world workplace experiences. Linked Learning ignites high school students' passions by creating meaningful learning experiences through career-oriented pathways in fields such as engineering, health care, performing arts, law, and more.

The Linked Learning pathway is defined as: A multiyear, comprehensive high school program of integrated academic and career technical study that is organized around a broad theme, interest area, or industry sector. Pathways connect learning with students' interests and career aspirations, preparing them for the full range of post-graduation options including two and four-year colleges and universities, apprenticeships, formal employment training, and military service.

In 2012, 63 districts and county offices of education in California committed to making Linked Learning a district-wide improvement strategy and participate in the state Linked Learning Pilot Program, authorized by Assembly Bill 790. Linked Learning is implemented through various models such as the California Linked Learning District initiative, which includes districts that have already implemented the Linked Learning approach:

Additional models include California Partnership Academies, career academies, National Academy Foundation academies, charter schools, and small-themed schools to name just a few. Today in California, 500 California Partnership Academies are organized around one of the state's California's 15 major industry sectors, and another approximately 300 career academies are in operation. Regional Occupational Centers and Programs (ROCPs) play an important part in many of these academies. In many other high schools, ROCPs are experimenting with innovative approaches to integrate academic and technical education.

An example of the CTE training at the community college level is one provided by the San Diego Continuing Education headquarters facility under the jurisdiction of the San Diego Community College District. A couple of years ago, I was given a tour of the facility by Dean Jane Signaigo-Cox and Vice President Brian Ellison. Continuing Education is the new name for what we used to call Adult Education where you could go back to school to get your high school diploma or take enrichment classes in art, cooking, foreign languages, sewing, etc.

While these types of classes are still being offered to adults over the age of 18, it is now possible to get technical job training and even certification in a variety of careers, such as automotive, computers, electronics, graphics, upholstery, pipe fitting, and welding. Unbelievably, these classes are free in California.

San Diego's Continuing Education program has been making history since 1914, when it started providing job training for returning military veterans from WWI. Year after year, more than 74,000 students are served annually by the seven Continuing Education campuses and many offsite community locations throughout the city of San Diego.

According to Dean Signaigo-Cox, "more than 1800 of the certificates awarded were for these Career Technical Education job training programs. Since students spend an average of 65 to 70 percent of course time using hands on tools and technology to learn relevant skills for today's jobs, they are prepared for an entry level position in their field after completing these courses."

My tour of the Educational Cultural Complex campus included the pipe fitting and welding training department. I was amazed at the number of Miller Electric welding stations they had to teach students in both MIG and TIG welding techniques. They even had one of the newer Lincoln Electric welding simulators that I got to try out at the FABTECH show in Las Vegas in 2012.

After certification, entry-level pipe fitters can earn $17/hour and welders can earn $19/hour, which is a very good entry-level wage in San Diego. Journeymen welders can make double this wage. These are no easy programs: both require 1,200 hours of training, completed in 48 to 52 weeks. The Continuing Education program provides Career Development Services (CDS) that helps students with resume preparation, interview tips, and specific information about companies that are looking for certain skills. Regular job fairs are hosted at various campuses. Students also have the opportunity to meet with a career counselor who can help with identifying and setting goals that will keep students on the right track toward employment.

Most of the career technical training requiring specific equipment is only available at the Educational Cultural Complex, but electronic technician training is only provided at the mid-city campus. Training for machinists is only available at the San Diego City College campus as a for-credit college class.

MiraCosta Career Technical Institute

For nearly twenty years, the only place to get the training in the San Diego region through the community college system to become a machinist was San Diego City College. Now, however, there is a second location for civilians to get training as a machinist in San Diego County at the Technology Career Institute (TCI) of MiraCosta Community College. MiraCosta College is a public California community college serving coastal North San Diego County

When I interviewed Linda Kurokawa, Director of Community Education & Workforce Development, in June 2017, she said, "The

Technology Career Institute officially opened in its current location in Carlsbad in March 2015, and it was actually my idea." She explained, "I started it because I felt that San Diego North County needed a technical training center to provide low cost and accelerated training. We wanted to get young people and Veterans trained for good paying jobs. For about five years, I had been asked by local manufacturers and the local chapter of the National Tooling & Manufacturing Association (NTMA) to start a machinist program. But, I had no money, no instructors, and no equipment.

I decided to see if there was a way it could be done. I worked with the City of Oceanside and asked if they had an empty building. They did since it was during the long-lasting recession. I talked to leaders in the local industry to see if we could raise the funds to get the equipment. The MiraCosta Foundation helped us get donations to buy some of the equipment. One donor even gave $50,000. I worked with Haas Automation®, Inc., and we got some automated machining centers through an 'Entrustment' arrangement."

Continuing, she said, "When we were in the planning stage for TCI, I was advised to make sure the course met the needs of the manufacturers, so we had manufacturers review our curriculum. We also visited training centers all over the country to learn about best practices. We started our machining program in the spring of 2013 at the Oceanside location. The program was very accelerated - the students went every day, five days a week, for eight hours a day. The local NTMA chapter helped me find our first instructor, a woman who was retiring from the Navy and had taught machining skills on board ship to sailors."

When I asked how they wound up at the current facility in Carlsbad, she responded, "I realized that with the small facility we had, we could only train a few students at a time. I heard about a grant available through the Department of Labor, and I hired a grant writer. We submitted our proposal and won a $2.75 million grant, which allowed us the funds to buy the equipment we needed to double the size of our machining program and also establish an engineering technician program.

We looked for a larger empty building and found one in the city of Carlsbad. We worked with city officials to get a low rent, as we are entirely funded by student fees. It was a mutually beneficial arrangement. Carlsbad is helping to fill the talent pipeline and helping residents in North County find technical training, and we provide the training in a low-cost building.

We moved into our 23,000-sq. ft. building in early 2015 and had the time and space to start night and weekend classes using modules from our daytime accelerated program. We are GI bill approved and funded through Workforce Innovation and Opportunity Act funds and state funds, which are only available about five months of the year before the funds are exhausted. Our fees are high per student (about $6,000), so I wanted to find another grant. The Girard Foundation did help out by funding one semester last year."

Next, Linda submitted a grant proposal for the America's Promise grants that were awarded on November 17, 2016 by the U.S. Department of Labor "to 23 regional workforce partnerships in 28 states to connect more than 21,000 Americans to education and in-demand jobs." They received a grant of $6 million over a period of four years. Linda, said, "We are six months into the grant, so we still have 3 1/2 years left. We are sharing some monies with Grossmont Cuyamaca College in east San Diego County and Chaffey College in Riverside. The grant funds have allowed us to eliminate tuition fees and reduce administrative fees down to a modest $375.

She said, "We are excited about launching our apprenticeship program for Machining Technician, CNC machine operators, engineering technicians, electronic assembly, and solar PV in the next few months that have been approved by the State of California Apprenticeship Standards. We will do the pre-training at our facility and monitor the students On the Job Training."

PLAYBOOK for Teens

In 2014, I wrote an article about the PLAYBOOK for Teens, created by Cari Lyn Vinci and Carleen MacKay, which is available in print and digital format on Amazon. In the PLAYBOOK, girls can meet fascinating women in STE@M (the "@" stands for "art") and follow the "plays" of successful young women to help them create their own "Dream Career." At the end of each story, the PLAYBOOK role models share heart-felt advice for girls to apply to their career path. Then, questions are asked of the reader to help them take the first step to writing their own PLAYBOOK. The PLAYBOOK is dedicated to the smart, talented teenage girls who will become the future business owners and leaders in STE@M industries. The PLAYBOOK can be used as a tool for organization and corporate partners to solve their future talent pool problems.

When I interviewed Ms. Vinci, she said, "We did extensive research before developing the STE@M™ Mentoring Program. Our discussions with middle school girls revealed there are several roadblocks that start to show up in Middle School. Students told us:

- STEM careers are only for boys
- STEM subjects are too hard. My teacher says I only need "fill in the blank class" to graduate.
- There are no girls in the science club
- I don't want to be viewed as the "smart one"
- My friends aren't interested in STEM
- My parents don't talk to me about or can't afford an education for me beyond high school

Our PLAYBOOK for Teens…STE@M Mentoring Program helps girls catapult those roadblocks by discussing the elephant in the room and helping girls see the truth and the possibilities. The 8th grade girls tell us these conversations are more open and beneficial in a "girls only" environment.

By seeing the necessary building blocks and seeing women who look like them that are happy and successful in STE@M careers, students understand what is possible for them. And, most important, students form a "techie tribe" of support to keep them motivated going forward.

When the program is delivered in 8th grade, students have the opportunity to take appropriate courses in high school based on their "PLAYBOOK for Success" which includes their education goals after high school of community college, a four-year college, military or other education option.

The mentoring program is a way to set the stories in motion by bringing more young women into the lucrative STEM arena. Teens explore STE@M careers, gain insights from the role model stories, journal and research educational options."

When I connected with Ms. Vinci on May 19, 2017, she said, " Since December 2015, we have been working with the Community College Chancellors office and County Offices of Education to conduct "Train the Trainer" programs for teachers/counselors/parents so that educators can bring the PLAYBOOK for Teens — STE@M™ Mentoring Program to Middle School students throughout California. Our long-term goal is to expand the mentoring program into middle schools nationwide."

Denver's Project DIY Encourages Girls in Advanced Manufacturing Careers

The first week of summer, June 5 – 9, 2017, the Community College of Denver (CCD) Advanced Manufacturing Center hosted their second week-long camp for high school girls to give them the opportunity to learn about advanced manufacturing, including machining and welding. The camp was sponsored by the Women's Foundation of Colorado, the Denver Public School's Career Connect, and Soeurs de Coeur Fund.

When I interviewed Janet Colvin, Manufacturing Pathways Campus Coordinator, at CCD, she said that they had two one-week summer camps in 2016 for nine girls each week, but this year, they had 28 girls in a one-week camp, so that two girls could participate in paid six-week internships after the camp with local companies involved with the Denver Public School Career Connect program.

I asked her how they selected the girls for the camp. She said, "We worked with the Denver Public School system to select girls who were already enrolled in the engineering, manufacturing and the "Maker" career pathway."

During our interview, Janet told me that each morning began with students watching TED talks from women in business, doing team building activities, and other exercises about how to handle difficult situations.

During the week, the girls visited an architectural company, RNLDesign, and one of the women architects spoke to the girls about careers in the field and gave them a tour of their design center. The girls did an Origami project and participated in an architecture photo scavenger hunt. They visited the CCD Mechanical Engineering Graphics lab, and each girl got to design her own "Fidget" device using Solidworks and then make it using 3D printing.

The girls toured two Advanced Manufacturing companies. At Sundyne, they met mechanical engineers and saw parts being made on a 5-axis CNC machining center. At Eldon James, a woman owned plastic injection molding company, they saw plastic parts being molded.

The students also spent a day at the Advanced Manufacturing Center at CCD doing some manual machining using mills and lathes to make a plasma-cut DIY sign in welding, and using a manual mill to drill a hole in a CNC-machined medallion. For welding, they used both simulators and actual welding equipment with careful supervision. They had the opportunity to interact with students at the AMC. In the afternoon, they also toured a welding company, Clear Intentions.

On the last day, they worked with two welding instructors to finish the projects started on Thursday in the morning. In the afternoon, there was a graduation ceremony where the girls had the opportunity to share their experiences. Women from the Women's Foundation and the Denver Public School Career Connect program attended the graduation ceremony.

Janet said, "The camp was a success because more than 25 professional women who are employed in advanced manufacturing companies participated in our camp, and 16 Community College of Denver staff, students, and faculty in architecture, machining, fabrication welding and engineering graphics helped design projects, presented, and coached girls. I can't say enough about the companies that participated. We have a very big MFG DAY event every fall, so we have built relationships with local manufacturers."

Janet added, "The biggest outcome of the camp was the change in the understanding of manufacturing skills. The girls' favorite activities were welding, machining, and 3D printing. One of the key outcomes is that the girls could visualize themselves in these manufacturing careers."

The Project DIY team had done a pretest before the camp and did a posttest to evaluate what the girls have learned. Janet later provided me the following results of the Project DIY summer camp:

- Two Project DIY attendees started paid internships with Denver Public Schools Career Connect after the camp
- Pre/post test showed **increased knowledge of manufacturing careers** and educational pathways; 74% of the participants agreed that the camp increased their motivation to pursue a career in Advanced Manufacturing.
- 100% of the campers indicated that they learned new skills; 91% stated that the camp helped them learn more about their career interest; 100% recommended the camp to others.
- Machining, welding, and the tours were listed among their favorite activities.
- Pre/post test showed an increased knowledge and skill level. For instance, 78% of the girls indicated that they could explain the basics of how to make metal parts with a machine, compared to 29% pretest.

- The post-test results showed that **none** of the girls thought Advanced Manufacturing was dirty work (compared to 39% in the pre-test)."

Janet said, " As a result of the camp last summer, one girl changed schools to attend a school that taught welding. We follow up with all of the girls during the school year. Two girls even came back to do the camp for the second time this summer."

Janet told me that the new CCD Advanced Manufacturing Center is a state-of-the-art 33,280-square-foot facility offering degree and certificate programs in machining and welding. CCD also offers continuing education courses for CNC machinists, 4/5/6 access, and wire EDM training allowing for workforce advancement.
Janet said, "CCD's manufacturing programs offer the ability to earn an Associate of Applied Science degree in fabrication welding, machining or engineering graphics & mechanical design. The college also offers a variety of basic and advanced certificate programs that are stackable —meaning students can earn a certificate and start working right away while continuing on towards more advanced certificates or associate's degrees in their field."

I asked Janet when they started the Advanced Manufacturing Center and how they were funded. She replied, "We opened July 21, 2015 after receiving a $3.5 million grant from the Department of Labor. Nine community colleges received this grant, called CHAMP. It enabled us to set up the center, buy the equipment, and develop the curriculum with the help of the local manufacturing industry. It was a three-year grant, so we have another year of funding. I am researching other opportunities for follow on funding for the center. We are a corporate training center, so we do training for a fee for local manufacturers."

There is a common thread among many of these innovative programs for attracting youth to STEM careers – one person had a vision and the long-term committed passion to bring it into reality. No one should ever say to themselves, "I'm only one person. What can I do?" As we have seen by these examples, one person can start a movement, change the course of an organization, and even change the course of a nation.

What a difference it would make if the founders of Workshop for Warriors, Vocademy, and Playbook for Teens could achieve their goals of expanding nationwide. Just these three programs would go a long way in solving the skills gap and attracting the next generation of manufacturing workers.

Chapter 9

What is being done now to rebuild American manufacturing?

After decades of warning by business and academic leaders about the value of manufacturing to our American economy, the Great Recession of 2007-2009 served as a brutal wake-up call to the country. The loss of 5.7 million manufacturing jobs and more than 65,000 U.S. manufacturing firms closing their doors between 2000 and 2011 led to the long-feared ramifications of damaged communities, stagnant wages, and shattered dreams.

Finally, business, academic, and government officials realized the need to revive American manufacturing and crafted a "once-in-a-generation investment in manufacturing that could serve as the centerpiece for a new high-tech industrial era in America." The result was the new National Network for Manufacturing Innovation, or NNMI, which was established by the passage of the Revitalize American Manufacturing and Innovation Act (H.R. 2996). Rep. Joseph P. Kennedy III, D-MA, and Rep. Tom Reed, R-NY, introduced H. R. 2996, but it was cosponsored by 51 Democrats and 49 Republicans. The Senate version also received bipartisan support, and the Act was signed into law in December 2014.

SME's recently released a report titled "Inside America's Bold Plan to Revive Manufacturing[101]," which describes the NNMI as "a moonshot—with lofty scientific ambitions—aimed at restoring America's leadership in manufacturing and securing it for the 21st Century."

SME's CEO Jeff Krause, said, "We're committed to communicating and sharing SME experience and expertise. The report describes in detail the climate that led to the creation of the Institutes; introduces the leadership and organizations involved and discusses the individual technologies being explored. It's a great introduction and overview of both the original problem and the innovative solution."

The report states that "part of the NNMI's goal is to bring even more manufacturing home and develop workers with high-demand advanced manufacturing skills. But the real heart of this effort is targeted at rebuilding America's strength in the manufacturing technologies that undergird today's modern manufacturing facilities, many of which are no longer "factories" in the classic sense."

SME's report points out that it wasn't just "low-wage countries and trade agreements that are to blame for the U.S. decline in manufacturing, the nation's diminished competitiveness in these technologies has also played an enormous role... America's lack of understanding about manufacturing technologies—what they are and what they do—was one reason why many dismissed the value of preserving the manufacturing industry in the U.S. years ago."

The report reminds us that it is "important to remember that manufacturing any part or product usually involves a series of distinct processes...Making an airplane, car, medical device or smartphone today, requires a series of highly engineered processes on the long path from converting raw materials into finished parts that will then be joined and assembled into a final product."

It states, "The advanced manufacturing technologies of today and tomorrow, and the companies that make them...are all in various states of maturity. Some are considered emerging technologies. That includes 3D printing, also known as additive manufacturing (AM). But it also includes "older technologies that have grown very sophisticated over time, with the help of software and other developments."

I thought it particularly important that the report highlighted that it takes "a deep understanding of these manufacturing technologies, and how they work together to make things, is actually necessary to design many of the cutting-edge products of today and the future."

The report noted that the above highlighted fact was one of the key arguments of the 2012 book, *Producing Prosperity: Why America*

Needs a Manufacturing Renaissance, by Harvard Business School professors Gary P. Pisano and Willy C. Shih. "Pisano and Shih argued that as America loses its so-called industrial commons, or communities of knowledge built around these manufacturing technologies, the nation will lose its ability to successfully innovate …the knowledge about how to make things is central to innovation — if it can't be made, it's just an idea—and usually it is the development of manufacturing technologies that actually leads to the new widgets and gadgets of the future."

Pisano and Shih wrote, "The United States has been losing its competitive advantage in those sectors and technologies that it needs to drive growth in the twenty-first century." They implored U.S. leaders to "abandon the grand experiment in de-industrialization before it's too late."

The report echoes what wrote in my own book, stating that "the U.S. was a leader in manufacturing technologies? But today, a sobering number of manufacturing technologies come from other countries, usually Germany, Japan, China, Italy, South Korea and Switzerland." It cites trade data from the U. S. Census Bureau showing that the U.S. imported $11.4 billion in metalworking machine tools in 2014, while exporting "just $7.5 billion, a decrease of about $189 million from the prior year." This is why the U. S. has gone from a trade surplus to a trade deficit in Advanced Technology Products, dropping from a surplus of $4 billion in 2001 to a deficit of $86 billion in 2014.

The next few pages of the report covers some of the technologies in which we have fallen behind, such as 3D printing, industrial robots, flat screen TVs, lithium-ion batteries, and solar panels. Even though we originated many of these technologies and have invested billions in them, foreign countries like China have spent trillions to take the lead. For example, "The U.S. supplied less than 16% of the industrial robots in the world in 2013, according to the International Federation of Robotics. About 60% of the world's industrial robots came from Asia, primarily China, Japan and Korea. Another fourth come from Europe, primarily Germany, Italy and Switzerland."

The report also states that is a question of priorities, because "the governments work as strong partners with manufacturers, providing consistent and high levels of financial backing for applied manufacturing research. And they are persistent in their efforts, without prolonged debates or whipsawing with the political winds. Germany's Fraunhofer Society is an often-cited example of other countries' commitment to these activities, and for good reason. That network of research institutes has an annual budget of 2 billion euros (about $2.27 billion) ..."

The report states that "Leaders in U.S. manufacturing have recognized for some time that if America does not want to be further sidelined in the critical, valuable manufacturing sector—after having a taste of the consequences—the nation would need to recapture leadership in a few key technology areas."

After taking office during the Recession, "President Obama commissioned a number of committees and reports, and meetings were held nationwide, as the depths of America's manufacturing challenge were explored.

"Although the NNMI was just one of many recommendations that came out of those sessions, it was a centerpiece proposal "because it prioritized reinvestment in manufacturing research," said Steven R. Schmid, a professor of aerospace and mechanical engineering at the University of Notre Dame in South Bend, IN Schmid served at the Advanced Manufacturing National Program Office, where he helped design the NNMI program. America's lack of investment in manufacturing research, he told SME, is "a key area where other countries are blowing us away."

Schmid added. "In a free-market world, manufacturing research investment is considered to be infrastructure, just like roads or airports. If we don't support our manufacturing infrastructure like these institutes, it gives other nations a competitive advantage."

What were the key provisions of the Revitalize American Manufacturing and Innovation Act[102]? Basically, it amended the

National Institute of Standards and Technology (NIST) Act to direct the Secretary of Commerce to establish a Network for Manufacturing Innovation Program within NIST. The Program purposes to: "(1) improve the competitiveness of U.S. manufacturing and increase domestic production; (2) stimulate U.S. leadership in advanced manufacturing research, innovation, and technology; and (3) accelerate the development of an advanced manufacturing workforce."

The Act required the Secretary to: "(1) establish a network of centers for manufacturing innovation, to be known as the Network for Manufacturing Innovation; and (2) award financial assistance to assist in planning, establishing, or supporting such centers."

The SME report states, "By the end of 2015, America will have nine of its own manufacturing research hubs in various stages of development. In addition to workforce development projects, their mission is to invest in applied research projects in technology readiness levels 4 to 7.

The initial pilot institute is America Makes, the Additive Manufacturing Center in Youngstown, OH. The report says it "is the furthest along and has worked through its start-up growing pains, such as intellectual property agreements with members, how to structure itself and deciding which projects to fund…America Makes has more than 140 members and has awarded funds to 47 projects in the area of additive manufacturing or 3D printing. Each applied research project matches public to private investment on a 1:1 basis and involves several companies and universities collaborating."

Other Centers currently selected are:

- Digital Manufacturing and Design Innovation Institute, (Digital Lab, Chicago, IL
- Lightweight Innovations for Tomorrow (LIFT), Materials Manufacturing, Detroit, MI
- Institute for Advanced Composites, Manufacturing Innovation, Knoxville, TN

- PowerAmerica, Semiconductor Technology, Raleigh, NC

Depending on additional funding for FY 2016 and beyond, "The National Network for Manufacturing Innovation may expand to as many as 16 institutes by the end of 2016. The vision is for an eventual total of 45."

Since the report was released, two other Centers have been launched:

- Manufacturing Innovation Institute for Integrated Photonics - Launched: July 27, 2015
- Flexible Hybrid Electronics Manufacturing Innovation Institute - Launched: August 28, 2015

Three more Centers are selected to be launched in the near future:

- Smart Manufacturing Innovation Institute
- Sensors and Process Controls
- The Revolutionary Fibers and Textiles Manufacturing Innovation Institute

Ed Morris, Executive Director of America Makes, said, "Given our competitive global economic environment, the U.S. is going to have to decide how to respond to continued long-term public funding by other nations in these key manufacturing technologies."

At the WESTEC show this past week, Jeff Krause, SME CEO, said "Advanced manufacturing and industrial-scale production are a big part of and contributors to our nation's proud history. This National Network for Manufacturing Innovation is the next great chapter in our story: a progressive partnership of public sector, private enterprise and academia working together to effectively explore and develop technologies and products that will inspire, revive and renew American manufacturing opportunity."

Mr. Krause added his opinion in why the investment in the NNMI's can work: "These new technologies hold such promise, but there is much effort and investment necessary. By combining applied research, product and process development, training and equipping a workforce, a partnership can collaborate and move more efficiently; invest more directly and produce quicker results than one entity."

With regard to the role SME can play in the NNMI, Mr. Krause, said, "SME and our leadership, members and staff value the opportunity to have participated with many of the Institutes from their beginning. We're advocates for manufacturing and engineering and have been for decades. We have the relationships and unique capability to bring together the right people with the right experiences and expertise to attack the challenge in support of advanced manufacturing. This is a really special, really entrepreneurial opportunity and we're proud to be a part of it."

The Manufacturing Extension Partnership (MEP) Provides Nationwide Training

The MEP website states, "Since 1988, the Hollings Manufacturing Extension Partnership (MEP[103]) has worked to strengthen U.S. manufacturing. MEP is part of the National Institute of Standards and Technology (NIST), a U.S. Department of Commerce agency…MEP is built on a national system of centers located in all 50 states and Puerto Rico. "Each center is a partnership between the federal government and a variety of public or private entities, including state, university, and nonprofit organizations. This diverse network, with nearly 600 service locations, has close to 1,300 field staff serving as trusted business advisors and technical experts to assist manufacturers in communities across the country."

In FY 2016, the MEP national network interacted with 25,445 manufacturers and achieved these results through their wide range of services:

- $9.3 Billion New and Retained Sales
- 86,602 New and Retained Jobs
- $3.5 Billion New Client Investments
- $1.4 Billion $1.4 Billion Cost Savings

I have personally met with the Jim Watson, head of the California Manufacturing Technology Consulting (CMTC), and had the pleasure of meeting with Scott Broughton, Director of the Advantage Kentucky Alliance (Kentucky's MEP), and David Linger, President & CEO of TechSolve, one of the Ohio MEP affiliates when I visited Cincinnati, in November 2016.

Jim Watson told me, "In 2016, CMTC was awarded a five-year agreement to be the California MEP. In 2016 CMTC served 1,065 small and medium-sized manufacturers, creating or retaining 8,575 high paying jobs statewide resulting in $169 million in cost savings, $647 million in total sales, and $305 million in total investment. For every manufacturing job, there are 3-4 full-time jobs created elsewhere in the United States to support manufacturers. Manufacturing is critical to the California economy, employing more than 1.2 million workers at more than 39,000 companies."

Scott Broughton told me, "AKA has generated over $88 million in impacts with 50 clients working with over 1,300 employees in the past 12 months alone. We are currently working with small manufacturers in Eastern Kentucky, who used to work in the coal industry to identify, vet, and implement change allowing them to work in non-coal industries and helping them to be sustainable in the future. These companies have worked with other entities with mixed results. AKA's programs are centered on AKA facilitators mentoring and training employees, allowing them to be the driver of change with continued support. This allows the employees to 'learn by doing' with the support and assistance of AKA's specialists. AKA's average engagements are over 12 months with monthly interactions allowing for sustainable support, change, and implementation."

He added, "For every federal dollar spent, it has resulted in $170K in impacts in Kentucky! Specific impacts in the past 12 months are below and that does not include the 762 new jobs created/retained:

- $9.9 million in new sales
- $21.6 million in retained sales
- $10.8 million in cost savings

- $40.3 million in investments made"

David Linger told me, "The Ohio Manufacturing Extension Partnership, located in Columbus, OH, provides technical services for small and medium-sized manufacturers to drive productivity, growth and global competitiveness; and can ultimately help Ohio's manufacturers become more profitable and competitive. From October 2015 – September 2016, the Ohio Manufacturing Extension Partnership served 439 Manufacturers resulting in new and retained sales of $277,900,000, created and retained 2,399 jobs, facilitated cost savings of over $41,700,000, and created new investments of $132,600,000."

This data illustrates why the nationwide Manufacturing Extension Partnership network is essential to the rebuilding manufacturing and growing the U. S. economy. The President and Congress should continue to approve funding for the MEP program in the federal budget.

NDSU Research & Technology Park Leads Region in Job Creation

On the first day of my visit to Fargo, North Dakota, I met with Chuck Hoge, Executive Director of the North Dakota State University Research & Technology Park (RTP), which is "dedicated to enhancing the investments in North Dakota State University by the citizens of North Dakota. The development of facilities and research centers conducive to cutting-edge research is also part of the NDSU Research and Technology Park." The Research Park operates a 50,000-sq. ft. technology incubator, which offers space, facilities, and services to technology-based entrepreneurs and businesses.

Mr. Hoge also serves on the Fargo Moorhead Growth Initiative Fund Board. Prior to the Research Park, he was president of the Ottertail Corporation Manufacturing Platform for six years, and before that, he was president and CEO of Bobcat Corporation.

Mr. Hoge said, "I was on the board of directors of the Park before I became Interim Director in 2013 and the Executive Director in 2016. The Research Park is a 501 (c3) corporation with its own Board of Directors. The Park is home to two NDSU research buildings, the John Deere Electronic Solutions building, and two buildings occupied by Appareo, one of our Incubator graduates."

Explaining the purpose of the research park, he said, "The Park's goals mirror those of the State of North Dakota. Our shared mission is to diversify the economy through high-tech STEM jobs, develop the workforce and provide valuable, in-state career opportunities for North Dakota students. In the past, many of NDSU's 15,000 students were seeking well-paid, high-tech positions out of state, so we made it our goal to create those opportunities for them in-state. The Research Park has created 1,339 direct jobs, of which 52% are held by graduates of North Dakota colleges and universities."

"In the Incubator, our mission is to help companies succeed faster, which is why we have two of our partner organizations in the Incubator; the Small Business Development Center (SBDC) and the Bank of North Dakota. The SBDC helps startups with anything from business plans to financial modeling and because the Bank of North Dakota is the only state-owned bank in the country, they have many programs aimed at helping startup companies."

When I asked for information about the founding of the Research Park and incubator, he said, "The Research Park was founded in 1999 and the incubator in 2007. Our funding sources were a combination of private donations, a State Centers of Excellence grant and an EDA grant."

Hoge, said, "The Bank of North Dakota isn't the only state entity creating programs for local startups. The Department of Commerce's Innovate North Dakota program provides up to $32,500 in startup funds to companies in four phases — $2,500, $5,000, $10,000, and $15,000. In the last couple years, we had over 50 companies in the Fargo area use the program to kick start their companies with a great success rate. The program doesn't only provide monetary support;

the company founders attend entrepreneur training boot camps to network with fellow founders and learn from world-renown entrepreneur, Dr. Jeffery Stamp of Bold Thinking, LLC."

He told me that the incubator has 12 current incubator clients and has graduated five companies: Appareo, Fargo 3D Printing, Intelligent InSites, Myriad Mobile, and Pedigree Technologies.

"In addition to programs designed to target local entrepreneurs, we also have a student competition called Innovation Challenge, where $27,000 is awarded to teams of NDSU students with the most innovative ideas. Through three rounds of judging by industry professionals, the students are challenged to pitch their innovations through a written proposal, a tradeshow scenario and a mock fundraising pitch. We want to inspire students to think about entrepreneurship as a career path and we use innovation as the gateway to entrepreneurship. We had three companies get their start in Innovation Challenge last year and we are hoping for more this year. The program is financially supported by a combination of a University Center EDA grant, state matching funds and contributions from local businesses and organizations.

The Incubator Manager, John Cosgriff, has a background in venture funds, and he assists companies with intellectual property, human resources and raising capital. We have monthly founder meetings where the entrepreneurs advise each other and 'Lunch and Learn' events where founders learn from and network with industry experts."

After I returned home, I was emailed an Economic Impact Study released November, 2016, and a few highlights are:
- Its companies support an estimated 1,300 indirect jobs in the Fargo-Moorhead area.
- Its companies employ 489 graduates of NDSU (37% of total RTP employment)
- Another 202 are graduates of other North Dakota University System schools.
- 107 student interns are employed by the RTP companies.

Why Universities are Important to Rebuilding U. S. Manufacturing

The fact that more and more manufacturers are returning manufacturing to the U. S. or keeping manufacturing here instead of moving to Mexico or Asia is good news, but on February 23,[104] 2017, President Trump met with two dozen manufacturing CEOs at the White House.

While they "declared their collective commitment to restoring factory jobs lost to foreign competition," some of the CEOs "suggested that there were still plenty of openings for U.S. factory jobs but too few qualified people to fill them. They urged the White House to support vocational training for the high-tech skills that today's manufacturers increasingly require...The jobs are there, but the skills are not," one executive said during meetings with White House officials that preceded a session with the president."

"We were challenged by the president to ... come up with a program to make sure the American worker is trained for the manufacturing jobs of tomorrow," Reed Cordish, a White House official, said after Thursday's meetings."

Training today's workers in the skills they will need for the jobs of the future in manufacturing is important, but we also need to educate the next generation of manufacturing workers. We need more engineers to rebuild American manufacturing, and universities play a key role in providing this education.

Last week, I had the opportunity to interview Dr. David B. Williams, Executive Dean of the Professional Colleges and Dean of The College of Engineering at The Ohio State University, located in Columbus, Ohio, to discuss the role universities are playing in rebuilding manufacturing and educating the next generation of manufacturing workers.

His official biography on the University website states, "Williams is involved in many university-industry economic development partnerships. He serves on the boards of ASM International, the State of Ohio's Third Frontier Advisory Board, Lightweight Innovations for Tomorrow (formerly American Lightweight Materials Manufacturing Innovation Institute), Columbus 2020, Metro Early College STEM School, EWI, Ohio Aerospace & Aviation Council, and the Transportation Research Center."

Dean Williams said, "Ohio State University is a manufacturing R&D and training Powerhouse. Manufacturing is a critical part of the state of Ohio's economy and accounts for 17 percent of the state's GPD. It is also the state's largest industry sector. We have partnered with over two hundred manufacturers in developing and funding research that can be used in their industries. It is a very important part of the college. We use the talent of our professors, graduate, and undergrad students and technology. OSU is committed to innovating applied research for product design, technology commercialization, and manufacturing for industry through its programs."

Dean Williams mentioned that on October 1, 2016 the Center for Design and Manufacturing Excellence (CDME) was designated as a new Manufacturing Extension Partnership (MEP) affiliate organization, and that Ohio State's MEP program will work directly with manufacturers to identify and execute growth strategies. Afterward, I was provided with information that states:[105] "The Ohio State University's Center for Design and Manufacturing Excellence (CDME) will receive up to $8.6 million in federal, state and industry funding over the next five years to lead a program facilitating growth of small- and mid-sized manufacturing companies in the 15-county central Ohio region. The program is funded by the National Institute of Standards and Technologies, with matching funds provided by the Ohio Development Services Agency, which administers operations through seven regional affiliates."

I found the information about Central Ohio's manufacturing very interesting: "The central Ohio manufacturing economy is comprised of approximately 3,350 self-identified manufacturing companies across the 15 Central Ohio counties. More than 90 percent of them have 50 or fewer employees. Many small and medium-sized manufacturing companies are aware of the growth challenges they face, but still require assistance to overcome them." The size of companies is similar to San Diego County, in which 97% have fewer than 50 employees.

Dean Williams told me that the Center's Executive Director, John Bair, is a successful entrepreneur, not an academic, and added that they had invited him to head up the Center after he had sold his company and semi-retired."

 He added, "We invite manufacturers to bring their problems to us, and then we put together teams of experts to work with them to solve these problems. The company gets to keep any of the Intellectual Property developed in the process of working together.

Dean Williams also said that Ohio State is home to the Ohio Manufacturing Institute[106], which "serves as a public policy mechanism for manufacturing within the state and nationally that facilitates the use of available technical resources for economic development." He said, "OMI acts like a clearinghouse for Ohio to provide manufacturers with the tools they need to collaborate with a statewide network of technical resources. Its state and national policy recommendations reflect a thoughtful response to industry problems and issues. OMI also engages in outreach programs that support manufacturers—from small to medium-size firms to original equipment manufacturers—by aligning with industries, academic institutions, technology support organizations and government."

As an example, Dean Williams said, "We have had a long relationship with Honda since they moved to Marysville in 1978, which is about 45 miles northwest of here. About five years ago, we started partnering with Honda to help them develop solutions to some of their manufacturing problems. Their high-end NSX brand is currently made with advanced engineered materials and is produced at only a rate of 7-8 vehicles per day. They want to produce the

Accord using the same materials and technology. At the Center, we have put together teams of experts to solve this problem."

Dean Williams said, "Hundreds of students study abroad for part of the education. Their experience abroad strengthens their performance and helps train the people necessary to maintain and repair the machines. They are still lots of manufacturers in Ohio. We graduate about 2,000 engineers per year and about half of them stay in Ohio. There are 14 engineering colleges in Ohio, and we have the educational base to drive the 21st Century manufacturing." Since the U.S. is only graduating about 50,000 engineers a year compared to the estimated 500,000 per year in China, Ohio State University is doing more than their fair share.

With regard to the next generation of manufacturing workers, he said, "A big part of the problem is that parents think manufacturing is like what it was in the past, so they don't want their children to get involved in manufacturing. I was at SpaceX recently and met the chief welding engineer, and she was a graduate of Ohio State with a degree in welding. Young men and women can even get a Master's Degree in 'joining' through Ohio State's online welding engineering master's program: This discipline includes a deep understanding of the properties and testing of materials that can be welded."

He said, "We are part of seven of the National Networks of Manufacturing Innovation (NNMIs). One of them is LIFT,[107] which I looked up and found that it is "an industry-led, government funded consortium. By reimagining processes and procedures, the highly linked and leveraged network is facilitating technology transfer into supply chain companies and empowering the lightweight metals workforce." Ohio State University, the University of Michigan in Detroit and EWI are the founding members of this NNMI consortium that was established February 25, 2014 following a competitive process led by the U.S. Department of Defense under the Lightweight and Modern Metals Manufacturing Innovation (LM3I).

Cincinnati Focuses on Re-industrialization to Create Prosperity

In November 2016, I spent two and a half days in Cincinnati, Ohio as the guest of Source Cincinnati, an independent, multi-year national social and media relations initiative that works to enhance perceptions of Cincinnati as a world-class Midwestern region. I met with Julie Calvert, Executive Director, during my visit, but my personal guide and host was Paul Fox, VP of Strategic Initiatives at Proctor & Gamble and "Executive on Loan" to Source Cincinnati for a year.

From Mr. Fox, I learned that Cincinnati is the third largest city in Ohio and had such interesting nicknames as "Porkopolis" in the past because it was the largest pork packing center in the world and the "Queen City of the West," for its ideal location on the Ohio River and its rich culture and heritage of a predominantly German population who settled Cincinnati in the late 1700s.

After arriving late Tuesday afternoon, Mr. Fox and I had dinner with David Linger of TechSolve, and Scott Broughton, Center Director for Advantage Kentucky Alliance at the WKU Center for R&D at Western Kentucky University in Bowling Green, KY. TechSolve is a 30-year old consulting firm that is a State of Ohio Manufacturing Extension Partner (MEP) affiliate, and Advantage Kentucky Alliance (AKA) is the MEP for Kentucky. Mr. Linger just took over the reins as President and CEO on September 1, 2016 after Gary Conley retired from 20 years of service.

Mr. Linger, said "There are about 2,500 manufacturers in the Ohio region of metropolitan Cincinnati, and Cincinnati used to be known as the "Machine Tool Capital of the U. S.", but very few machine tool companies exist today, including its most well-known machine tool company, Cincinnati Milacron," after its machine tool line was sold to Unova. TechSolve provides manufacturing and health care consulting. It has a focus and strength in process improvement, machining, and innovation -- applying these skills to help businesses find long-term solutions and promote problem-solving cultures.

Mr. Broughton said, "AKA is a not-for-profit partnership that provides assistance and training to help manufacturers of all sizes grow, improve their manufacturing and business strategies and processes, adopt advanced technologies, increase productivity, reduce costs, and improve competitiveness. Manufacturing in Eastern Kentucky was mainly related to the coal mining industry, and two-thirds of the companies have gone out of business. We have focused on helping the remaining manufacturers to understand their core competencies to market to new industries, such as aviation and automotive. Our services include: business growth services, continuous improvement services, and workforce solution services."

On Wednesday morning, we had breakfast with Laura Brunner, President/CEO, and Gail Paul Director of Communication Strategy of the Port of Greater Cincinnati Development Authority. She told me that the Port Authority was established by the City of Cincinnati and Hamilton County in 2001 and is the second largest inland port covering 26 miles from the Indiana/Ohio border. In 2008, the Port Authority was reformed and empowered to take a leadership position in regional economic development. It is a quasi-public agency that operates collaboratively with dozens of economic development, community and corporate partners.

Ms. Brunner presented me with a report prepared for me, titled "Manufacturing in the Greater Cincinnati Region. As background, "The Port Authority leverages its infrastructure strengths and development-related expertise to design and execute complex projects to improve property value, catalyze private investment and promote job creation."

I was astounded when she told me, "The Cincinnati region has lost 67% of its manufacturing jobs." The report states, "Manufacturing was a primary component of Cincinnati's economy until its peak in 1969 when 43 percent of the workforce in Hamilton County was employed in manufacturing jobs. Today, lower-wage service-providing jobs far outnumber manufacturing jobs by about 7:1...From 1969-2015, the number of people employed in manufacturing decreased from 146,000 to 48,000."

She said that the Port Authority Board of Directors has established a vision to transform Cincinnati to prosperity by 2022 through "repositioning undervalued properties and re-building neighborhoods." The report she gave me states that the strategies for success are:

- "Industrial Revitalization – redevelopment of 500 acres of underutilized industrial land along key transportation corridors
- Neighborhood Revitalization – transform ten communities for lasting impact, including residential properties and commercial business districts
- Public Finance Innovation – cultivate a nationally-recognized public finance program that supports economic and community development efforts

The projected Return on Investment for these strategies is:

500 industrial acres redeveloped	10 revitalized communities
8,000 new jobs	300 quality homes
$565 million in annual payroll	50 commercial acres with 400K SF
$550 million in capital investment	130 new businesses
$8 million in income taxes	Increased property & income taxes
$14 million in real estate taxes	Improved lives of residents

In June 2015, the PGCDA Board approved establishment of the industrial and neighborhood strategy, development of internal resources, communication strategy, and the financing and fundraising plan to support the strategies."

The report states, "The proposed redevelopment of approximately 2,000 acres of industrial land through Hamilton County for

Manufacturing uses will have a considerable impact on the Greater Cincinnati Region."

The first sites for the Redevelopment Pilot program have been selected, and the first funds have been obtained for acquisition of land parcels, demolition/remediation of existing buildings, and site preparation. The first site is assembled and is scheduled to open in 2017.

In the meeting with Ms. Brunner and Paul, I was also provided a "Manufacturing Attractiveness Study" by Deloitte Consulting LLP presented on October 3, 2016 to the Greater Cincinnati Port Development Authority, TechSolve, and Cushman and Wakefield. The study states, "The **current lack of easily developable real estate** (cleared, access to utilities, free from environmental concerns, etc.) **in the Cincinnati area likely puts the city at a significant disadvantage for attracting manufacturing investments. The Port Authority's** operations focus on transportation, community revitalization, public finance and real estate development makes it **especially well-equipped to evaluate and address opportunities to redevelop and reposition sites** formerly occupied by industrial operations."

The Port Authority seeks "**to achieve the following objectives:**
- **Analyze the last 5 years of manufacturing deployments** in the Ohio Region (Ohio and surrounding states)
- **Understand trends in urban manufacturing** through case studies
- **Identify demand-side location factors that drive location decisions** in the advanced manufacturing, food and flavoring, and Bio-Health (Life Sciences) industries
- **Understand the strengths/ weaknesses** of Cincinnati as business location"

In analyzing the Manufacturing Investments for the Ohio Region from 2011-2016, the study revealed: "Indiana, Ohio and Kentucky saw the most number of project announcements along with largest amounts of capital investment over the past five years."

States	# of Project Announcements	Capital Investment	Jobs Created
Indiana	350~	~$13.4	~37,000
Ohio	271	~$17.6	~34,000
Kentucky	230	~$9.0	~24,000

"The majority of the manufacturing investments in Ohio over the past 5 years are spread throughout rural areas within commutable distances of large metropolitan areas (Cincinnati, Dayton, Columbus, Akron and Cleveland.) Based on FDI data, 14 manufacturing projects were announced in Cincinnati within the past 5 years."

The Deloitte study stated "Advanced manufacturers are highly interested in labor quality and availability as well as minimizing risk related to site development and neighboring use concerns." The two highest factors are: "Labor Quality and Availability (engineers, technicians and operators) and Real Estate (Site readiness, Capacity and availability of utilities, and Neighboring use/pollution). Labor quality, labor availability and supply chain tend to be the key drivers for food industry in making location decisions.

The study showed that "A 1-hr drive time from downtown Cincinnati allows access to a significant labor force, with over 2.5 million in population." The manufacturing industry represents 14.34% of the Cincinnati Metro economy. Persons with Associate degrees (20.12%), Bachelor degrees (11.97%), and graduate degrees (8.42%) represent 50.51% of the population, and another 45.71% of workers have a high school diploma (26.08%) or some college (19.63%).

Other advantages are: "When compared to the states surrounding Ohio, Ohio has a relatively low average industrial electricity price;" and "Cincinnati is located right in the heart of the most utilized truck routes in the country and has a relatively low percentage of roads requiring significant maintenance when compared to nearby states…"

The summary findings of the report were:

- **"Cincinnati has an advantage in the presence of industrial engineers, machinist and tool/ die makers,** as well as a **large supply of lower skilled production workers,** giving the area a talent proposition to attract manufacturing deployments
- However, **a key driver of the evaluation process for manufacturing deployments is developable sites... Cincinnati currently lacks suitable real estate options** to entice most manufacturing operations
- Given **Cincinnati's availability in key manufacturing skill sets and low/average cost in several talent segments, an investment program to prepare site options would enhance its ability to attract manufacturing investment."**

Our next meeting was with Kimm Coyner, V. P. Business Development & Project Management of REDI Cincinnati, which was spun out of the Cincinnati Chamber in 2014 with the support of Jobs Ohio. REDI Cincinnati covers 15 counties — five in Southwest Ohio, seven in northern Kentucky, and three in Southeast Indiana, through which the Ohio River runs in the center.

Ms. Coyner said, "REDI is solely focused on new capital investment and attracting and expanding manufacturing to create good paying jobs. We have 165 public and private members. Our team identifies opportunities to attract businesses to the region by developing relationships with companies and new markets - domestically and across the globe. We provide connections to the resources that take startups to the next level and grow existing businesses. We connect companies to the region's assets, advantages and business leaders to secure Greater Cincinnati's place as one of the world's leading business centers."

She told us that railroads were the key to industrial development of the region in the 19th Century to provide transportation beyond the river. She said, "While Cincinnati arguably stayed too long in the manufacture of carriages and missed out on being a primary automotive manufacturing center like Detroit, we remain a major tier 1 supplier to that industry with hundreds of manufacturers and a significant talent base. We have five key industry clusters: Advanced Manufacturing, Information Technology, Food and Flavorings, BioHealth, and Shared Services. Advanced Manufacturing is made up of automotive, aerospace, chemicals and plastics and additive manufacturing/3D printing. Our region is the #1 supply state to Boeing and Airbus. We have nine Fortune 500 companies headquartered in Cincinnati, and four of the nine are manufacturers: AK Steel Holding, Ashland, Kroger and Procter & Gamble."

I was subsequently emailed a list of the top ten employers, nine of which are manufacturers:

- Kroger - 21,646 employees
- GE Aviation - 7,800 employees
- AK Steel Holding Corp. - 2,400 employees
- United Dairy Farmers - 2,029 employees
- Ford Motor Co. - 1,650 employees
- Mubea NA - 1,360 employees
- Bosch Automotive Steering - 1,300 employees
- Intelligrated Inc. - 1,100 employees
- Hillenbrand Inc. - 1,080 employees
- Milacron LLC - 1,020 employees

She added, "We participated with JobsOhio in a booth at the IMTS show in Chicago and focused on promoting Cincinnati as a site destination to companies from Germany." She noted that Cincinnati has the second largest Oktoberfest outside of Munich, Germany. I told her that we have a strong German-American club in San Diego that puts on a good Oktoberfest featuring a band they bring from Germany.

It is obvious to me that Cincinnati leaders recognize the important role that manufacturing plays in a local and state economy. I had mentioned to everyone I met that manufacturing is the foundation of the middle class, and if we lose manufacturing, we will lose the middle class. Cincinnati learned this lesson the hard way, but I am confident that their new vision to re-industrialize Cincinnati will create good paying jobs for residents and restore prosperity to the Cincinnati region.

Chapter 10

What needs to be done to rebuild American manufacturing?

In September 2012, the Information Technology and Innovation Foundation (ITIF) released a report[108] titled, *"Fifty Ways to Leave Your Competitiveness Woes Behind: A National Traded Sector Competitiveness Strategy,"* by Stephen Ezell and Robert Atkinson in which they stated, "A comprehensive strategy aimed at strengthening U.S. establishments competing in global markets is needed for the United States to boost short-term recovery and long-term prosperity…"

The report, presents 50 federal-level policy recommendations to help restore U.S. traded sector competitiveness, along with 13 state-level recommendations. The recommendations are organized around federal policies regarding the "4Ts of technology, tax, trade, and talent, as well as policies to increase access to capital, reform regulations, and better assess U.S. traded sector competitiveness."

The report stated, "A nation's traded sector includes industries such as manufacturing, software, engineering and design services, music, movies, video games, farming, and mining, which compete in international marketplaces and whose output is sold at least in part to nonresidents of the nation. They are the core engine of U.S. economic growth and face unique challenges."

 Because these industries face competition in the global market that non-traded, local-serving industries (retail trade or personal services) do not, their success is riskier. "The health of U.S. traded sector enterprises in industries such as semiconductors, software, machine tools, or automobiles—all far more exposed to global competition than local-serving firms and industries—cannot be taken for granted."

If a company like Boeing loses market share to Airbus, thousands of domestic jobs at Boeing, its suppliers, and the companies at which their employees spend money will be lost. In contrast, a local grocery store may compete for business with other supermarkets, but it is not threatened by international competition. If Safeway loses market share to Wal-Mart, the jobs remain in the United States.

Ezell and Atkinson corroborate what I have written previously: "every lost manufacturing job has meant the loss of an additional two to three jobs throughout the rest of the economy. The 32 percent loss of manufacturing jobs was a central cause of the country's anemic overall job performance during the previous decade, when the U.S. economy produced, on net, no new jobs....at the rate of growth in manufacturing jobs that occurred in 2011, it would take until at least 2020 for employment to return to where the economy was in terms of manufacturing jobs at the end of 2007."

The reasons why the authors emphasize the importance of manufacturing as a "traded sector" are:

- It will be difficult for the U. S. to balance its foreign trade without a robust manufacturing sector because manufacturing accounts for 86 percent of U.S. goods exports and 60 percent of total U.S. exports.
- Manufacturing remains a key source of jobs that pay well.
- Each manufacturing job supports an average of 2.9 other jobs in the economy.
- The average wages in U.S. high technology are 86 percent higher than the average of other private sector wages.
- Manufacturing, R&D, and innovation go hand-in-hand.
- The manufacturing sector accounts for 72 percent of all private sector R&D spending.
- Manufacturing employs 63 percent of domestic scientists and engineers.

- U.S. manufacturing firms demonstrate almost three times the rate of innovation as U.S. services firms.
- Manufacturing is vital to U.S. national security and defense.

They contend that "the engines of a nation's competitiveness are in fact not mom and pop small businesses, but rather firms in traded sectors, high-growth entrepreneurial companies, and U.S.-headquartered multinational corporations. Although such firms comprise far less than 1 percent of U.S. companies, they account for about 19 percent of private-sector jobs, 25 percent of private-sector wages, 48 percent of goods exports, and 74 percent of nonpublic R&D investment. And, since 1990, they have been responsible for 41 percent of the nation's increase in private labor productivity."

The report notes that "traded sector businesses improve the local economy in three ways:

1. Traded sector businesses bring money into a region by selling to people and businesses outside the region.
2. They help keep local money at home through import substitution, which occurs when local residents and businesses purchase locally produced products instead of importing goods and services.
3. They improve economic equity since "their productivity and market size tends to lead them to offer higher wage levels" and "jobs at traded sector companies help anchor a region's middle-class employment base by providing stable, living wage jobs for residents."

While the authors believe all 50 recommendations are needed, they believe the 10 most critical recommendations are:

1. Create a network of 25 "Engineering and Manufacturing Institutes" performing applied R&D across a range of advanced technologies.
2. Support the designation of at least 20 U.S. "manufacturing universities."

3. Increase funding for the Manufacturing Extension Partnership (MEP).
4. Increase R&D tax credit generosity and make the R&D tax credit permanent.
5. Institute an investment tax credit on purchases of new capital equipment and software.
6. Develop a national trade strategy and increase funding for U.S. trade policymaking and enforcement agencies.
7. Fully fund a nationwide manufacturing skills standards initiative.
8. Expand high-skill immigration, particularly which focuses on the traded sector.
9. Transform Fannie Mae into an industrial bank.
10. Require the Office of Information and Regulatory Affairs (OIRA) to incorporate a "competitiveness screen" in its review of federal regulations.

I support all of their other top 10 recommendations, as well as many of their other 40 recommendations, especially the following:

- Lower the effective U. S. corporate tax rate - As of April 1, 2012 (when Japan lowered its corporate tax rate), the United States took the mantle of having the highest statutory corporate tax rate at almost 39 percent (when state and federal rates are combined) of any OECD nation.
- Combat foreign currency manipulation
- Better support and align trade promotion programs to boost U. S. exports.
- Better promotion of reshoring.

I also support their recommendation that Congress should broaden the R&D tax credit's scope to make it clear that process R&D (to develop better ways of making things) qualifies for the tax incentive and that Congress should expand the R&D credit to allow expenditures on employee training to count as qualified expenditures.

Ezell and Atkinson state, "Implementing the policies recommended in this report will make the United States a more attractive investment environment for traded sector enterprises and their establishments. The technology policies will help spur innovation in advanced manufacturing, upgrade the technology capacity of manufacturing and other traded sector firms, help restore America's industrial commons, and support the productivity, innovation, and competitiveness of traded sector SMEs. The tax policies will stimulate a favorable climate for private sector investment by making the overall U.S. corporate tax code more competitive with that of other nations and also by leveraging tax policy to incent private sector R&D and investment."

In conclusion, they urge that U.S. policymakers understand that "manufacturing is not some low-value-added industry to be cavalierly abandoned." Manufacturing is vital to U.S. competitiveness. I highly recommend reading all of this comprehensive, well-researched, well-documented report to be able to evaluate all of their recommendations and benefit from the details that are the basis for each recommendation.

Create a National Manufacturing Strategy

Businesses must have a strategic plan to start and grow. This strategic plan guides the business with regard to product development, finance, marketing, production, procurement, etc. Many other countries have an economic strategy to grow their economy. A country's strategy guides their economic, fiscal, trade, innovation, finance and monetary policy, so that they all work together to enhance their competitiveness as a nation.

The United States has no comprehensive strategy — just a hodgepodge of laws and rules. Trade negotiators have had no strategic plan to guide them, and neither has the administrative agencies relevant to manufacturing, agricultural, and use of natural resources. The United States needs a comprehensive competitiveness strategy that clearly expresses exactly what we want to achieve for our country... not for an industry or special interest... but our country as a whole.

For several years, one business or government leader after another proposed developing a national manufacturing strategy. For example, the Information Technology& Innovation Foundation (ITIF) released a report,[109] "The Case for a National Manufacturing Strategy," in April 2011 that built the intellectual case for why the United States needs a serious national manufacturing strategy.

The Alliance for American Manufacturing was a strong proponent of a national manufacturing strategy, and repeatedly put forward a "Plan to Save Manufacturing," calling for a national manufacturing strategy to reverse the decline in U.S. manufacturing and the good jobs that come with it.

A bill to set up a process to develop a national manufacturing strategy was introduced by Rep. Dan Lipinski and even passed the House of Representatives in 2010 by a vote of 379 to 38, but died in the Senate.

In 2012, Illinois Reps. Dan Lipinski (D) and Adam Kinzinger (R) introduced "The American Manufacturing Competitiveness Act" (HR-5865), which passed the House Energy and Commerce Committee on June 20, 2012 and was passed by the House, but a similar bill in the Senate was not brought up for a vote.

Rep. Lipinski never gives up, and in June 20, 2013, he introduced HR 2447, the American Manufacturing Competitiveness Act, and the Senate companion (S. 1709) was introduced by Sen. Kirk, but was not brought up for a vote. In April 2014, the Senate Commerce Committee marked up S. 1468, the Revitalize American Manufacturing and Innovation Act (which would authorize the National Network of Manufacturing Institutes), and the manufacturing strategy text was added as an amendment by Sen. Mark Pryor.

The House SST Committee marked up House version of S. 1468 (HR 2996), the Revitalize American Manufacturing and Innovation Act, and the Rep. Lipinski amendment to insert revised manufacturing strategy language was adopted. The House approved HR 2996 by voice vote. Instead of passing the Senate bill, the text of the manufacturing strategy (HR 2447, as revised) was included as Section 704 of the omnibus spending bill, HR 83. Both the House and Senate passed HR 83, and the President signed it December 16, 2014.

Perhaps because it was incorporated into HR 83 that is thousands of pages long, nothing has been done to develop a national manufacturing strategy, as far as I have been able to discern. This may be why Rep. Lipinski is a co-sponsor of the Chief Manufacturing Officer Act (H.R. 1092) introduced by Rep. Tim Ryan (D-OH) on 02/15/2017 to the House Energy and Commerce Committee.

"This bill: (1) expresses the sense of Congress that a well-designed national manufacturing strategy would benefit the U.S. economy, and (2) directs the President to appoint a United States Chief Manufacturing Officer, which shall be a member of the National Economic Council.

The Officer's duties shall include developing, by May 1, 2018, a national manufacturing strategy, which shall incorporate: (1) the national strategic plan for advanced manufacturing developed under the America COMPETES Reauthorization Act of 2010, and (2) the strategic plan developed for the Network for Manufacturing Innovation Program under the National Institute of Standards and Technology Act. The Officer shall provide annual updates on progress made toward achieving the objectives of such strategic plan for advanced manufacturing and carrying out the strategy developed under this bill."

The Coalition for a Prosperous America Proposes a Competitiveness Strategy for the U. S.

The Coalition for a Prosperous America is an unprecedented alliance of manufacturing, agriculture and labor working for smart trade policies. CPA represents over three million households through our member associations and companies. Members include farmers, ranchers, associations, and businesses in copper, steel, livestock, row crop, textile, tooling, machining, electronics, software, and other industries. CPA members hold education and advocacy meetings across the country informing business owners, local elected officials, service organizations, and trade associations of problems and solutions to trade problems.

CPA works hard to develop trade policy solutions that benefit the entire economy, not just a particular sector. Every solution we present has been agreed to by agriculture, manufacturing and organized labor as good for the entire country.

On November 11, 2015, the Coalition for a Prosperous America (CPA) released a White paper,[110] entitled "A Competitiveness Strategy for the United States - America at a Crossroads," which addresses other sectors of our economy in addition to manufacturing. "America needs to start winning again," said Michael Stumo, CEO of CPA. "That is why the mission of the Competitiveness Strategy is to:

- 'Win the international competition for good jobs, sustained real economic growth and prosperity with a national strategy to counter foreign mercantilism, balance trade and grow strong domestic supply chains.'

"Across the USA, localities and states employ plans to attract jobs," said Brian O'Shaughnessy, CPA Chief Co-Chair and Chairman of Revere Copper Products. "Other countries have sophisticated national strategies to acquire industries and bring good paying jobs to their countries. The USA has no comprehensive national strategy for domestic production and good paying jobs to guide trade negotiators and administration officials."

CPA's Competitiveness Strategy argues that: "The United States is losing an economic competition against other nations whose mercantilist strategies are destroying our manufacturing jobs, critical industries, our standard of living, our national security, the security of our food supply and our children's futures.

The threat to the US economy and national security is grave. Other trading nations are using comprehensive strategies to import jobs across all economic sectors but are particularly focused on strategically significant technologies and industries. US companies in these sectors face not only wide-ranging mercantilist practices and non-tariff trade barriers such as currency manipulation, tariffs and subsidies but also much more sophisticated and specific strategies aimed at identifying, acquiring or otherwise controlling critical technologies. Tactics used include unusually large direct and indirect subsidies, joint ventures—with both corporations and US universities-- requiring transfer or licensing of technology, corporate acquisitions and, for certain countries, systematic theft of intellectual property."

CPA's competitiveness strategy shown below is succinct, yet comprehensive:

STRATEGIC OBJECTIVES

"Identify and counter foreign mercantilist strategies that grow their economies at the expense of other countries through achieving a persistent trade surplus

- End both currency exchange rate imbalances and the accumulation of excessive US dollar holdings by non-US public and private entities.
- Impose offsetting tariffs to neutralize foreign government subsidies to industries and supply chains that compete with ours.

- Counter foreign government policies that force offshoring by conditioning access to their markets on transfers of technology, research facilities and/or production to their countries, as well as compliance with export performance and domestic content requirements, while their exporters have access to US markets without these conditions.
- Ensure that foreign greenfield investments in the US and acquisitions of existing US companies provide a clear "net benefit" to the US with special scrutiny in cases of state influenced foreign entities.

Balance trade

- Offset cumulative trade deficits of recent decades and excessive accumulations of dollar reserves through sustained trade surplus to ultimately achieve a long term overall trade balance.
- Insure that the composition of trade includes a substantial trade surplus in high value added and advanced manufactured goods.
- Make the US workforce more cost competitive by promoting fair pay, rising living standards and safe working conditions for workers everywhere.
- Reduce US producers' trade disadvantage through tax reform which finances the reduction of payroll taxes and health insurance costs with a border adjustable consumption tax in a revenue and distribution neutral manner.
- Lower corporate tax rates and end corporate inversion and profit shifting tax avoidance by taxing the income of unitary business groups, whether domestic or foreign, based upon proportion of global sales in the US.

Grow Domestic Supply Chains

- Preserve and develop domestic manufacturing and agricultural supply chains to maximize value added production in the US.

- Develop, build and maintain a world-class land, water, air, communications and energy infrastructure.
- Safeguard our military strength and national security by insuring that critical technologies, weapons & IT components are developed and manufactured in America by American controlled companies.
- Develop, commercialize, and retain strategic and economically significant advanced technology and grow their manufacturing supply chains in the US.
- Increase public support for, and incentives for, private investment in, basic and applied research, infra-technologies and new product and process technologies.
- Continually raise the competitiveness of American workers by improving Science, Technology, Engineering and Math (STEM) education available at all levels, systematically enhance lifelong learning for existing workers, and fostering a national system of apprenticeship and paid internships through collaborative public-private endeavors that are connected to actual opportunities in the labor market.
- Raise the competitiveness of small and medium sized domestic enterprises by increasing long-term private sector financing, the sharing of research on common issues and the diffusion of new technologies and production methods.
- Preserve our right to adopt and enforce domestic policies that insure the quality of our food and goods, and protect the health, safety and general welfare of our citizens without restrictions from international trade agreements.
- Ensure that domestic manufacturing and agriculture benefit fully from an expanded supply of low cost US produced energy"

The brilliance of CPA's strategy is that it is not limited to manufacturing and is not a "to do list" of actions to take. The Competitiveness Strategy will work best when pursued as a whole. The three objectives are interrelated because, for example, we cannot balance trade without growing domestic supply chains to produce more, and add more value in the U. S. We cannot grow domestic supply chains unless we neutralize foreign mercantilism (trade cheating) that offshores otherwise competitive industries that we started and developed in the U. S. We cannot address foreign mercantilism without the guidance of a balanced trade objective.

Ways to Revitalize American Manufacturing

On June 7, 2016, The Wall Street Journal, published an opinion article[111] by Bob Tita, "How to Revitalize U.S. Manufacturing." In the article, Mr. Tita briefly outlined "some of the strategies for getting U.S. manufacturing back on track."

Make Exports More Valuable: "Under a plan proposed by investor Warren Buffet, companies that export goods form the U.S. would accumulate certificates equal to the value of their exports. But companies that wanted to import goods would have to purchase certificates from exports…foreign-made items imported into the U.S. would become more expensive…As exports increase, though, more certificates would flow into the market, and their cost for importers would fall. The price could eventually slip to zero if a trade surplus was achieved."

Impose a Value Added Tax: A similar idea for lowering the trade deficit is imposing a value-added tax. The tax, which is used by more than 130 countries, is applied to each step along a production chain as a product or material increases in value or is consumed. How does this help domestic manufacturing? Almost all countries with VATs waive them on exports but impose them on imports, at an average rate of about 17%...

A VAT would need to be coupled with an elimination or reduction of existing taxes on businesses, including payroll taxes for Social Security and Medicare. Likewise, consumers would need tax relief to make up for the higher prices they would face for most purchases.

Deal with an overvalued currency: "Lowering the U.S. dollar's status as the world's reserve currency is killing demand for U.S.-made goods in global markets…Lowering the value of the dollar is difficult…" [see below for detail on how to lower value of currency.]

Look at True Cost of Offshoring: "When companies decide to offshore production, they often simply seek the lowest initial price per unit. If they were required to take into account the hidden costs of foreign production, U.S.-made goods would become more cost competitive…"

Purge Duplicate Regulations: "When federal agencies impose new rules, they rarely repeal old ones or check to see if another agency has a similar or conflicting regulation. Over decades, this has resulted in layers of rules for environmental protection, workplace safety and financial reporting that are often redundant or outdated. The National Association of Manufacturers estimates that regulatory compliance costs manufacturers about $139 billion annually…"

Look at More than Jobs: "State and federal governments typically view manufacturing as employment generators. But economic-development policies that place too much emphasis on boosting head counts risk missing the broader trend coursing through manufacturing even in low-cost locations: automation. Countries that give short shrift to robots and other manpower-reduction technologies won't be desirable destinations for manufacturing in the future."

Analysts say policy makers should do more to encourage investments in manufacturing technology and automation, even if it initially seems to undermine manufacturing-employment growth. U.S. incentives for investments in factory automation and research generally lag behind other countries' efforts…Boosting tax breaks to the levels of other large, developed nations is crucial, advocates say."

Turn Community Colleges into Career Factories: "While community colleges offer programs for skilled trades business executives' complain the course work is often too generalized to suit companies' needs...Some companies are collaborating with community colleges to design job-training programs specifically for the companies' needs..."

Spend More on Manufacturing R&D: "The fledgling National Network for Manufacturing Innovation is the U.S.'s best attempt so far at closing the gaps in homegrown applied research...Eight of the 15 institutes have opened with the bulk of the funding coming from corporate participants..."

Create Regional Centers of Expertise: "In this approach, a region looks to leverage an existing set of skills or an industrial legacy, such as machining or casting metal...These centers typically start with an intermediary group – a chamber or a regional development agency – that assembles businesses, schools, and government agencies into a network that can work together to attract new businesses and, in general, improve the competitiveness of businesses..."

What is amazing to me is how many of these recommendations I have written about in blog articles from 2011 to the present time and are now contained in this chapter. I created the outline for this book and the Table of Contents in December 2015 and selected articles I had already written to go in the various chapters. Since then, I have written articles that would fit in the chapter topics I selected. chapters of this book.

Recommendations for Trump Administration by ITIF

On January 31, 2017, the Information Technology and Innovation Foundation (ITIF) released a report,[112] "Ten Principles to Guide the Trump Administration's Manufacturing Strategy" by Robert D. Atkinson and Stephen Ezell.

The report summary states, "The Trump administration has a real opportunity to do that by ignoring both supercilious criticism and tired laissez-faire thinking, but it also runs the risk of overreacting and thereby making things worse, not better. Therefore, to help guide the new administration's manufacturing policy efforts, this briefing paper first unpacks four key policy debates on manufacturing (why jobs were lost; why jobs went offshore; what's the right amount of manufacturing for America; and whether manufacturing can return) and shows how the conventional economics position that the media reflectively recycles is wrong on each of them." The paper then presents strategic principles that should guide the administration's efforts to restore U.S. manufacturing:

(1) "Focus on traded sectors, not just manufacturing;
(2) Focus on high-value-added, defensible sectors and segments;
(3) Focus on the trade deficit, not jobs per se;
(4) Recognize what should stay and what shouldn't;
(5) Understand that when U.S. companies succeed in overseas markets it can help U.S. employment;
(6) Focus on attraction rather than compulsion;
(7) Move beyond one-off deals and a low-cost business climate;
(8) Change the playing field through technology;
(9) Support the defense industrial base; and (10) Pay attention to where advanced production is located in the United States."

To emphasize three key components of the above report, Adams Nager and Robert D. Atkinson, of the Information Technology and Innovation Foundation wrote a follow up article[113] "Can US Manufacturing Be Made Great Again?" that was published by Industry Week on February 22, 2017.

They wrote: "First, President Trump should focus on high value-added, defensible sectors. Not all manufacturing sectors and functions within sectors provide the same value. Some industries and occupations are more important than others... more targeted policies to encourage more production in middle- and higher-wage industries, which the Carrier deal in Indiana represents, would increase U.S. living standards."

"Second, enticing American—and even foreign—manufacturers to create or maintain manufacturing production in the United States represents a laudable goal, but one that's best pursued by following an "attraction" strategy, which emphasizes implementing a coordinated set of public policies relating to taxes, high-skill talent, technology, trade, regulations and competition, finance, and digital and physical infrastructure, rather than a "compulsion" strategy."

"Third, the U.S. manufacturing strategy should be broader than working on individual deals with particular firms because the extent of the challenge is too great for a piecemeal, scattershot approach."

To implement these strategies, they recommend the following tactics:

- "Push for legislation such as the 2016 "Made in America Manufacturing Communities Act," a no-cost bill that designates "Manufacturing Communities" to assist regions in thinking strategically about how they fit into emerging industries and value chains and where they can be competitive.
- Champion the Export-Import Bank, an important component of the fabric that supports American manufacturing competitiveness.
- Push to increase funding for the Manufacturing Extension Partnership, which raises the technical and innovation capacity of America's small- to medium-sized manufacturers.
- Expand Manufacturing USA, a public-private partnership network of innovation institutes that are focused on U.S. leadership in advanced manufacturing.
- Quickly implement the newly enacted Manufacturing Universities program."

Concluding, they wrote, "In short, it's time to change the narrative that U.S. manufacturing jobs are being lost to robots in a rapid shift to high-tech "factories of the future" that pushes U.S. manufacturing output to an all-time high. This kind of Pollyannaish thinking keeps policymakers from focusing on what is really needed: a robust U.S. manufacturing strategy."

New Recommendations from the Coalition for a Prosperous America

How to Fix the Dollar's Overvaluation & Exchange Rate Misalignment: On July 11, 2017, the Coalition for a Prosperous America released a paper[114] titled, "The Threat of U.S. Dollar Overvaluation: How to Calculate True Exchange Rate Misalignment & How to Fix It" by Michael Stumo (CEO), Jeff Ferry (Research Director) and Dr. John R. Hansen, a 30-year veteran of the World Bank and Advisory Board member. The purpose of the paper is to explain the problem of the dollar overvaluation, to show how to accurately calculate the dollar's misalignment against trading partner currencies, and to propose a solution to this serious threat to America's future.

The authors point out that "In past centuries, the only reason that people would choose to hold a foreign currency would be to trade with it... But in the last few decades, and especially since the early 1990s, international speculators and traders have invested in dollars, including stocks, bonds, and cash, at the rate of hundreds of billions of dollars a year. The dollar investments of private investors now far outweigh the investments of government investors." These private investments shrunk from $1 trillion in 2007 down to $200 billion in 2010 during the recession and have grown back up to about $400 billion.

The authors explain that private investors buy dollars for many reasons: to purchase goods that are priced in dollars (like oil), "as a hedge against depreciation of their own local currencies," to invest in the U.S. economy, to make a speculative investment, and "in many cases simply because in an uncertain world, the U.S. dollar is viewed as a rock of reliability and stability."

In economic terms, the authors explain that the current account deficit is "the trade deficit with overseas remittances and other small items added in." In the past when currency markets still maintained a link between exchange rates and balanced trade, the value of the dollar and the account deficit affect each other; i.e., "When the dollar rises, the current account worsens (larger negative figure as a percent of GDP), and when the dollar falls, the current account improves."

However, the authors point out this hasn't been happening for years. For example, "The current account deficit has been strongly negative throughout the last ten years, yet the dollar has not fallen to bring trade back into balance. On the contrary, in mid-2014, despite a trade balance close to -3% of GDP, the dollar suddenly rose more than 15%, and stabilized in 2016, only to rise yet again after the November election."

The consequences are: "A dollar that is too high keeps our exports too expensive and makes imports too cheap, prompting Americans to consume more imports and to export less. The impact of an overvalued dollar is hard to overstate."

Why this is critical is: "According to Fred Bergsten and William Cline, both of the Peterson Institute, "every 10 percent rise in the dollar adds about $350 billion to the trade deficit and reduces the level of U.S. economic activity by about 1.65%, with a corresponding loss of about 1.5 million jobs." Since the U.S. has had a more than $500 billion trade deficit[115] since 2003, except for 2009, this helps explain why we lost 5.8 million manufacturing jobs between 2000 – 2010.

Calculating the Currency Misalignment: In 2008, Fred Bergsten and his Peterson Institute for International Economics colleagues developed a methodology to calculate a Fundamental Equilibrium Exchange Rate (FEER) of a currency that will enable a country's trade to balance (i.e. exports and imports equal) in a reasonably short timeframe. The authors state, "The traditional FEER methodology generally targets getting a nation's current account to within plus or minus 3 percent of balance…In 2015, Peterson suggested targeting absolute, true-zero trade balances and recalculated FEER levels based on targets of balanced trade. Moving from a target of +/-3% of GDP to a true-zero balance is very important for the United States. Our present current account deficits equal to 3% of GDP cost us the needless unemployment of about three million American workers, according to most estimates of the job cost of imports."

After "the Peterson Institute issued new global FEER estimates in May using the traditional +/- 3% balance target methodology," Dr. John Hansen "converted these FEER estimates into true-zero FEER estimates using a methodology agreed with Peterson."

According to his calculations, **"The U.S. dollar is currently 25.5% overvalued compared to its FEER,"** which makes it "more seriously misaligned than the currency of any other major trading partner country. "

In contrast, "Germany and Japan – are misaligned in the opposite direction. They are undervalued while the U.S. dollar is overvalued." Japan's currency is undervalued by 25% and Germany's by 23.6%.

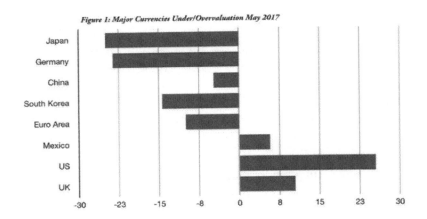

Figure 1: Major Currencies Under/Overvaluation May 2017

As a consequence of the misalignment of the dollar against the currency of two of our major trading partners and to a lesser degree with other countries, "The dollar's gross overvaluation imposes a tax on the selling price of all U.S. products that can be traded internationally – even if they are not actually traded. It is a tax on U.S. producers trying to export. On U.S. producers competing with imported goods. And it is even a tax on U.S. producers who face the threat of imports. For example, the threat of imported shirts from China can force a New England shirt manufacturer to sell his shirt for 25 percent less than he would otherwise be able to charge if the dollar were not so overvalued."

Because this is a tax on the selling price and not on profits like the income tax, "…the dollar's overvaluation is such a serious threat to the survival of manufacturing and farming in the United States. The dollar's overvaluation threatens not only the existence of these two critical sectors. It also threatens the entire economy because these two sectors are by far the most important sources of the exports we need to pay for our imports."

Contrary to popular opinion, the overvaluation of the dollar is not caused by government currency manipulation The authors assert that "The dollar's misalignment is primarily caused by the buying and selling decisions of private traders…the dollar is overvalued because private investor decisions are unrelated to the fundamental performance of trade or production in the U.S. or any other economy, and the global monetary system no longer has a mechanism to bring exchange rates back to levels consistent with balanced trade."

What is the solution?

Dr. John Hansen has developed a Market Access Charge (MAC) "as a system to discourage overseas private investors and return-sensitive official investors such as sovereign wealth fund managers from excessive speculation and trading in U.S. dollar assets."

He believes that "By reducing the incentive for foreigners to invest in dollars, we can gradually and safely reduce its overvaluation, benefiting the U.S. economy and restoring control over our own currency."

His proposal is to initiate the MAC with a 0.5% charge "on any purchase of U.S. dollar financial assets by a foreign entity or individual…As a one-time charge, the MAC will discourage would-be short-term investors, many of whom hold dollars or dollar-denominated securities overnight or even for minutes for the sake of a tiny profit.

The MAC rate would operate on a sliding scale, geared to the value of the trade deficit as a percentage of GDP. The MAC tax would rise if the trade deficit rose, and fall as the trade deficit falls… Most importantly, the MAC would have a substantial impact on the dollar's value, moving it gradually and safely to a trade-balancing exchange rate and keeping it there, regardless of what other countries do. If the trade deficit goes to zero, so would the MAC."

Dr. Hansen and the Coalition for a Prosperous America believe that this small charge "would be sufficient to discourage foreign inflows of hot money, with no material impact on foreign direct investment in factories and other directly productive activities."

They agree that, "if properly implemented, the MAC could eliminate the full 25% overvaluation of the dollar, and this could lead to the complete elimination of the trade deficit over the subsequent three to four years."

How could it be implemented?

The authors believe the MAC could be implemented unilaterally by the U.S. federal government. because "it does not violate IMF rules, which explicitly allow member nations to implement policies needed to rectify international financial imbalances [and] It does not violate WTO rules either."

However, they "recommend a period of international consultation with G20 members to reduce the risk of misunderstandings and, hopefully, to get them to implement their own versions of the MAC...[which] would benefit the U.S. and the world by restoring a stable foundation for balanced, sustainable global growth."
They envision: "The MAC would be a self-financing system since it would generate revenue. We expect the MAC would generate at least $1 billion in annual revenues, and probably more, depending largely upon how much foreign exchange trading in the dollar declines due to increased transaction costs from the MAC.

Because the goal of the MAC is "to reduce and ultimately eliminate the trade deficit," the revenue would be temporary and would go to zero when the goal is achieved. They propose that at "MAC revenue be earmarked for a "U.S. Competitiveness Fund" supporting short-term spending projects such as infrastructure investment."
They also clarify that "no Americans would pay the MAC charge. Only foreign-based individuals and entities are liable to pay the MAC." Until the MAC achieves its goal, the Government will enjoy increased tax revenue because the MAC will greatly stimulate U.S. competitiveness and thus overall output, profits, wages – and thus the tax base."

They "believe the MAC could eliminate the trade deficit entirely over a period of several years," but emphasize that "there is still a clear need for other U.S. trade policies focused on eliminating unfair trade practices and non-tariff barriers. The MAC should be seen as complementary to, not competitive with, such trade policies. Though in remission now, currency intervention and manipulation by governments is likely to resume, and the U.S. government should not hesitate to act to stop or counteract such activities."

The Coalition for a Prosperous America "favors actions to strengthen the monitoring, definition, and enforcement of remedies to counteract currency manipulation, dumping, and other unfair trading practices."

Imposing VAT Could Help Rebuild American Manufacturing and Create Jobs: Over 150 countries in the world have shifted a significant portion of their tax mix to border adjustable consumption taxes – value added taxes (VATs) or goods and services taxes (GSTs). Consumption taxes are "border adjustable taxes" and allowed under World Trade Organization rules. Consumption taxes are a tax on consumption - as opposed to income, wealth, property, or wages. Consumption taxes are called goods and services taxes in Canada, Australia, New Zealand or value added taxes in other countries. They are usually a tax only on the incremental value that is added at each level of the supply chain to a product, material or service. Most countries VATs or GSTs are tariff and subsidy replacements, mimicking a currency devaluation if a country raises the VAT or GST and uses proceeds to lower purely domestic taxes and costs.

After 40 years of multilateral tariff reduction, other countries replaced tariffs with VATs but the U.S. did not. American exporters face nearly the same border taxes (tariffs + consumption tax) as they did in the early 1970s. Foreign VATs are export subsidies as they are rebated to companies that export their goods. For example:

- Mexico established a 15% VAT after NAFTA
- Central American countries established a 12% VAT after CAFTA
- Germany raised its VAT to 19% in 2007 to fund business tax reduction for trade competitiveness

The rates range from 12% to 24% and average 17% globally. This means that virtually all foreign countries tax our exports at 17% on top of tariffs. They subsidize domestic shipments abroad with the average 17% tax rebate. The figure below illustrates how it works.

U.S. Local Price = $100	China Local Price = $100
U.S. Price PLUS 17% VAT = $117.00	Chinese Price MINUS 17% VAT rebate = $85.47

The map below shows which nations have consumption taxes (red) and which do not (blue).

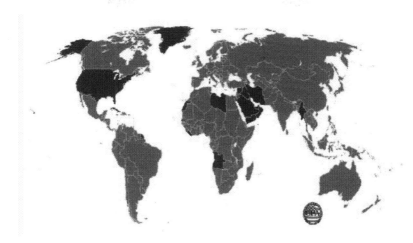

Because foreign consumption taxes are border adjustable, companies that export are double taxed. They pay U. S. taxes and the foreign border tax. Importers can sell cheaper products because they receive a consumption tax rebate from their home country and do not pay U. S. VAT.

Eliminate Payroll Tax Burden with the most efficient VAT in world: In written testimony[116] to the House Ways and Means Committee of the U. S. House of Representatives on May 18, 2017, the Coalition for a Prosperous America (CPA) recommended "**a new border adjustable consumption tax (Goods and Services Tax) that funds a full credit against all payroll taxes.**"

Highlights from the testimony paraphrased or quoted include: "A new U.S. *goods and services tax* (GST) of approximately 12% should be enacted to shift taxation to consumption using the credit/invoice method. The proceeds should be credited against payroll taxes paid by all workers and businesses. GST proceeds should be applied as a full credit against the 15.3% rate of payroll taxes to reduce the cost of labor in the US while increasing after tax wages.

Exported goods and services would receive a full rebate. Imports would pay the GST. Small business with less than, for example, one million dollars could be exempted without sacrificing significant tax revenue."

CPA's written testimony explained, "Domestic prices vs. wages would not worsen because the payroll tax is embedded in the cost of all goods and services. Thus, eliminating the payroll tax lowers the prices for goods and services or increases wages depending upon the particular competitive forces in each product sector. A GST raises goods and services prices, but the GST/payroll tax combination would largely cancel each other out thereby holding the domestic economy harmless.

The more modern GSTs implemented by free market economies are in Canada, Australia and New Zealand. The compliance and administration burdens are relatively low in comparison to other taxation methods. The U. S. can learn from those and other countries' experiences to implement the most modern, streamlined GST in the world."

In summary, the proposed GST would:

- Reduce the cost of labor in the U. S.
- Give every worker a raise
- Lower price of U. S. exports
- Levy a tax on imports

The following are some of the benefits of a payroll tax credit for manufacturers, ranchers, and farmers:

- Regressiveness of VAT offset by elimination of regressive payroll tax
- VAT costs on all domestic producers are offset
- No impact on prices of domestic goods/services

- Imported goods/services prices increase
- Cost of production for exports reduced

Change to a Sales Factor Apportionment (SFA) Border Adjustable Profit Tax: In 2016, I wrote an article[117] about corporate tax reform at the federal level based on the Sales Factor Apportionment Framework proposed by one of the members of the Coalition for a Prosperous America, Bill Parks. Mr. Parks is a retired finance professor and founder of NRS Inc., an Idaho-based paddle sports accessory maker. He asserted that "Tax reform proposals won't fix our broken corporate system… [because] they fail to fix the unfairness of domestic companies paying more tax than multinational enterprises in identical circumstances."

He explained that multinational enterprises (MNEs) can use cost accounting practices to transfer costs and profits within the company to achieve different goals. "Currently MNEs manipulate loopholes in our tax system to avoid paying U. S. taxes… MNEs can legitimately choose a cost that reduces or increases the profits of its subsidiaries in different countries. Because the United States is a relatively high-tax country, MNEs will choose the costs that minimize profits in the United States and maximize them in what are usually lower-tax countries."

Sales Factor Tax Apportionment is the bi-partisan tax reform legislation that states passed to address the problem of getting corporations to pay a fair share of taxes in their state. The solution was "apportionment" of corporate income taxes that is a share of taxes to be paid by a corporation to a state based on a particular formula. According to a Policy Brief[118] by the Institute on Taxation and Economic Policy, all but the five states that don't have a corporate income tax (Nevada, South Dakota, Texas, Washington, and Wyoming) have adopted some type of formula for state apportionment of corporate taxes.

Mr. Parks has proposed that Sales Factor Tax Apportionment be implemented on a national basis to ensure that multinational corporations are paying their fair share of taxes. The way his plan would work is that the amount of corporate taxes that a multinational company would pay "would be determined solely on the percent of that company's world-wide sales made to U. S. customers. Foreign MNEs would also be taxed the same way on their U. S. income leveling the playing field between domestic firms and foreign and domestic MNEs."

For example, if a MNE's share of worldwide sales in the United States is 40%, then the company would pay taxes on 40% of its sales. Mr. Parks states that the advantages of his plan are:

- "Inversions [and transfer pricing] for tax purposes become pointless because the company would pay the same tax no matter what its base.
- It would encourage exports because all exports are fully excluded from corporate income tax.
- It simplifies the calculation for federal, state, and local taxes because the profit to be taxed by the U. S. is determined by a simple formula.
- Reduces or eliminates the tax incentives to locate jobs, factories, and corporate headquarters offshore, boosting employment and U. S. tax revenue.
- Ends the disguised income taxes which are actually royalty payments.
- Allow Congress to raise revenue without raising rates because it stops U. S. and foreign multinationals from being able to place their profits offshore to avoid U. S. taxes."
- "Removing the incentives for multinational corporations to leave their profits in off-shore tax havens.
- Maintaining Congress' ability to lower rates and/or increase revenue."

Mr. Parks concludes that "Sales Factor Apportionment is simpler and more effective than our current system which attempts — and often fails — to tax the worldwide business activities of U. S. corporations. Because it is based on sales, not payroll or assets, it is a difficult system to game. Companies can easily move certain business operations and assets out of the U. S., but few, if any, would be willing to give up sales to the world's largest market."

The Board of the Directors of the Coalition for a Prosperous America chose to support Sales Factor Tax Apportionment and included the following in their testimony to the House Ways and Means Committee:

"The US corporate tax system harms America's trade competitiveness, over taxes income from wages, under taxes consumption, and is bad at actually collecting what is owed. It also enables rampant base erosion through transferring profits to tax havens or countries with lower corporate tax rates. Full reform centered around destination based, border adjustment principles can result in an efficient, trade competitive, and largely tamper-proof tax system.

SFA is a destination based profit tax. Pretax income is allocated to the US in proportion to the percentage of a company's total sales in the U. S. Pre-tax income earned outside the US is not taxed. Tax rates can be lowered substantially while still meeting revenue targets."

The Coalition for a Prosperous America (CPA) favors "a border adjustable business tax (for all entity types) which allocates pre-tax income based upon the destination of sales. Formulary apportionment based upon a single sales factor (sales factor apportionment or SFA) is well established at the state level. It solves most of the base erosion/profit shifting and tax haven abuse problems facing tax writing committees. SFA eliminates the disparate tax treatment between domestic companies (who pay the full income tax burden on worldwide income), multinationals (many of which shift profits to tax havens), and foreign companies (which pay a territorial income tax).

A broad based 12% GST could raise $1.4 trillion in new revenue. Payroll tax revenue in 2015 was 33% of total tax revenue at $1.056 trillion."

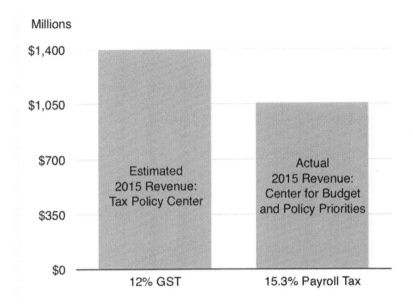

CPA asserts that U. S. "trade competitiveness would be substantially improved because exports are freed from both the GST and payroll tax burden. Imports never include the cost of the U. S. payroll tax, but would pay the GST. This effect has been called Fiscal Devaluation because it mimics a currency devaluation for trade purposes. It only works if you combine a new GST with a ubiquitous domestic tax or cost reduction. The optimal domestic tax reduction is the payroll tax burden."

The reason for CPA's support is that "SFA taxes pre-tax income allocated to the U. S. but not profits allocated to foreign sales. Domestic firms can legitimately 'avoid' taxation by exporting more. Profits from imports are subject to tax. Domestic, multinational and foreign firms are on an equal tax footing.

The current corporate tax system cannot be fixed because it allows the fiction of intra-firm transactions to erode the tax base. Multinational companies use them to self-deal, strictly for tax purposes, shifting income to tax haven jurisdictions. Companies sell products or services to themselves, governed only by an 'arm's length' principle which allows them to create their own pricing terms subject to a nearly unenforceable 'fair market value' constraint.

The intra-company transactions are not free market, 'arm's length' or true third-party transactions. The only economically meaningful 'sale' is one to a true third party outside the company. As much of 30% of tax revenue may be lost from profit shifting to tax haven jurisdictions which have effective tax rates of 0-4%. These include Bermuda, Netherlands, UK Caribbean Islands, Ireland, Luxembourg, Singapore, and Switzerland."

The CPA testimony provides the following example: "Assume a multinational corporation has worldwide sales of $100 billion, $50 billion sales in the U. S. and company-wide pretax income of $10 billion. Fifty percent of the profits, under SFA, are apportioned to the US. So, the profits to be taxed in the USA in this case are $5 Billion. Using a 20% corporate tax rate yields a SFA tax of $1 billion. Intra-company transactions with a Bermuda subsidiary would be irrelevant.

Merely lowering the U. S. corporate tax rate for example to 15% without further reform would not eliminate the tax competition with tax haven jurisdictions. SFA would make tax havens irrelevant because true sales to any foreign country would be ignored. IRS litigation centered around the proper fair market value of intra-firm transactions would disappear. Only profits allocated to the US in proportion to true third-party sales would be taxable."

CPA asserts that "SFA would allow a significant reduction in the business tax rate while collecting similar revenue because base erosion is largely fixed. By one estimate, a 13% corporate tax rate under SFA would collect the same revenue as the current system..."

In conclusion, CPA recommends, "The U. S. tax system should shift to more border adjustability through destination based taxation. If the House GOP Blueprint does not gain Senate or White House support, the Ways and Means Committee has solid alternatives to meet their goals. CPA supports enacting (1) a new GST to fund a full credit against payroll taxes, plus (2) a shift to sales factor apportionment of global profits as an alternative to our current corporate income tax system."

While all of the proposed recommendations by various organizations would benefit rebuilding American manufacturing, I believe the proposals of the Coalition for a Prosperous America would have the most immediate effect in accelerating this rebuilding.

Proposals Made in my book, *Can American Manufacturing Be Saved? Why we should and how we can*

The chapter "How Can We Save American Manufacturing?" contains a summary of the recommendations of many organizations as well as my own recommendations, which I have incorporated into articles and presentations whenever possible in the past several years. As chair of the California chapter of CPA, I also incorporate CPA's competitiveness strategy into articles and presentations whenever possible.

One of the recommendations I made is that Congress should strengthen and tighten procurement regulations to enforce "Buy America" for all government agencies and not just the Department of Defense. All federal spending should have "Buy America" provisions giving American workers and businesses the first opportunity at procurement contracts. New federal loan guarantees for energy projects should require the utilization of domestic supply chains for construction. No federal, state, or local government dollars should be spent buying materials, equipment, supplies, and workers from China as was done for the San Francisco-Oakland Bay bridge in 2011.

My other recommendations for creating jobs are based on improving the competitiveness of American companies by improving the business climate of the United States so that there is less incentive for American manufacturing companies to outsource manufacturing offshore or build plants in foreign countries. The proposed legislation would also close tax loopholes and prevent corporations from avoiding paying corporate income taxes. They are:

- Reduce corporate taxes to 25 percent
- No negotiation or ratification by Congress of any new Free Trade Agreements
- Make the capital gains tax of 15 percent permanent
- Increase and make permanent the R&D tax credit
- Eliminate the estate tax (also called the Death Tax)
- Improve intellectual property rights protection and increase criminal prosecution
- Prevent sale of strategic U.S.-owned companies to foreign-owned companies

I still strongly advocate that the above recommendations would benefit rebuilding American manufacturing, but if Sales Factor Tax Apportionment and a Cost of Goods tax were adopted to create additional federal revenue, we could reduce the corporate tax rate to 15 percent.

Since I started writing the first edition of my previous book, *Can American Manufacturing be Saved? Why we should and how we can* in 2007, I have made it my mission for the rest of my life to do as much as possible as I can to rebuild American manufacturing to create jobs and prosperity. The future of the American middle class and, more importantly, our national security depends on the choices we make and the actions that are taken by the Trump Administration.

About the Author

Michele Nash-Hoff has been in and out of San Diego's high-tech manufacturing industry since starting as an engineering secretary at age 18. Her career includes being part of the founding team of two startup companies. She took a hiatus from the high-tech industry to attend college and graduated from San Diego State University in 1982 with a bachelor's degree in French and Spanish.

After returning to work full-time, she became Vice President of a sales agency covering 11 of the western states. In 1985, Michele left the company to form her own sales agency, ElectroFab Sales, to work with companies to help them select the right manufacturing processes for their new and existing products.

In 1998, The National Business Incubation Association published her first book, For Profit Business Incubators.

Michele has been president of the San Diego Electronics Network, the San Diego Chapter of the Electronics Representatives Association, and The High Technology Foundation, as well as several professional and non-profit organizations. She is an active member of the Soroptimist International of San Diego club. Michele is currently a director on the national board of the American Jobs Alliance and San Diego Inventors Forum. She is Chair of the California chapter of the Coalition for a Prosperous America.

She has a certificate in Total Quality Management and is a 1994 graduate of San Diego's leadership program (LEAD San Diego.) She earned a Certificate in Lean Six Sigma in 2014.

Michele is married to Michael Hoff and has raised two sons and two daughters. She enjoys spending time with her two grandsons and eight granddaughters. Her favorite leisure activities are hiking in the mountains, swimming, running, gardening, reading, and taking tap dance lessons.

End Notes

[1] https://en.wikipedia.org/wiki/Manufacturing_in_the_United_States
[2] http://www.freerepublic.com/focus/f-news/947266/posts
[3] https://www.bea.gov/newsreleases/industry/gdpindustry/gdpindnewsrelease.htm
[4] http://www.kiplinger.com/article/business/T019-C000-S010-gdp-growth-rate-and-forecast.html
[5] https://www.nist.gov/sites/default/files/documents/2017/05/09/1-Manufacturing-Insecurity-ES-V2-1.pdf
[6] http://behl.berkeley.edu/files/2013/02/BEHLWP2013-04_olneypacitti_2-26-13.pdf
[7] https://www.bis.doc.gov/index.php/forms-documents/doc_view/641-national-aeronautics-and-space-administration-nasa-industrial-base-post-space-shuttle
[8] http://usatoday30.usatoday.com/money/economy/employment/story/2012-07-15/space-workers-jobs/56234378/1
[9]http://www.amtonline.org/ReadTheNews/PressReleases/usmtonewsreleaseforaugust2017manufacturingtechnologyorders.htm [9]
[10] http://www.newequipment.com/technology-innovations/manufacturing-predictions-2016-hype-free-edition
[11] http://www.industryweek.com/strategic-planning-execution/manufacturing-recovery-real
[12] http://www.nam.org/Newsroom/Press-Releases/2017/03/Manufacturers--Optimism-at-20-Year-High--According-to-New-NAM-Survey/
[13] http://www2.itif.org/2013-restoring-americas-lagging-investment.pdf
[14] http://www.armed-services.senate.gov/Publications/Counterfeit%20Electronic%20Parts.pdf
[15] http://armed-services.senate.gov/press/SASC%20Counterfeit%20Electronics%20Report%2005-21-12.pdf
[16] http://www.manufacturingnews.com/news/2015/New-Era-For-Defense-Industry-0520151.html
[17] http://www.manufacturingnews.com/news/2015/New-Era-For-Defense-Industry-0520151.html
[18] https://ca.news.yahoo.com/exclusive-u-waived-laws-keep-f-35-track-204531422--sector.html
[19] http://itif.org/publications/impact-international-technology-transfer-american-research-and-development
[20] http://www2.itif.org/2012-enough-enough-chinese-mercantilism.pdf
[21] http://www.ipcommission.org/report/IP_Commission_Report_052213.pdf
[22] http://www.forbes.com/sites/emmawoollacott/2013/05/23/us-should-get-tough-on-chinese-ip-theft-committee-warns/#471a011def04
[23] http://dailycaller.com/2015/09/24/china-is-stealing-american-property/
[24] http://www.cnn.com/2015/07/24/politics/fbi-economic-espionage/

[25] http://www.bbc.com/news/world-asia-china-31503967

[26] http://www.aipla.org/advocacy/congress/aia/Pages/summary.aspx

[27] http://www.independentinventorsofamerica.org/wp-content/uploads/2015/06/Googled-HR9-V3.pdf

[28]

http://books.google.com/books?id=ThJT5CcmCBUC&pg=PA1009&lpg=PA1009&dq=Friedrich+List,+wrote,+%E2%80%9CThe+power+of+producing+wealth+is+%E2%80%A6infinitely+more+important+than+wealth+itself.%E2%80%9D&source=bl&ots=J1BXvD9jIj&sig=cCEgrVqYyTfhfJXg7FVy-mDUJ_I&h

[29] http://nationalhogfarmer.com/business/shareholders-approve-smithfield-foods-merger

[30] http://en.wikipedia.org/wiki/The_Hoover_Company

[31] http://articles.chicagotribune.com/2014-01-30/business/chi-motorola-cell-phone-unit-near-deal-to-be-bought-20140129_1_yang-yuanqing-lenovo-motorola-mobility

[32] http://money.cnn.com/interactive/economy/chinese-acquisitions-us-companies/

[33] ibid

[34] http://www.census.gov/foreign-trade/balance/c5700.html

[35] http://www.abc.net.au/news/2013-06-07/chinese-market-develops-growing-appetite-for-sydney-real-estate/4739992

[36] http://www.britannica.com/EBchecked/topic/126972/Columbia-Pictures-Entertainment-Inc

[37] http://www.nytimes.com/1988/03/18/business/bridgestone-in-deal-for-firestone.html

[38]

https://www.google.com/url?sa=t&rct=j&q=&esrc=s&source=web&cd=1&cad=rja&uact=8&ved=0ahUKEwjXvqO3hPjUAhVD9mMKHdc5BXQQFggrMAA&url=https%3A%2F%2Fwww.whitecase.com%2Fpublications%2Falert%2Fcfius-annual-report-shows-uptick-foreign-direct-investment-and-decline-mitigation&usg=AFQjCNGYrhq9vvuE_h0UZA9kOcRJKOGHCQ

[39]

http://origin.www.uscc.gov/sites/default/files/annual_reports/Executive%20Summary.pdf

[40] http://nypost.com/2013/12/15/why-are-we-letting-china-buy-american-companies/

[41] http://americanmachinist.com/web-eclusive/calling-free-trade-what-it

[42] http://www.businessdictionary.com/definition/free-trade.html#ixzz3Z1KEJSww

[43] https://www.census.gov/foreign-trade/balance/c0015.html

[44] http://en.wikipedia.org/wiki/General_Agreement_on_Tariffs_and_Trade

[45] https://www.census.gov/foreign-trade/balance/c5700.html

[46] http://www.census.gov/foreign-trade/balance/c0007.html

[47] https://www.citizen.org/documents/NAFTA-at-20.pdf

[48] https://www.census.gov/foreign-trade/balance/c2010.html#1993

[49] https://www.census.gov/foreign-trade/balance/c1220.html#1993

[50] http://www.bls.gov/opub/mlr/cwc/american-labor-in-the-20th-century.pdf
[51] http://www.newrepublic.com/article/trade-secrets
[52] http://georgegoens.com/todays-major-issue-is-the-deck-stacked-against-the-common-man/
[53]
http://www.prosperousamerica.org/press_release_cpa_to_us_trade_rep_overhaul_nafta_or_walk_away?utm_campaign=170911_pr&utm_medium=email&utm_source=prosperousamerica
[54] http://www.epi.org/publication/growth-in-u-s-china-trade-deficit-between-2001-and-2015-cost-3-4-million-jobs-heres-how-to-rebalance-trade-and-rebuild-american-manufacturing/http:/www.epi.org/publication/growth-in-u-s-china-trade-deficit-between-2001-and-2
[55] http://www.citizen.org/Page.aspx?pid=5411&frcrld=
[56] http://getliberty.org/leaked-pacific-trade-pact-exempts-foreign-firms-from-u-s-law/
[57] http://savingusmanufacturing.com/blog/category/general/
[58]
http://www.cargroup.org/assets/files/the_effects_a_u.s._free_trade_agreement_with_japan_would_have_on_the_u.s._automotive_industry2.pdf
[59] http://stopthetpp.org/the-trans-pacific-partnership-an-attack-on-u-s-jobs/
[60]
http://www.prosperousamerica.org/cpa_letter_regarding_currency_manipulation_issues_in_trade_agreements
[61] http://www.treasurydirect.gov/govt/reports/pd/histdebt/histdebt_histo5.htm
[62] http://en.wikipedia.org/wiki/Most_favoured_nation
[63] http://www.bcg.com/documents/file84471.pdf
[64] http://www.bcg.com/media/PressReleaseDetails.aspx?id=tcm:12-104216
[65] http://www.bcg.com/media/PressReleaseDetails.aspx?id=tcm:12-100750
[66] http://www.economist.com/news/special-report/21569570-growing-number-american-companies-are-moving-their-manufacturing-back-united
[67] http://www.thehackettgroup.com/research/2012/reshoring-global-manufacturing/hckt2012-reshoring-global-manufacturing.pdf
[68] https://www.atkearney.com/operations/ideas-insights/manufacturing-reshoring#sthash.CtB7nhip.dpuf
[69] http://www.bcg.com/news/press/10december2015-2015-manufacturing-survey.aspx
[70]
https://www.bcgperspectives.com/content/articles/lean_manufacturing_globalization_shifting_economics_global_manufacturing/
[71] http://www.iedconline.org/web-pages/resources-publications/understanding-reshoring/
[72] http://www.iedconline.org/web-pages/resources-publications/tools-for-reshoring/

73 http://www.iedconline.org/web-pages/resources-publications/reshoring-in-the-media/

74 http://www.iedconline.org/clientuploads/Downloads/Reshoring/Reshoring_American_Jobs.pdf

75 http://acetool.commerce.gov/

76 http://www.edastayusa.org/

77 http://www.clustermapping.us/

78 http://www.nam.org/Data-and-Reports/Manufacturers-Outlook-Survey/2016-Manufacturers--Outlook-Survey---Third-Quarter/

79 http://smallbusiness.chron.com/tax-breaks-offshoring-21655.html

80 http://usatoday30.usatoday.com/money/perfi/taxes/2008-03-20-corporate-tax-offshoring_N.htm

81 http://usatoday30.usatoday.com/money/perfi/taxes/2008-03-20-corporate-tax-offshoring_N.htm

82 http://www.brookings.edu/research/reports2/2015/02/03-advanced-industries#/M10420

83 https://www.brookings.edu/research/americas-advanced-industries-what-they-are-where-they-are-and-why-they-matter/

84 http://us6.campaign-archive1.com/?u=bda8170a38ff902659605b718&id=2661d1a913&e=58bbe58865

85 http://www.manufacturing.net/news/2015/03/liquid-printer-turns-3d-manufacturing-upside-down

86 http://www.senvol.com/database

87 https://www.manufacturing.net/blog/2017/07/five-trends-future-manufacturing

88 http://wardsauto.com/keydata/historical/UsaSa01summary

89 http://www.sbnonline.com/2011/07/what-the-shortage-in-skilled-manufacturing-workers-means-to-a-hungry-industry/?paging=1

90 http://www.sbnonline.com/2011/07/what-the-shortage-in-skilled-manufacturing-workers-means-to-a-hungry-industry/?paging=1

91 https://www.google.com/url?sa=t&rct=j&q=&esrc=s&source=web&cd=6&ved=0ahUKEwiY6sSm1-3UAhUS52MKHbVZAGoQFghEMAU&url=http%3A%2F%2Fwww.manpowergroup.us%2Fcampaigns%2Ftalent-shortage%2Fassets%2Fpdf%2F2016-Talent-Shortage-Whitepaper.pdf&usg=AFQjCNEBwaMACxcnGH9NyoBZgkzkNWUeGw&cad=rja

92 http://www.gao.gov/products/GAO-11-92

93 http://ppc.toolingu.com/readiness-1/

94 http://www.sbnonline.com/article/what-the-shortage-in-skilled-manufacturing-workers-means-to-a-hungry-industry/

95 http://www.nam.org/Newsroom/Top-20-Facts-About-Manufacturing/

96 http://www.smeef.org/prime/page/prime-schools

[97] http://smeef.org/

[98] https://www.pltw.org/

[99] http://www.cde.ca.gov/ci/ct/sf/

[100] http://linkedlearning.org/about/where-linked-learning-is-happening/

[101] http://advancedmanufacturing.org/manufacturing-information-center/inside-americas-bold-plan-revive-manufacturing/

[102] https://en.wikipedia.org/wiki/Revitalize_American_Manufacturing_and_Innovation_Act_of_2013

[103] http://www.nist.gov/MEP

[104] http://www.manufacturing.net/news/2017/02/us-factory-ceos-trump-jobs-exist-skills-dont-0?et_cid=5845685&et_rid=394077683&location=top&et_cid=5845685&et_rid=394077683&linkid=http%3a%2f%2fwww.manufacturing.net%2fnews%2f2017%2f02%2fus-factory-ceos-trump-jobs-

[105] https://engineering.osu.edu/news/2016/10/ohio-state-center-will-help-regional-manufacturing-companies-grow

[106] https://omi.osu.edu/

[107] https://lift.technology/

[108] https://itif.org/publications/2012/09/20/fifty-ways-leave-your-competitiveness-woes-behind-national-traded-sector

[109] http://www.itif.org/publications/case-national-manufacturing-strategy

[110] http://www.prosperousamerica.org/a_competitiveness_strategy_for_the_united_states

[111] https://www.wsj.com/articles/how-to-revitalize-u-s-manufacturing-1465351501

[112] https://itif.org/publications/2017/01/31/ten-principles-guide-trump-administrations-manufacturing-strategy

[113] http://www.industryweek.com/competitiveness/can-us-manufacturing-be-made-great-again?page=1

[114] https://d3n8a8pro7vhmx.cloudfront.net/prosperousamerica/pages/2764/attachments/original/1499708589/170623_working_paper_currency_v5_MCS.pdf?1499708589

[115] https://www.census.gov/foreign-trade/statistics/historical/index.html

[116] http://www.prosperousamerica.org/cpa_testimony_how_tax_reform_will_grow_our_economy_and_create_jobs

[117] http://www.industryweek.com/legislation/bipartisan-tax-reform-possible

[118] http://itepnet.org/pdf/pb11ssf.pdf

42966497R10161

Made in the USA
Middletown, DE
21 April 2019